I felt so inspir[ed]... d his wonderful family—and ... unt of their story brings back the very same feelings. For in the midst of a fierce storm named cancer, they have continually managed to find their way to a place of trust, hope, and worship. Ellie writes in a raw yet reverent tone—not avoiding the crazily tough moments they have had to face as a family, but each time recounting them with a deep and heartening sense of faith. Chase is a very brave boy, and this is a very courageous book. I know it will encourage and inspire so many others who find themselves navigating the storms of this life.

MATT REDMAN
Songwriter, UK

To see a child suffer is grievous, but when it is your own child, the pain is unbearable. And yet this true story of a young mother and her son Chase, who was diagnosed with cancer... that there can be a sliver of sunshine even... st night.

DR. ERWIN W. LUTZER
Pastor Emeritus, Moody Church, Chicago

Written with honest emotion and depth, this book gives every parent reason to count their blessings, and every family with a child fighting cancer inspiration to make each day count.

KATHLEEN RUDDY
CEO, St. Baldrick's Foundation, Conquer Childhood Cancer

I love books that are deeply encouraging and yet brutally honest. I love writers who don't insist prayer is a magic wand and yet believe God is amazingly all-powerful. *Chase Away Cancer* is one of those books, and Ellie Poole Ewoldt is one of those writers. This story made me fall in love with her little Chase and deeper in love with our very big God. I think you will too.

LYNN EIB
Author of *When God & Cancer Meet*

The Lord gives us all a journey. It takes an anointed one to traverse the "cancer journey." Chase and his family join the ranks of Spider-Man and Batman as superheroes in their epic battle against this enemy. Only one that has walked in these shoes can truly guide another along this road. Ellie does an amazing job of always pointing to the Lord as the guidepost that leads them in their conquest. Since cancer is an enemy that touches all of us in some way, I would encourage everyone to read this book to gain an insight of a life well lived in the battle against this foe.

REGGIE ANDERSON
Author of *Appointments with Heaven*

Chase Away Cancer is for anyone who is looking for hope, courage, or strength while battling through some of life's great challenges. It offers encouragement to others, and it focuses on living moment by moment—relying on God's grace to get through some of life's hardships. Ellie takes the reader into her world with her realistic accounts and transparency, walking the reader through the trenches of her family's battle, with Jesus as her primary source of strength. This book helps the reader remember that one is never alone through life's journey, and it empowers the reader to keep fighting and believing, even when circumstances are not what is wanted or expected. *Chase Away Cancer* helps the reader see the "beauty in brokenness." This book is a must-read for all, no matter the season of life.

GAVIN FLOYD & DR. LEANNA FLOYD
MLB pitcher; Doctor of Clinical Psychology

CHASE AWAY CANCER

A POWERFUL TRUE STORY OF FINDING LIGHT IN A DARK DIAGNOSIS

ELLIE POOLE EWOLDT

TYNDALE®
MOMENTUM

An Imprint of
Tyndale House Publishers, Inc.

Visit Tyndale online at www.tyndale.com.

Visit Tyndale Momentum online at www.tyndalemomentum.com.

Tyndale Momentum and the Tyndale Momentum logo are registered trademarks of Tyndale House Publishers, Inc. Tyndale Momentum is an imprint of Tyndale House Publishers, Inc., Carol Stream, Illinois.

Chase Away Cancer: A Powerful True Story of Finding Light in a Dark Diagnosis

Designed by Dean H. Renninger

Edited by Bonne Steffen

The stories in this book are about real people and real events, but some names have been omitted for the privacy of the individuals involved. Dialogue has been recreated to the author's best recollection.

Library of Congress Cataloging-in-Publication Data
Names: Ewoldt, Ellie Poole, author.
Title: Chase away cancer : a powerful true story of finding light in a dark
    diagnosis / Ellie Poole Ewoldt.
Description: Carol Stream, IL : Tyndale House Publishers, Inc., 2016. |
    Includes bibliographical references.
Identifiers: LCCN 2015050121 | ISBN 9781496411693 (sc)
Subjects: LCSH: Ewoldt, Chase. | Cancer—Religious aspects—Christianity. |
    Cancer—Patients. | Hope--Religious aspects—Christianity.
Classification: LCC BV4910.33 .E93 2016 | DDC 248.8/6196994—dc23 LC record available
at http://lccn.loc.gov/2015050121

Printed in the United States of America

22   21   20   19   18   17   16
7   6   5   4   3   2   1

For my precious children Darcy, Aidan, Chase, and Karsten—
know you are fearfully and wonderfully made,
and your stories are extraordinary.

For my darling husband, Robert, my perfect counterpart,
who believed I could write when I didn't believe it myself.

For all those who have gone before us in this cancer fight and
stand battered and broken, some with empty arms.

"Weeping may last through the night,
but joy comes with the morning."

PSALM 30:5

CONTENTS

Introduction: Learning to Let Go xi

1. The Joy in Changing Plans *1*

2. Trusting When There Aren't Answers *7*

3. Absorbing the Shock *23*

4. Jesus Is Near *31*

5. Being Transparent *37*

6. Learning to Laugh *45*

7. Love Believes All Things *49*

8. We Were Never Created for Separation *57*

9. Feeling Inadequate *65*

10. Learning to Live in Grace *73*

11. When Life Stops but We Keep Breathing *79*

12. Searching for Shelter *91*

13. Preparing for Loss *113*

14. Searching for Purpose *123*

15. When There Is No Relief *135*

16. Practicing Thankfulness *145*

17. Celebrating in All Circumstances *153*

18. Love Can't Stop Death *159*

19. When Joy Is Confusing *169*

20. Slaying Guilt *179*

21. Facing Fears *189*

22. Acknowledging Anger *199*

23. Accepting Weariness *211*

24. Learning to Persevere *223*

25. We Can't Protect Them *227*

26. Practicing Endurance *233*

27. Finding Peace without Being Free *243*

28. The Most Perfect Identity *257*

29. Learning to Love *267*

Afterword 273
Photo Gallery 278
Acknowledgements 284
Sources of Comfort, Strength, and Inspiration 285
Notes 287
About the Author 289

LEARNING TO LET GO

It was a perfect June evening for a family walk. Going as far as several sets of little legs could go, we'd made it down the sidewalk that bordered the busy street along our condo complex to the corner and back, and now it was time to start thinking about cleaning grubby palms and feet and getting little ones tucked into bed.

The setting sun played with us, flooding our backs with warm, end-of-the-day light as our family turned into a drive that led to our building. I was last in the line of six, pushing seven-month-old Karsten in his stroller as he watched the cars excitedly and banged his fists on the tray in front of him. Six-year-old Darcy and three-year-old Aidan held hands as they stayed near my husband, Bob, chattering about who had counted the most cars, and Bob, at the front, held on to two-year-old Chase's hand. We made quite the procession.

I could hear the voices of neighbors as a slight breeze rustled the trees, birds called to one another, and someplace far off, a dog barked. At the other end of the drive, Bob and I noticed a delivery truck making several stops, and we moved everyone to the side of the small lane and into the grass to stay out of its way. But neither Bob nor I realized that Chase had broken out of his hold and was no longer standing next to us. The heavy truck lumbered down the pavement, slowly picking up speed as it drove toward us, directly into the blinding glare of the setting sun. And standing in its path, just barely taller than the truck's front bumper, was a small boy . . . *our* small boy.

Tiny, barrel-chested Chase stood in the middle of the drive with his feet planted wide in his scuffed shoes and stared down the truck. He had no plans on moving.

This isn't happening . . .

Bob and I both screamed in a desperate plea for action. "Chase! Come here *now!*" I had been in enough showdowns with him that I knew just by looking at the back of his unturned, unmoving head, that he had heard us but chose not to respond and was most likely scowling.

Bob lunged forward, his long legs propelling him into a running dive, and scooped up Chase just seconds before the truck passed us and exited the drive. The driver never slowed or turned to look at us; perhaps he never even saw the small boy in front of him, but it didn't matter—Chase was safe.

As we stood in the grass, everyone took a deep breath, and we absorbed what had felt like a near miss. Darcy and Aidan appeared as horrified as Bob and I were, and Darcy found her voice before we could collect our thoughts. "Chase! You could have been badly hurted!"

Aidan stepped up next, chiming in. "Yeah, Chase!"

Chase ignored them, his face still twisted into a scowl, as he spun around to face Bob and exclaimed, "Dad! You picked me up! You can't do that! I was fine!"

I marveled at the confidence of the small boy in front of us. *He genuinely believes he has the power to stop moving vehicles with his presence alone.* With his few, feisty words, he made it clear that he had no need for rescue.

Chase's self-assurance and determination surfaced early in life. Whether he was challenging his older brother, Aidan, while they played with trains at the living room table, or comfortably stuffing his hands into his pockets, rocking on his heels as he talked to adults as if he were one of them, he was a strong, old soul from the start. In everything he did, this boy was full tilt. His siblings sensed this in him, and for better or usually worse, they almost always fell into line behind him. For Chase, no activity held any middle ground; it wasn't any fun if it wasn't a challenge.

Just like that, I started spotting gray hairs mixed into my usually redheaded frizz. There were almost weekly occurrences that ended with a gasped prayer and the full heartbeat-in-my-eardrums knowledge that if his foot had slipped, if I hadn't walked into the room at that exact moment, if he'd jumped, gotten that drawer open, that window open, I would have been grabbing my purse and heading to the emergency room—not, as those moments often ended, holding him in a bear hug and talking about making better choices.

One night, just a few short weeks after his attempted standoff with the delivery truck, I stood over his crib and watched him sleeping. It was late, and the moon was high and full, shining in through the window coverings, making his face luminous. I stroked the short hair off his forehead, and as I watched him, I felt a strange stirring in my heart. *"Are you prepared to let him go?"*

Images of daredevil stunts on a motorcycle or being parachuted into an overseas assignment crossed my mind as I pictured a tall, sandy-haired man with his father's brown eyes and infectious smile. The thought of my baby risking his life as an adult hurt my heart, but as all mothers of little children do, I comforted myself that the days of letting go were eons away. I didn't need to answer that question just yet. I found myself mentally thanking God for the reminder and moved on. Kissing Chase's cool forehead, I tucked the blanket in around his shoulders and tiptoed out of the room.

I would forget that late-night moment for several weeks. It was summer and wonderful, and the days were spent across town at Grandma's house, running in the yard and playing in the pool and sprinkler.

Once that idyllic June, Chase slipped and fell out of the pool, scratching his side pretty badly. After tending to him, I didn't give the moment much thought; after all, he was such an active boy. Shortly after this, on July 4, he fell again. This time he was standing next to the hot grill and burned his hand. He was curious, fascinated by the open fire, and had gotten too close. But with a little ice, he was okay. He tripped and fell several times in the house, too, but those incidents all seemed to be okay because he was always running and I was always telling him to slow down. Later he contracted what appeared to be the stomach flu twice in one month, vomiting early in the morning and then wanting to sleep for the rest of the day. The flu was short-lived and strange, but I thought maybe having four children introduced more germs into the house, and he was the unfortunate recipient.

Occasionally, I could feel a knot growing in my stomach but I told myself it was all going to be okay. I'm a first-class, worst-case-scenario worrier, and so I began to wonder about allergies and sensitivities as my brain pieced together these seemingly random incidences with Chase, things the other children were somehow not affected by. But I could not and did not see these things as pieces of a whole yet. I could not see them for what they were—an unprecedented, breathtaking nightmare of truck-sized proportions that was gathering on the horizon, preparing to tear us apart. We were standing in the middle of the road, staring it down, and we didn't even realize it yet.

Let go . . .

1
THE JOY IN CHANGING PLANS

I had a feeling something was going to happen that Saturday morning. I sat quietly on the edge of the bed, my swollen ankles and feet barely visible over my distended, very pregnant stomach. My arms and legs ached far more than they had been recently, and it felt as if every nerve were coming alive, as if my body was preparing for something. December 12, 2009: Chase's due date. My firstborn, Darcy, had been nine days late, followed by Aidan, who was eight days early, but as I felt these subtle changes, I wondered, *Will Chase actually come on the predicted day?*

It had all gone by so quickly. Nine months earlier, when Aidan was barely a three-month-old in my arms, I began to notice that certain colors made me feel queasy. Like my mother before me, the women in our family find certain colors nausea-inducing when we are pregnant. As I stood in my tiny kitchen and stared at the food label on the can in front of me, the chartreuse border made me want to run to the bathroom and give up my lunch.

This is crazy, I thought. *I can't be.* I laughed it off quickly. *It's more than likely my body is still recovering from Aidan's birth.*

That night, after the kids were asleep, I sat on the edge of our bed as my husband, Bob, hung up his tie in the closet. "How was your day today, love?" he asked.

"It was okay, but I had a really weird experience. I was looking at this can with a green label, and it made me feel physically ill."

Bob stopped what he was doing and looked over at me. "The smell made you feel sick?"

I shook my head. "No, the color did."

I saw that Bob was confused. "Do you remember me saying that happened when I was first pregnant with Aid and Darcy too?"

Bob had been listening as he was hanging up his clothes, but as soon as I said "pregnant," his head snapped up.

"Do you think it's possible?" I asked. "What will we do?" I left the questions hanging in midair, almost afraid to say aloud what I suspected, lest it prove true.

He sighed, running his hands through his hair as he often did when he was tired. "I have no idea, but there's one way to find out." Bob has always been good at stating next steps when I get emotionally existential.

"Okay, I'll take a test. Are we ready for this?"

He sighed again. "It doesn't matter. If this is really happening, we will figure it out." I took heart in the certainty of his tone. He crossed the room to sit next to me on the bed and took my hand in both of his. "For now, don't worry about things we don't know about yet. We'll take one thing at a time."

Shortly later, we stared at double pink lines on the white plastic stick. We slowly caught our breath and exhaled a prayer for wisdom and strength. Two pregnancies in less than two years, and the children would probably only be about a year apart. This definitely wasn't part of the plan.

I felt the new life inside me early in my pregnancy, weeks earlier than either of my other two. This baby never seemed to stop moving, and it may have been my imagination, but he or she seemed to respond to my moods and feelings, kicking me when I was hungry, thrashing when I felt anger, and of course, dancing wildly whenever I felt joy or tried to sleep. This was a child with such high energy that at times, I grew worried for what life would look like after delivery. If the baby was this active before birth, how would I possibly handle such energy after it was born?

By the end of the summer, we learned it was another boy. Baby Aidan would have a younger brother, and I, the girl who grew up in a household of sisters, would now mother a family in which Darcy and I were fast becoming outnumbered. My father, the sole male in a household of sisters, felt that life had finally righted a great injustice to him, and he was irrationally thrilled over the addition of another grandson.

God help me.

With little else under our control, we turned to something we could decide: the baby's name. I picked his middle names from the maiden names of his grandmothers, and Bob voted early and often for the first name *Chase* because it mirrored our prayer that this son would run hard after God.

I felt more than a little annoyed when Aidan's first birthday came and went without me going into labor. There was a silly part of me that really wanted the bragging rights to two sons born less than a year apart. But no, Chase was his own person who did things his way, in his own time.

And so it was in the early hours on that second Saturday of December, as my feet dangled off the bed and I felt my spine curl around a wisp of the pain that was yet to come, I wondered how much longer I'd wait before holding this special surprise boy in my arms.

Bob went to work as he always did on Saturday mornings, and my mother picked up three-year-old Darcy for some one-on-one time. Aid and I settled in for whatever the day might bring.

When the pain increased in the early afternoon, I put Aidan in his crib because I could no longer hold him. He began crying pitifully, so I poured some Cheerios into a bowl for him, hoping that would quiet him. He cried harder. He didn't want food; he wanted me to hold him. As I hunched over the crib, I cried with him, feeling helpless and alone. I couldn't help him understand what was happening or how our lives were about to change. All I could do was apologize and try to hug him as he stood at the rail of his crib.

"I'm so sorry, buddy, I'm so, so sorry. I love you so much, and I'd hold you if I could." Stroking his white-blond head, I continued, "It's going to be okay. You'll be okay. I'm so, so sorry."

Distractedly picking up my phone to call Bob, I remembered that he didn't get cell service in his office at the church, and so I limped to the computer between contractions to send him a chat message on my Google e-mail account.

"Bobby, I think it's time. My contractions are getting worse, and they're already every seven minutes apart."

He responded, "I'm just finishing up some stuff here, and I don't want to be there too early—can you just call me back when the contractions are closer together?"

We laugh about it now, but believe me, I wasn't laughing much at the time. I sent him another message—this time in all capital letters—asking him to please consider coming home, and sensing my "tone," he came quickly.

My mom was still several minutes away with Darcy, but she called my sister Meg, who just happened to be stopping for gas at the station right down the street from our house, for temporary backup. Meg arrived to watch Aidan so that we could leave for the hospital. Sometimes God has the perfect timing, even in the craziest moments. As Bob and I got on the road, rushing toward the hospital, we passed my mom and Darcy. We both waved, and I blew her kisses. She and Aidan wouldn't be allowed in the hospital due to a flu season guideline, so we'd be separated for at least two days.

Once we arrived at the hospital, everything happened quickly. The familiar pain intensified. *Hadn't I just gone through labor with Aidan seconds ago?* Within a few short hours, the wonderfully agonizing relief finally came as the labor ended and my tiny new son slipped into the world.

The doctor caught him in both hands, exclaiming, "It's a *boy*! Did you know it was a boy?" And then he nearly shouted, "And he's holding his head up on his own! This kid is strong! Look at this!"

Grabbing a towel to place him in, the doctor laid Chase, still purple and blue, on my chest, and I wrapped my arms around him as the oxygen raced into his body, fueling his initial screams against the harsh and cold.

He was beautiful. "Oh, my darling boy. Momma is here now."

I gently rocked him. "I'm here, I'm here, I'm here . . . don't cry. It's going to be okay, my darling boy," I whispered in a songlike cadence as I held him close.

"He's perfect, Bob, isn't he?"

Bob smiled at me, his eyes full of pride as we shared those first joyful moments. I wiggled my now-visible toes under the covers. "And I can see my feet again!" Bob laughed. After two years of nearly continuous pregnancy, this season was finally over, and a whole new one was beginning. Sometimes the moments that break the carefully constructed mold of your life plan turn out to be the greatest ones. Although we hadn't considered this for ourselves, it was clearly God's plan for our lives. And I believe he knew that Chase Stratton Elliot Ewoldt needed to be part of this world for very special reasons.

2

TRUSTING WHEN THERE AREN'T ANSWERS

Chase lived up to his action-packed name. Almost completely bypassing the crawling stage, he began walking around Halloween of the following year at only ten months of age. He not only learned to speak early, but he also was very articulate, and from his first birthday on, it became increasingly apparent that he was most happy when he was being challenged. Every interaction was a chance for competition, and his energy was astounding, inexplicably replenishing after only a very few hours of sleep each night. Chase was a force to be reckoned with.

During this time, I became pregnant with our youngest son, Karsten, who joined our family in the fall of 2011, completing the stair-step lineup of small boys. As Karsten grew, I noticed that Chase's behavior began to change. At first, the issues were subtle, happening so slowly that sometimes we wondered if we were imagining things. In the spring after Chase's second birthday, everything turned into a standoff, with mealtimes being the worst. Chase grew tired and irrational easily but would not want to sleep, and when he finally did sleep, he'd only be down for a short amount of time, even less than usual. And then, in the early summer, he started grinding his teeth and would even occasionally drool when he talked. There was always the chance that he was taking the most destructive path through "the terrible twos," but one day, something different happened.

He wandered into the kitchen where I was working and said, "Mommy, can I have a snack?"

Glancing at the clock on the stove, I said, "Of course, sweet boy."

He pointed to the container of pretzels that sat on top of the fridge. "Can I have some of those?"

There was something in the way he said *those* that made me pause. I baited him just a little, trying to get him to ask for the pretzels by name as he always had before. "Can you tell me what you want, Chase?"

His brown eyes were alert, but he seemed to be searching for the word in his mind. It hit me. *Why can't he remember the word?* His pudgy little arms were outstretched, and he stood next to the fridge on tiptoes, as if coming closer would somehow help him make the connection.

"The uh, the uh, hamburger?"

I could tell by the look on his face that he knew it wasn't the right word. Tamping down a growing sense of panic, I coached him until he said it and sent him on his way with his snack. Maybe it was a chance thing, his forgetting a word that he knew, but I was still scared.

As soon as Chase left the kitchen with his pretzels, I snuck into the bedroom, shut the door, and called Bob.

"You aren't going to believe what just happened." I told him the story, then said, "Bob, I really think he needs to go to a doctor."

I heard a long sigh on the other end of the phone. "I really don't think it's that big a deal, love. So he forgot a word. We all do that."

"Bob, please." Even though I was almost always the panic to his calm, I needed him to see this particular situation from my perspective. "It isn't just about forgetting a word. He's struggling. He's not wanting to sleep. He's been sick twice this month, refused to eat lunch the last two Sundays, and there's that weird drooling thing." I knew I was bombarding Bob with information, but for some reason I felt desperate for him to see why this was so frightening to me.

He waited until I had exhausted my list. "Okay. Why don't you set up an appointment with the pediatrician and have Chase checked out?"

I closed my eyes. "Thank you, honey; thank you so much."

Within twenty-four hours, Chase and I were sitting in the waiting room of the doctor's office. Bob stayed at work, asking me to call him as soon as the appointment concluded, and I'd dropped the other three children off at my mom's, so I was free to focus on Chase. Our regular pediatrician was unavailable that day, but I'd opted to see someone else on staff rather than waiting an extra day.

The office was under construction because the practice was expanding, and so when Chase's name was called, the nurse ushered us to what looked like a supply room with floor-to-ceiling storage cabinets and mounted cupboards along three of the walls. One area next to the sink had been turned into a makeshift exam room with a table and instruments, while the other side of the room was lined with cardboard boxes. The nurse apologized for the inconvenience and disarray.

When the doctor came in, I described what we'd been seeing over the last several weeks. Were they anomalies? But instead of providing answers, after he examined Chase, the doctor asked more questions.

Had I let him eat spare change? *No.*

But could I be sure? *No. He's a two-year-old boy.*
Had he been eating dirt? *Unlikely.*

But could he have eaten some dirt and picked up a parasite? *Possibly, but I hadn't seen him do it, and I think I'd see evidence that my son had eaten dirt.* Chase wasn't exactly known as being a tidy eater, often wearing more than he swallowed.

This new pediatrician freely admitted to being as puzzled as we were and suggested starting with an X-ray of Chase's stomach to rule out his having ingested anything extraordinary. Somewhere in a box I still have that X-ray showing his perfectly clean stomach with no coins or dirt or parasites . . . or answers. Later that day, I received the results of the scan. The radiologist had noted that Chase might be a little constipated, so the doctor prescribed a heavy laxative and suggested we call back in a few days with a progress report.

After a stop at the pharmacy and picking up the other children, we arrived home and I gave Chase the suggested medicine, following the directions carefully. But within an hour of ingesting it, Chase started complaining of stomach pain. I called my mom and asked if she could come over in case I had to take Chase back to the doctor. Her voice sounded concerned as she confirmed that she was on her way. As I ended the call, my phone flashed a message that the power was nearly gone, so I hurried back to the kitchen to plug it in and recharge it.

I could hear Chase crying; he was getting worse. By the time I crossed the few feet to the kitchen, he was on the floor, clutching his stomach and screaming. Darcy and Aiden stood a few feet away watching him, clearly more curious than afraid.

Hurrying them out of the room, I then reached for my cell phone. The screen was frozen, and it may as well have been dead. *Come on, come on, come on . . . work!* My hands were shaking as I tried to power it off and back on, trying anything I could think of to make it spring to life. It was no use.

As Chase lay crying near my feet on the rug, I threw the phone back on the counter. My mind seemed to race in a million directions at once, all within seconds. *Should I leave Chase to run to a neighbor's and make the call?* I couldn't leave him. *Should I pick him up and try to carry him with me?* The thought seemed crazy, but I had no idea what to do. It could not have been more than two or three minutes before my mom arrived, but those minutes felt like hours, as if I were trapped in a nightmare where I screamed and no sound came out. As I heard the sound of my mom's key in the dead bolt, Chase doubled over and vomited on the rug.

"Mom! Thank God! I need your phone now!"

Her eyes widened as she saw Chase on the floor and grasped the gravity of the situation. She fumbled in her purse for her phone, and I quickly punched in the number I knew by heart. The office was closed for the day, and the wait for the answering service to page the on-call doctor felt like more nightmarish years. Once connected, we were instructed to go directly to the emergency room.

I called Bob, who was on his way home, and moments later, we rushed out of the house together. When we finally got Chase to the hospital, there were more questions. To me, the doctor in the emergency room seemed abrupt, and he appeared irritated by our decision to give Chase the medicine.

"It's simply a stomach virus," he lectured us. "You just need to push fluids and let it run its course." The implication was clear: In his opinion, we'd been foolish to listen to the pediatrician. And while we wanted to believe this simple diagnosis, we couldn't help but want to question this doctor as well. If it was only a virus, why did it come and go over weeks at a time, and in a household of four small children, why was Chase the only one who had gotten sick? He had no answers for us other than to let it play out. In our hearts, we felt that our questions remained unanswered.[1] So we went back to our usual pediatrician, and this time, Bob came with us.

Another day passed, and this time my favorite family physician, Dr. O'Donnell, the man who cared for me when I was a child, sat in the room with us and just watched Chase. Hand on his chin, his white-haired head bent in thought, he silently watched. He didn't say it, but I knew what he was looking for: seizures. After nearly twenty minutes of observing Chase, Dr. O'Donnell said he hadn't seen anything that might present a red flag. There were no signs pointing to loss of consciousness or muscle weakness. *Nothing.* He told us he'd look into some things and follow up shortly.

We would learn much later that he contacted a specialist and voiced deep concerns, thinking what Chase was experiencing might be signaling something serious, possibly even a brain tumor. The specialist had advised him not to burden us with unnecessary worries. Instead, he suggested that speech therapy was needed.

This was the message that I received. "We advise you to call this office and set up an appointment. He's a normal two-year-old, and he needs speech therapy."

I did it. The appointment was set for nearly three weeks out—such a long time to wait for answers. But something in my gut said this didn't add up. What about the drooling and vomiting? Was that speech-related? I thought therapy helped you develop vocabulary and skills, but would it help Chase replace the words he was starting to lose?

My phone rang a lot in that week, and there were still so many questions. Unsatisfied himself, Dr. O'Donnell had kept pushing behind the scenes, advocating on our behalf. He finally arranged for Chase to get a test to monitor his brain waves—one that would determine once and for all if Chase was having seizures.

The test was scheduled for 1:30 p.m. on Monday, July 30, 2012.

The day before the test was the first Sunday I'd been to church in weeks. The pastor's sermon was taken from Philippians 4. Jesus was near, Pastor Dave said, anxiousness could be given to Him; we could find peace even without our circumstances changing. I sat in the lobby outside the sanctuary with a lethargic Chase draped across my lap and took notes like crazy. Dave's words that day seemed tailored for me, and I drank them in. "Don't be afraid. . . . Jesus is near."

That afternoon, I drove to Meg's to borrow a bunch of movies. Chase would need to sleep during the next day's EEG (electroencephalogram), as seizures often occur during changing moments in the brain—like waking and sleeping—and because of this, the test required significant sleep deprivation the night before. We decided to make it fun and planned to pop popcorn and watch movies late into the night.

Darcy and Aidan stayed up for one, maybe two films, and then I slept for twenty minutes while Bob walked Chase down the street to the convenience store to get some M&M'S. I heard that they'd munched the candy together all the way home. The night was cool and quiet, and Bob needed to sleep, so I took the next shift. Chase thought it was all great fun. And it kind of was.

The later the night dragged on, the more active and unsteady Chase became. Even his speech seemed vaguely jumbled. We sat together on the old blue love seat facing the couch when he exclaimed, "Mom, watch this!" and suddenly tucking his head, he did a somersault before I could react or stop him. His trajectory should have landed him further up the soft leather of the low armrest, but instead, he seemed to weaken and twist, crashing onto his side on the cream-colored carpet by my feet.

I gasped. "Chase! What are you doing? Be careful, Son, please!"

Had I imagined it or was he a little off balance? Completely unfazed and uninjured, he wanted to do it again, and I let him while moving my body to block a fall, just to see what would happen. This time he nailed the landing, and I breathed a sigh of relief.

My overactive, overtired mind had probably been playing tricks on me. Chase was fine. I was exhausted.

The next afternoon, I lay on the exam room bed next to him as they dimmed the lights and told me that he should try to sleep. It's strange how you can pass through tiredness into an exhausted wakefulness. I remember not being able to sleep and wishing I could. Chase dozed off briefly, but I could feel him fidgeting for most of the test. He whispered to me in the darkness, "I can't sleep, Mommy. I just can't." The promised post-scan animal crackers were far too wonderful to be able to really sleep deeply.

Somehow, we made it through the test and back home, and as I stood in the hall and took off my shoes and helped Chase take off his, I noticed that his hand was trembling. *This is real. I am not imagining this.* But for the moment, I had to dismiss it. As Bob always said, things should be taken one at a time. The answers would come with the results soon enough. *Maybe even tomorrow.*

The evening passed in a blur of dinner and early bedtimes after our crazy, pre-test lateness the night before. My head hit the pillow and I finally slept. Sometime after midnight, I heard heavy rain, and my heart sank. A thunderstorm. Darcy hated thunder and would shortly be awake. *So much for sleep.*

The storm came and went in the earliest hours of the predawn. With a little coaxing, Darcy had gone back to bed, but as I passed back into unconsciousness, I heard her come back in.

"Daddy?" She knew better than to come and wake me.

"Darcy . . ." I heard the exhaustion in Bob's voice as he rolled over in the bed. "It's okay. Listen to the thunder; it's getting farther away. Go back to sleep, Sister."

"But, Daddy! Chase is awake and he won't be quiet. I can't sleep. He just keeps moving around in his bed, and he won't let me sleep. Can you please come in and talk to him?"

I heard Bob get up, and knowing he would handle the situation, I closed my eyes again, praying for peace. I was nearly asleep when Bob shook my shoulder. "Babe, get up. I think Chase is having some kind of a seizure. Come quick."

I was out of bed and walking before he finished speaking, before I was fully awake. I stood over Chase in the crib. The moonlight and the streetlight streaming through the blinds illuminated his face with a dim, surreal quality.

I had only ever seen a seizure once in my life. I was twelve, and I'd been awakened in the early morning by the sound of my mother crying frantically for my father to come quickly. Jumping out of bed, I ran out of my room to the doorway of the room next to mine and stood frozen in horror, as I watched my five-year-old sister's body shake the bunk bed. Mom cried out to God as she dialed 911, and Dad knelt by the bed, speaking to my sister Carrie in a half-firm, half-terrified voice that I'd never heard before. He held her upper arms and kept calling for her to wake up. I could hear my mom give the operator directions to our house, as she tried to tell my dad, through tears, that my sister couldn't wake up even if she could hear him. Carrie's eyes rolled back, and her whole body convulsed the way possessed people do in movies. She heard nothing and saw nothing, and it seemed to go on and on. It wasn't so much the sight of a convulsing child, but the sound of fear and helplessness in my parents' voices that terrified me the most that day.

But Chase wasn't displaying anything like what I remembered. His eyes were focused; he could see me. He lay on his back, and his right arm and leg moved in rhythmic dissonance as he tried to cry. I'd never heard anything like the sound he made—half whine, half grunt. The expression on his face seemed to say *I want to talk to you but I can't.* His eyes seemed to beg us to make it stop, but we couldn't.

"Call 911!" Bob ordered me hoarsely, and I fled the room for my phone. "Please work, please work." It rang once before Bob shouted to me that Chase had stopped seizing, so I quickly hung up. It seemed silly to bother paramedics if the danger had passed, and we could get him to the hospital on our own. Just as my father had tried to awaken his seizing child, I hesitated to believe my own child was in trauma.

Bob carried a limp, lethargic Chase into the living room and laid him on the couch. He seemed very weak and didn't speak. My phone rang. My aborted call had still been enough to connect to dispatch before I'd hung up, and the operator wanted to know if we were okay. I remember very little of the conversation other than the man telling me to stay where we were and that they'd feel better if they sent people to at least check on us. I hung up the phone and called my mom, her voice thick with sleep on the other end of the line. "Mom, Chase just had a seizure."

I could hear her gasp. "Oh, Jesus, no." Her words were not a curse, but a prayer. "I'm on my way."

Within a few minutes, there was a police officer at our door. He asked to come in and see Chase as we explained to him what was happening, and with one hand on his belt and the other on his radio, he stood over the couch where Chase lay and radioed the emergency responders to guide them into our condo complex.

An entire crew joined the officer in our condo, and I could tell by the flashing lights through the blinds that they'd even sent the fire truck. They surrounded Chase on the couch and asked Bob and me lots of questions. When did it start? How long did it last? Has he ever had a seizure before? The questions washed over us as the paramedics prepared Chase to be moved. I heard my mom walk in the open door, and she whispered that my dad was parking the car.

I was aware that Darcy and Aidan crouched near the door of the dark bedroom they shared, peering into the hall. When I walked by, they called out for answers in small, scared voices. "Mommy, what's happening?" I stopped for just a second in the dark doorway. I could not ignore them, but I felt the pressure to keep moving. I heard the snap of the gurney being locked into place and realized I only had seconds before we left. "I have no idea right now, but it's going to be okay," I tried to reassure them. "I can't talk right now. Please, please stay in your beds."

Two of the paramedics began to lift Chase, still weak and lethargic, onto the gurney, and he whimpered in fear. He looked so small and scared. I offered to lie on the bed and have him lie on me, and they quickly agreed.

I cradled Chase to my chest as someone handed me an oxygen mask and instructed me to hold it to his face.

"Why does he need the oxygen?"

One of the men standing at the foot of the gurney looked up. "Oh, he's okay. His 'O₂-SAT' is fine." Catching himself, the paramedic said it in terms I could understand. "His oxygen saturation is okay. This is just a precaution. It doesn't even have to be against his skin. Just keep it close."

Chase and I were rolled out of the living room and into the still-dark foyer of our condo. For some reason, nobody had turned on the lights, as if leaving the house in as natural a state as possible would make this less terrifying. I could still hear my two older children crying, and I called to them as calmly as I could, "Grammie is here now. I love you so much, and I'll see you soon, okay? It's going to be all right." I choked on the last words a little as we crossed the threshold of our condo and were hurried down the first floor hall. As we rounded the corner in the lobby, we nearly collided with my dad. I saw the vulnerability on his face and had to look away. This wasn't the time to cry. Not yet.

Chase stirred on my chest and hoarsely whispered, "Bapa" into the oxygen mask—his pet name for his grandfather. One of the paramedics leaned closer at the sound of his voice. "Good. Chase recognized him."

The gurney was loaded into the ambulance headfirst, and one of the crew swung himself up with practiced ease onto a bench next to us. As I held Chase, the rig's powerful engine rumbled, and we started to move; I could see our home disappear through the back window. The paramedic riding with us was asking for a medical history, and I answered him somewhat absently as I stared at the oxygen mask and the top of Chase's head. It must have been sometime around 5:00 a.m., and the roads were nearly deserted. I could hear the echo of the sirens off the top of the cab as we approached intersections. The hospital was only six or seven minutes from our house, yet on that morning it seemed to take two to three times as long to get there. My heart willed us there faster. Questions flitted through my mind. Why had the paramedic said it was good that Chase recognized his Bapa? Why wouldn't he?

Please God, get us there. Please God, be near.

I felt the gears of the engine shifting as the truck slowed and drove into the bay closest to the emergency room. *Finally.* With a slight jolt and the hiss of brakes, we stopped and the doors swung open into a huge garage structure with doors on either end. We went through sliding glass doors in the side of the building and entered the hospital. Chase remained limp and quiet in my arms, and not being able to see his face, I wasn't sure if he was awake, asleep, or even conscious.

The pediatric side of the emergency room wouldn't be open for a few hours, so Chase and I were rolled through a series of halls to the main emergency room. One paramedic good-naturedly ribbed his partner's sense of direction. "We really do know where we're going around here," he assured me.

Finally, we arrived at our destination. It was a large beige room across from the nurses' station, and as they wheeled us in, I saw rumpled sheets on the bed and a small silver table that held papers and wrappers, as if the room hadn't been fully cleaned from the last procedure. One of the paramedics looked around. "Hang on. Let me get someone in here to clean this up before we move you." He disappeared out the sliding glass doors and reappeared a moment later with a member of the cleaning staff.

Several minutes later, they gently lifted Chase off my chest, placing him in the now-fresh bed, and I hopped off the gurney to stand by his side. As the paramedics turned to leave, the last one out the door stopped. He looked at Chase for a moment and then looked at me. His eyes spoke volumes, like he was hoping for the best and had seen too much of the worst.

"I have a little one, too. Let us know how it goes."

And with that, they were gone. I never saw that man again, and I've often wondered if he ever found out what happened to Chase that day.

Almost immediately, an emergency room doctor walked into the quiet room. He was tall and freckled, wearing a white coat over his scrubs, and he carried a white Styrofoam cup filled with what I guessed was coffee. His tone was relaxed and upbeat, and though I felt he meant to be nice, in my anxious state, it grated on me.

"Hey there, Chase! So we think there may have been a seizure, huh?" I nodded silently. His voice seemed too loud for the quiet room. "Okay," he said to me, "we're gonna get you all set up in here, and then we'll do a CT scan and go from there, alright?" He shook my hand, smiled, and was gone.

Bob arrived shortly after, and we whispered softly as Chase lay in the bed before the nurse came in to take down his medical history and prepare him for the CT scan. Only one person was allowed to accompany a patient into the scan area, so Bob volunteered to go with Chase. While I waited for them to return, I called my mom to let her know what was happening with Chase and go over instructions for the children's morning routines. As we talked, I wandered into the deserted hallway and stood outside the test chamber, absentmindedly staring at a glowing blue art installation that ran the length of the wall. Tiny bubbles lazily floated upwards in backlit clear tubes, and the light from the display washed over the partially lit hallway with an almost eerie glow.

I could hear the worry in my mom's voice. "Where is Chase now? Where are you?"

"He's in a CT chamber right now; Bob's with him. I'm just standing out here in the hall. Only one parent could go in. Pray for him, okay? They said the scan takes only a couple of minutes, and they didn't want to sedate him."

"Why?"

"I don't know . . . maybe something to do with the seizure? I didn't even think to ask. Anyway, they're trying to do it now, so just pray he lies still and they can get it done quickly."

"Of course. How are you doing?"

"I don't even know. I feel numb."

"Okay. Keep me updated. Love you, sweetie." I hung up the phone, realizing that I'd been staring at the floating bubbles for several minutes.

"O God, O God, O God," I repeated over and over in my mind.

I tried to pray but could only repeat His name like a refrain. It was so still in the hall, and I had no words or coherent thoughts. I felt oddly peaceful and yet at the same time like everything was waiting to explode with no telling what the trigger would be. *Is this what trust looks like when there are no answers?*

The double doors swung open and the nurse wheeled Chase out, with Bob a few steps behind. We headed back to the room to wait for results. Bob let me know how things went, reporting on behalf of Chase. "Mommy, you would have been so proud of

Chase. Chase lay so still for his picture in there, and he wasn't afraid at all."

When I gasped in exaggerated surprise with funny faces and praise, I received a wan smile from my second son. I detected a tiny spark in his eyes again, which was definitely progress. It was clear that whatever had caused the seizure was still overshadowing him since he wasn't completely snapping out of this little fog. The nurses made him comfortable with oxygen and blankets and turned down the lights as he drifted off into a light sleep. Bob and I hovered near Chase's bed and waited—for what, we didn't know. But we waited, praying and trusting, because there was nothing else we could do.

3

ABSORBING THE SHOCK

There was a quiet knock on the glass door and my parents' friends Monica and Charlie stood outside. Because of Charlie's job, they were used to getting up very early, and they'd been my mom's first call for help. They gave us long hugs, and we all sat quietly for a minute as Chase slept.

Then Charlie stirred in his chair. "What do you guys need? Write us a list, okay? We'll go get you breakfast, coffees, whatever you need, just write us a list."

The idea of feeling hungry seemed suspended in all that had occurred, but I knew a caffeine headache would lay me out in a few hours if I didn't at least get coffee. I realized that I was still in the T-shirt and sweatpants that I'd gone to sleep in the night before— or a hundred years ago . . . I could hardly remember. I felt terribly vulnerable and undone, and I couldn't tell if it was my clothes or my heart. Caring about mundane things felt crazy and trivial in the face of a seizure, but I knew I should at least get dressed, so I added a change of clothes to the list.

Monica and Charlie left, and silence filled the room once again. I could hear my heart beating, and I had no idea how much time was passing. Bob leaned his head back against the wall, closing his eyes while I stood up and paced, staying close to Chase's bed. I knew it was a waste of energy, but I couldn't seem to make myself sit down.

"Is this taking a long time? It feels like it's taking a long time."

Bob opened his eyes. "These things take a while. We'll know soon enough."

After a while, the emergency room doctor reappeared, but it was as if he were a completely different person. Gone was the cup of coffee and loud voice, and his shoulders were slumped as he began to walk slowly into the room. Pausing, he looked at us and his eyes had an unreadable expression. My pulse began to race. *Why isn't he saying anything?*

When he finally spoke, his voice was low and unsteady, and it may have been my imagination but his eyes looked watery too. He cleared his throat and looked at Chase, who still dozed in the bed against the wall. Standing a distance from the bed, he motioned us closer and spoke in low tones, making certain Chase could not even subconsciously hear his next words.

Bob and I drew closer to each other as we saw such a change in the doctor, and looking from the bed back to us, he jumped right in. "The CT showed a large mass in your son's head." He hurried on, raising a hand to stop us from interrupting as he sensed the questions that were to come. "That's all we know for now. The CT just detected it. We have no information at this time, but I'm going to be honest with you, it's a significant size . . . I'd guess at least two or three centimeters. This doesn't look good."

This is not happening . . .

Suddenly, every part of my body felt both weighted and weight-less. My mind went into both a deep blankness and a hyperaware state simultaneously.

The doctor spoke of needing more answers and wanting to call the children's hospital downtown. He stood silently with us, as if he wanted to say more but knew words were insufficient in the shock and dawning grief. And then he touched my arm and said he'd leave us for a moment.

As the door closed, Bob and I turned to each other, almost afraid of what we'd see in each other's faces. I burst into tears and as he held me close, I felt Bob's chest heave too. Shock tore us open. My husband almost never cried . . . at least, not around me. They were unusual, these tears. They were momentary, not prolonged, because even though they stemmed from heartbreak, they were laced with the tiniest hint of relief.

I straightened up and wiped my eyes, looking straight into Bob's. "Can I just say?" I had to stop and take a breath. "This is a ter-rible thing to even think right now, but . . . *I wasn't crazy*. We weren't imagining things. Something was really, really wrong. I feel . . . jus-tified." It's strange how even tragedy can bring vindication when it comes with justification. Bob nearly smiled as he held me at arms' length. Only I would think of such a crazy thing to say at a time like this.

The lighter moment passed, and the painful disbelief hit fresh. This was heartbreaking . . . a huge mass. *How can the same thing shock you more than once?* There was a searing pain like a burn on the skin. I could feel it in my chest as I tried to breathe past it.

Why had the doctor touched my arm?

When people stand in line at a wake, they pay their respects to the bereaved, and they touch the arm of the grieving and say their condolences. The arm touch left me terrified . . . *Is this the doctor's way of saying Chase is dying?*

The doctor returned and asked us if we wanted to see the CT images. Bob and I took turns—one person staying with Chase, one going to the nurses' station to view the pictures.

Bob went first, leaving with the doctor and returning by himself only a moment later, his face drawn.

"How was it? What did it look like?"

He shook his head. "You have to see it. The doctor is waiting. Go."

Alongside the nurses' station was a small alcove. On one side was a cupboard, and on the other was a desk with a computer. Someone directed me to the computer. I stood as close to the hallway as I could, as if somehow *not* entering the alcove would make what I was about to see less horrifying. On the screen in front of me was the outline of Chase's head, and just as the doctor had explained, even though everything was hazy in this scan, there was an unmistakably large white area—the mass. As we talked, the doctor again mentioned his estimation of the size, holding his fingers to the screen, spanning the area like a measurement, but freely admitted that only an MRI would reveal the most information.

I rejoined Bob in the room, and we both just stared at Chase, sleeping peacefully. Other than being lethargic, on the outside our son looked virtually unchanged, the same Chase who, just last week, had been running through the backyard and splashing in the pool. The idea that he had terrifying, even deathly, internal issues just didn't seem real. There was a small part of me that wanted to insist it couldn't be so, though I already knew in my heart that it was true. Somehow, all those random things over the last several weeks added up to this answer, even though I didn't yet know how.

A moment later, the doctor put his head around the corner of the door. "So I've been talking to the children's hospital and we all agreed. This isn't really something we have the capacity to treat here, so we're going to send you to them for some consults and tests." He had arranged for hospital ambulance transport, and we'd be leaving shortly.

As we started to gather our things, he came back again. "Okay, so there's been a bit of an update. They don't want us to move you guys. They're sending their own team to take you, so just stay put for now. Someone will update you as soon as we know what to expect." With his words, everything entered a new level of surreal.

Why couldn't Chase be moved? Who was this special team that was coming? Just how serious was Chase's condition that he couldn't be treated here?

Nobody had answers, and so we waited.

Bob stayed with Chase as I stepped into the hall to make some phone calls. Sitting on the floor, my back propped against the wall of a deserted corridor, I heard myself say the words aloud: "There's a large mass." It somehow made everything more real as I choked them out, and my throat began to close tightly.

This is real. This isn't a dream.

Chase woke up and we must have talked to him, but I don't really remember what we said. Something about a ball inside his head that was making him sick, that he'd be okay, that he'd need to see a few more doctors.

How do you explain something to a child when you don't understand it yourself?

We told him the ambulance was coming, and he started crying because he was afraid. He didn't seem to remember riding in an ambulance earlier that morning. One of the nurses brought him a gray plush elephant to keep him company on his fun ride. Another nurse started giving us papers to sign and discharge instructions, and while I was signing the discharge papers, a third nurse stuck her head into the room. "The transport team just called in. They're about five minutes out."

Monica and Charlie arrived with our breakfast and stood against one wall, out of the way of the hurrying staff, just waiting in case we needed anything. I could see the horror on their faces.

The children's hospital team arrived with their crisp, white-and-blue uniforms. There were five of them, and they seemed encouraged to see how responsive Chase was. I couldn't help but wonder what they'd been told to expect. There were many more papers to sign, and then Chase was strapped to another gurney, alone this time, with a bunch of portable machines to monitor him.

I was riding on the transport again, so I hugged Bob good-bye. "You'll be with us soon, right? I'll need you there." He nodded.

We walked down the hall and back through the huge bay doors into the garage, and a wall of heat hit me as I squinted against the sunlight radiating off the translucent panels that made up the space. I'd forgotten the day and the weather and even the year. They swung open the doors to the ambulance, and I noticed the insignia of a child's hand etched on the window. To this day, it is a symbol of both the greatest hope and grief to me.

What we saw inside was truly astounding. The entire back of the ambulance was the most beautiful, unclinical sight I've ever seen. Every available inch not covered with medical supplies and machines was decorated with colorful decals of Disney characters. You can't feel sad when you're riding with Princess Belle and Woody the cowboy.

Chase had been somewhere between silent and whimpering, dreading the upcoming ride, but as the back doors of the ambulance swung open, he gasped.

"Chase, look! It's Buzz Lightyear!"

I pointed to a picture above the supply cabinets. "And look, Chase! Lightning McQueen is in here too!" It was going to be okay after all.

Staying closest to the door, I was harnessed into a seat with parachute-like straps that went over my shoulders and legs. Riding sideways next to two paramedics, I faced the opposite wall full of characters and supplies, and as the huge metal doors shut, I could peer through the hand insignia on the back window and see where we were while being close to Chase. We traveled in "sirens and lights" mode—the highest priority protocol, needing to cover miles as quickly as possible.

As we accelerated on roads I now know by heart, Chase heard the muffled sirens and whimpered. "Chase, don't cry. Do you know what those sirens are saying?"

Looking frightened, he shook his head. "They're saying, 'Get out of the way, get out of the way for Chase!' Those sirens are telling people to move for *you*."

My words caused the transport team to smile, and even Chase smiled just a bit. He straightened up on the gurney where he was strapped. Seizure aside, it was obvious he felt important.

I remember talking to the three women from the team who sat in the back of the rig with us. I believe we talked most of the way down to the hospital, but to this day, I don't remember what we said. Everyone was so nice, and the cadence of our conversation was only broken by the occasional "Truck!" as Chase would point out the large vehicles we passed on the highway.

We made it from the suburbs into Chicago in record time, familiar streets and landmarks flashing by. There were muffled sounds of radio communication from the cab as the ambulance slowed, and I caught a glimpse of the creamy stones of the Water Tower on Michigan Avenue as we circled past it, turned, and stopped. I could hear the sound of a large garage door opening, and the metallic alarm so often found in large cities warning sidewalk traffic to stand clear. "This is it, we're here."

As the ambulance inched forward, I glimpsed a woman standing on the sidewalk waiting for us to pass. Her long, dark hair swirled in the breeze, revealing earbuds. She readjusted her shoulder bag as she peered at our barely visible faces through the handprint on the window with frank curiosity. Her face was the last thing I saw as we pulled into the dark garage. This change in perspective was significant, and I promised myself to remember this moment.

Once I belonged to the outsiders, the sidewalk crowds who saw a passing ambulance, caught glimpses of faces inside, and maybe offered up a prayer that God be with them whatever they were going through. Now, I was the face on the inside who, for better or worse, would never know what it was like to stand on the outside again.

4

JESUS IS NEAR

The transport team led us up a winding ramp and through several hallways, each one more white and pristine than the last. The hospital had only opened the doors to this building six weeks before, and everything was shiny and new. Wheeling us through the hall of a large ER and then into a room with a wall-to-wall picture of clown fish on one side, they left us as new nurses and doctors took over, and I began to answer questions and tell the story of the seizure all over again. I knew from texts that people from church who were in or near Chicago were trying to get to us as quickly as possible, but for that first little while, Chase and I were alone.

Bob, who had not had the benefit of sirens parting traffic for his commute to the city, finally joined us, and his arrival coincided with Chase reaching his saturation level for the medical teams that surrounded him. About three doctors into the morning, Chase lost it completely and began screaming and kicking anytime anyone approached him or tried to touch him, despite the staff bending over backwards to be sweet and kind. They talked to him and cajoled him. They befriended him and bribed him and still he screamed as a preemptive first strike.

This was my healthiest child, the one who never had so much as an ear infection, and he was suddenly in a state of near constant medical triage—people and machines all around—everybody needing to touch him, checking him. He was being called to perform again and again.

"Chase, can you watch my finger? Follow it with your eyes . . . no, not your head, your eyes . . . like this . . ."

"Chase, how many fingers am I holding up?"

"Chase, can you squeeze my fingers? Hold on to my hands and squeeze as hard as you can."

"Chase, how old are you? Can you tell me when your birthday is?"

I wonder what Chase saw on that day, how we seemed to him, what it felt like to have everything change and be the subject at the center of every test and conversation at two and a half years of age.

All I remember is he just kept asking to go home.

We couldn't. There were more tests to be done. Someone said that they had to place an IV. They needed to take blood, and Chase would need fluids to stay hydrated, since it was unclear how long it would be before he'd be allowed to eat. Bob was asked to help hold him, and the nurse also called an orderly for backup. The first IV was not for the faint of heart, and everyone knew before it started that Chase would fight it as if he was fighting for his life.

I looked at Bob. His face was unreadable, his expression giving no hint of what he was thinking as he rolled up his sleeves and prepared to lay his body across Chase. There are some things that only a father can do. I couldn't watch; I had to leave. I was Chase's mother, the person who was supposed to keep pain away from him, not stand back and allow it.

The sound of Chase's hysterical screams echoed off the walls as I wandered down the hall and found a small conference room with three chairs, a small table, and a sizable window that looked down onto the street.

I perched on the wide blue windowsill of that temporary hideaway, taking in the view and trying not to think about the frenzied screams floating down the hall. Calling my mom with an update, I stepped to the doorway, phone in hand. "Can you hear that?" I asked her.

She gasped, "Oh, sweet boy, oh, Jesus, please be with him and Bob! Give them peace . . . please! Oh, Father, let them get the needle in quickly, please . . ." I could hear the tears in her voice as her feelings tumbled out in a desperate prayer, and I was filled with a frenetic, terrifying energy as my heart physically responded to the sound of one of my own children in pain.

I spoke the secret, scary words that hovered beneath the facade of adulthood: "I can't. I just can't."

Mom's voice came through the line with the strength of conviction I'd heard so many times in my life, and it was as if I were a small child all over again.

"You can and you will because you are not alone."

The screaming continued. Chase did not give up easily, but then, he never had.

While I was on the phone, Dave, the same pastor who'd spoken Philippians 4 over us on Sunday, walked past me on his way to Chase's room. Seeing him gave me a needed sense of peace. He stopped, turned around, and when I finished my call with my mom, he and I stood in that little room and talked, waiting until the IV was in place.

One of the strangest experiences is to have a conversation about a situation for which there are no good words. There was nothing he could say to comfort me, nothing I could hear to be comforted;

nothing he could ask, nothing I could adequately answer—it was all still too big and new for words. And yet, I was so glad that he'd come. Our church was like our family, and having them around us was comforting, like a thrown rope to the drowning.

Dave passed me a slip of paper with the words he had quoted at the end of his sermon. I'd loved it when I heard it, and I couldn't believe I had it in my hands right at the moment of having no good words. It felt so timely, this poem poured out from the heart of a nineteenth-century Scottish pastor, poet, and hymn writer who had lost five of his children in their youth. The words expressed something I could hardly dare to believe, but hoped to be true. *This is what I want to think when I can't think at all.*

> *I stand upon the Mount of God*
>   *With sunlight in my soul;*
> *I hear the storms in vales beneath,*
>   *I hear the thunders roll.*
>
> *But I am calm with thee, my God,*
>   *Beneath these glorious skies;*
> *And to the height on which I stand,*
> *No storms, nor clouds, can rise.*
>
> *O, this is life! O, this is joy!*
>   *My God, to find thee so;*
> *Thy face to see, thy voice to hear,*
>   *And all thy love to know.*[2]

As I absorbed those words afresh, Dave took the paper out of my hand, turned it over, and wrote "Phil. 4:5—Jesus is near." This most simple truth never ceases to be a profound and needed reminder.

I folded the paper into the pocket of my jeans and would often reach my hand in and touch it, mulling over the lines during the longest hours of what was yet to come. I couldn't bring myself to articulate the hope in conscious thought, for it was too awful to even consider thinking, but I knew it in my heart: If Jesus could stay near this pastor while he grieved the loss of five children, He would surely stay near me if I lost one.

The IV was finally in, and Dave and I went to Chase's room, only to hear from Bob that the orderly had been kicked plenty during the procedure. That poor, sweet man brought Chase another stuffed animal because, as he told us, he felt so terrible for having to hold Chase down. We sheepishly began to apologize, but the orderly waved off our words, saying something we'd hear hundreds of times more. He simply smiled at Chase with compassion.

"No, it's fine. . . . It's good, really. He's two and I'd do the same thing if I were him. Let him kick. The fight is good."

It was as if the staff knew that all they were doing to ensure Chase's well-being was also actively stripping away his sense of safety. Very suddenly, doctors and nurses had gone from the people who gave stickers after looking in your ears to people who, of necessity, had to examine and even use needles. With the insertion of the IV, they had essentially asked us to let them hurt him and to calm him and help throughout. Pain was never the goal, but it was a very real side effect, and even though it was their job and ultimately for Chase's good, they knew how agonizing it was for all of us and felt terrible for it, so they apologized.

At first, it felt odd to hear "I'm sorry" over something that was their responsibility, but I began to see that this was part of their reaching into our grief and shock and participating in the newness of it with us. As emergency room staff, they'd been through this countless times, but they knew it was very fresh and hard for us. As they absorbed our news with us, they were part of something much bigger than an IV needle or another round of tests: In the hospital emergency room that day, there was a dynamic shift in our relationship with our son. We could no longer protect him from pain. We had entered a time in which we would not only allow it, but at times, even choose it for a far-reaching good that Chase could not yet comprehend.

And Chase, a fresh needle tethered and taped to his chubby hand, with tears on his cheeks and the red of his flushed face still visible, held up his new stuffed animal prize and seemed quite pleased with himself. Despite the IV splint immobilizing one of his arms, the proud and satisfied look on his face spoke volumes as he began to understand how this was going to work. He was going to get lots of presents for enduring difficult things.

Within the first hour in this new ER, it became apparent that the tests and consults would be continuous and that Chase, though stable, was considered fragile and would therefore not be discharged, but rather, admitted until further notice. After several hours in that first room with the clown fish, Chase was finally moved to a different floor and a beautiful room overlooking Lake Michigan. Everything that had happened and was going to happen seemed to hinge on pending test results. While we waited, more friends dropped by. They brought food and big, long hugs, and they just sat with us because that was the only thing that we seemed able to do. The most important thing we needed to know for the day had already been spoken. No matter what we knew or didn't, no matter what we felt or didn't, Jesus was near.

5

Being Transparent

Later in the early afternoon, Bob accompanied Chase for another EEG as I sat with two friends—Jody and Nicole—in Chase's room. Jody had brought snacks and she encouraged me to eat something, so while I ate and we stared out at the lake, I asked Nicole, who was getting married in less than two weeks, to tell me about the wedding plans.

She laughed nervously. "Ellie, you don't want to hear about that right now, do you?"

Peeling the top off a room-temperature yogurt, I nodded. "Please. Tell me anything other than this." I gestured to the room. "It would be a welcome break for a minute."

A break I desperately needed.

"Tell me about your dress."

Nicole's eyes sparkled as she described the design. "I found it at a boutique. It's simple and perfect. And so beautiful! And you should see how Raynie is decorating the church gym for the reception. It's going to be transformed."

We talked through a few other fun details, and after a little while, they encouraged me to try to sleep, gave big hugs, and left. Grabbing a stiff hospital blanket off the end of Chase's bed, I leaned back in the faux leather recliner, made sure my phone was on in case Bob called, and willed my exhausted brain to slow into slumber.

The moment my eyes closed, there was a sound at the door. A tall man in a gray lab coat peered through the window, and when he saw me, he knocked and entered respectfully. "I hope I'm not disturbing you."

He sat down and spoke to me about a study he was doing on pediatric brain tumors and many other things that seemed in my tired brain to have no correlation to our situation. He said he was an oncologist; I wasn't even sure what that was. Remembering that Chase was in a teaching hospital, I thought this was a random piece of information, like a medical survey, so I put off this man who was interrupting my one chance to sleep.

"Could you leave the papers with me, and I'll talk to my husband?" I said. "One of us will get back to you." He passed his business card to me along with the stack of papers and left. I did not know that I'd just met a man who would become a dear and trusted lifeline for Chase and our entire family.

Sleep eluded me. Time passed and more friends from church came by, interspersed with more hospital staff with further questions. Everything and everyone seemed to be moving like a revolving door until the phone rang and Bob's voice was on the other end. He spoke steadily, but with urgency, and his tone was calm—*too* calm.

"Chase is seizing almost constantly on the table down here. They're moving us to the ICU."

"Oh, dear God . . . what? I don't understand! Is he conscious? What is—"

"I don't know. I don't know anything right now." His voice conveyed the frustration and fear we both felt.

"What floor are you on? Should I come find you?"

"No." I could hear muffled voices filtering through the phone as someone in the room with Bob passed on instructions to a medical staff person. "No, just stay where you are. Someone is coming to get you and will bring you to us—probably when we get to the ICU, and then we can . . ."

With that, he was gone, the phone connection too weak to continue our conversation. But I still had questions. *What did Bob mean by "seizing constantly"? How would they be able to transport Chase if that was happening? Should I be preparing to . . . ?* The thought of what could come next was too much.

As I dropped the phone and pushed myself out of the recliner, my legs felt like they were going to give out. *I don't think I can take any more bad news.* There were still friends in the room with me. *What should I tell them?* I could be open, or I could choose a show of strength. This was the time to either appear strong or be real and transparent. *This is it. Tell them.* It would be the first of many moments when the battle between polished faith and rugged reality would present itself. In the quietest voice, I felt a clear challenge to be real in suffering.

I repeated what Bob had just told me and then, with trembling legs, I said, "I am so scared right now, more than I've ever felt before. I can't stop shaking. Can we pray? Can you pray for me right now?"

In the middle of the room high atop the city and overlooking the shining lake, we stood in a tight circle with arms around each other, and each one of us prayed for God to be with Chase and hold us up, to give us strength when we had none. And when we finished, I was still weak and scared, but I was also known.

Hastily gathering the few possessions we'd accumulated, I was ready to go. Moments later, led by a hospital orderly, I entered Chase's new room in the ICU with trepidation. The nurse greeted me warmly. She wore a lavender scrub shirt decorated with Winnie the Pooh graphics. Surely, nothing terrifying could happen in a place where people dressed as if they had emerged from the Hundred Acre Wood.

In the middle of the big white bed, bare legs crossed under his hospital gown, sat Chase, looking just as I'd left him—perfectly stable. The only indication that anything had happened since I'd last seen him was that his head was wrapped in a turban of white gauze and there was a camera monitoring him. It was mounted on a large black tripod that stood more than five feet tall, effectively blocking one side of the bed.

He was seizing constantly? There must be a mistake.

But no, as in so much of the rest of life, appearances don't tell the whole story, and he was indeed in trauma. The EEG had revealed that his brain was having almost continuous small seizures, a reaction to the mass pushing out, like one country invading another. Unlike the seizure we'd witnessed earlier that morning, these had no outward symptoms whatsoever, and it was surmised that he had probably been having these hidden spasms for quite some time. So now they had hooked him up to a round-the-clock monitor, and a whole team of neurologists would watch video feed somewhere else in the hospital that would both confirm and track his tiny, invisible "subclinical" seizures.

I flashed back to all the times in the last few months that I'd inwardly cursed the "terrible twos"—all of that behavior during all of that time—not knowing that something had been growing and his brain had been seizing. The realization of his silent struggle was tormenting, and yet, the picture before me now was calming.

For the first time in an hour, my heartbeat slowed to something approaching normal. "Mom, they have Lightning McQueen!"

Chase had just discovered that his favorite movie—*Cars*—was available on the TV in the room. He happily sucked his thumb and tried to get comfortable on the bed, despite dozens of colored electrodes that attached him to a machine. His head was on a veritable leash of cords that kept him from moving too far.

"They have Lightning McQueen? Sweet! Hey, how are you doing there, Chasey Bear?"

The thumb came out for a brief moment, though his eyes never left the screen. "Good."

"Um, so what's with your new hat?"

"Sssssh! No talking! The movie is on!" Chase had his priorities, and even though his tone was a little bossy, I had to smile. Right there, right then, he began to adapt.

This last day in July stretched on and on. They took us down to yet another floor for an MRI, and I know Chase must have been sedated for it but I don't remember it at all. I remember being on the staff elevator going down for the scan and the tall doctor who told me about the brain-tumor study got on. He saw us and when I apologized that we hadn't gotten back to him yet, he just smiled as he got off at his floor and said he was sure he'd see us again and not to worry.

While Chase was in the MRI, I sat down and tried to gather my thoughts. We needed to make some kind of official statement to our friends and family. People were shocked and grieving for us; we were shocked and grieving for ourselves. But where would I start? What could we possibly say? There are no good words to describe a day like this day.

A nurse came in to drop off supplies while Bob and I talked. "I couldn't help overhearing," she said. "I know a lot of families like to use those medical update websites. That way, their families can log in and read anytime."

Thanking her, I turned back to Bob. "We could do something like that."

Bob shook his head. "I really don't think we need more than one thing. Let's just use the family blog."

The blog was our little place where we'd tuck funny anecdotes and family pictures. It had started as an experiment of sorts when Chase was a baby, but I'd quickly grown to love it and love writing, and Bob had encouraged me to keep it up. For me, the blog had become a way to actively practice reflection and thankfulness in thankless and busy seasons, and now it would support what was unfolding into the story of Chase.

Bob sat with me on the bench in the ICU room as we waited for Chase and commented as I wrote. We began with the obvious things: We were sitting watching the lake, waiting for Chase in his MRI, and it had now been nearly fourteen hours since the seizure and the 911 call. We found ways to list facts even though we knew nothing conclusive: The hospital was keeping him stable, there was swelling, a large mass, and there would be surgery soon.

And then, because just the very few things we did know made us short of breath, we talked through and wrote down the words of truth that we needed to keep in front of our own eyes and hearts as reminders: that God could handle our fears, that God promised peace, and that God knew and loved Chase and had known about this mass and this day since forever.

As we finished talking, I stared at the blank space awaiting a title. "What do I call this?" We both sat for a moment, stymied by the thought of summing up this life-altering day in a few words.

Bob leaned forward, looking at the iPad propped on a hospital pillow in my lap. "What about how the seizure is a blessing? If Chase hadn't seized, we wouldn't have known . . ." He left the sentence hanging, as we both felt too raw to call this terrible thing good. But he was right.

I typed the title "When a Seizure Is a Blessing," and the blog went up for everyone to read. Now our thoughts were public and live. It felt scary to let people see what was unfolding and even more terrifying to consider that we had opened ourselves up to others while we had no answers. But in that moment, we knew that what was happening to Chase was too big and too intense for us to carry by ourselves. We would need others around us to carry this and, at times, carry us. In this, transparency would be our salvation.

6

LEARNING TO LAUGH

Shortly after Chase returned from his MRI, we were joined by a group of neurologists who would follow Chase through those first days. They filled the ICU room, led by a man who was more than six feet tall, with a crisp white lab coat, an engaging British accent, and a vague resemblance to U2's Adam Clayton. As Chase ate a hot dog and french fries—his first real meal since dinner the previous evening, nearly twenty-four hours earlier—he watched his movie and tried to ignore the new doctor and team who circled him. It was not the easiest task in the world when they kept asking him to do things, like give them high fives.

The doctor explained that Chase's seizure, the one we had witnessed at home, could very well have been caused by the tumor pushing one hemisphere of the brain into the other, but that the frequent seizures that he'd had for some time were buried deep in his brain. "Not even a trained neurologist standing in this room watching him would know that he was seizing."

Just then, the doctor's pager buzzed. He excused himself momentarily, scanned the screen, and said, "You know there are other doctors watching this video feed?" He smiled. "Well, I just got a message saying, 'eating a french fry and having a seizure.'"

Immediately, all eyes shifted to Chase sitting completely unfazed on the bed, giggling at a Disney movie while eating comfort food. Even though the neurologists behind the scenes confirmed that the electrodes attached to Chase's skull registered a seizure, "seeing" how it affected Chase was both incomprehensible and quite comical.

If I ever found myself in a situation of severe neurological trauma, I'd probably want a fistful of french fries too.

"Hey, Chase, can I steal one of your fries?"

He looked at us for a second before a giant grin broke out. "No way, Jose!"

Once again the tension was eased for a moment by Chase, not the first time we found ourselves smiling. I thought back to the early hours in the ambulance, whipping through our little city's downtown. Chase, who had been quiet and lethargic, suddenly locked in on something he spotted through the window. Raising his arm, he pointed and yelled, "Starbucks!"

His outburst shocked everyone on the rig, and we all burst into laughter, a needed humorous relief filling the space. It felt good to laugh, and it felt good to hear Chase's voice and have it be something so normal. Of all the places to recognize, this boy, so clearly the child of my genes, would recognize the nearest coffee shop.

I was glad that my cousin Emily, who had been with us since we'd been admitted, was there to experience the french-fry moment firsthand. Emily was a speech pathologist at another hospital in the city, and when she had burst into the ER—my father's side of the family has a gift for grand entrances—she pulled out her pad of paper and list of questions, and made it clear that she was there for the express purpose of maintaining order and taking names. Though she said it in such a way to make me smile, I knew she really would start interviewing people if I asked. Her knowledge of hospitals and her ability to understand "medical" would prove to be a great comfort.

As we continued to converse, there was a knock on the sliding glass doors, and the neurosurgery team entered. The room was getting crowded with medical staff, and Chase's nurse joked that he must be pretty impressive, indeed, to warrant not one, but two attending physicians in his room at the same time. And we laughed again as Chase, less impressed by credentials than the rest of us, continued to ignore all the white coats around him as he wiggled around on his bed, trying not to pull the IV too tight. Dr. Alden, the man who was to be his neurosurgeon, laughed at the high-level drive emanating from his patient and explained that he'd grown up with quite a few brothers. We knew instantly that we'd like him because he understood Chase's energy.

Once the doctors left and the shifts changed, the ward became much quieter. It was after 7:00 p.m. and we were getting hungry. Emily suggested a pizza place near the hospital, then added, "Dinner's on my dad. I've been keeping him updated throughout the day, and he gave me his credit card number to get dinner for us wherever, whenever."

I couldn't hide my astonishment. "*What*? Your dad is buying dinner?"

Emily's dad, Jeff, and my dad are brothers, and there are long-standing family jokes about how far the brothers will go in regard to saving money and refusing to spend it. Family legend has it that once upon a childhood, my father, the older brother, convinced Jeff to trade his dimes for nickels because "the nickels were bigger." To this day, my father, a retired schoolteacher, swears that he's been maligned and misrepresented while Jeff, who is still active in the world of business and sales, claims that not only is the story true but he also has a bank full of nickels to prove it. The same dear uncle who taught me when I was seven how to steal a slice of pie from the freezer rather than buy candy with my allowance was generously offering to buy dinner now.

The act was bighearted and kind, and the laughter was a release valve. When my dad heard about his baby brother's gesture, he got tears in his eyes. And I think he probably would have returned all the dimes if he could have.

We had laughed in the ambulance, we had laughed with the doctors, and we were laughing in the ICU. Ambulances and intensive care wards are not funny places, but the lives that occupy them can be joyous even in the most crushing circumstances. Each time we found a reason to laugh, it felt guilty and normal and just a little like we weren't taking things seriously. However, I was reminded that where a capacity for life exists, there also exists a capacity for joy, even in seasons of intense pain. And this would prove to be a lesson to keep close in the coming days.

7

Love Believes All Things

"Has anybody shown you the MRI yet?" It was after nine o'clock, and the surgical resident dressed in mint-green scrubs and a white coat was standing at the door, asking the question. When we replied that we had not, he said that we would meet with our neurosurgeon again tomorrow and review it in detail along with a plan for surgery, but that we could see it tonight if we liked. Emily had already left for the night, and Chase had fallen asleep, so we answered that yes, we wanted to see it, for we were finding that the greatest torment was the unknown.

He typed instructions into the small computer in the corner of the room, which was mounted to a shelflike desk against the wall, and began scrolling through large black-and-white images. His deft fingers moved quickly, and the speed at which the picture slices passed was slightly disorienting. I have always had trouble understanding scan images, even needing someone to point out my growing babies on ultrasound screens, but this time, I could at least tell by the shape of the head from the CT scan that we had seen earlier that it was Chase. The resident was explaining the position of Chase's head when he stopped on a particular slice and moved the cursor arrow around the image filling the screen, but I no longer heard him speaking.

In the middle of the computer screen was the mass in Chase's head, and it was huge, bigger than anything I'd ever imagined. The white "ball" seemed to take up one whole side of his brain, so large that it had actually pushed the diseased side of Chase's brain into the other side, just as the teams of doctors had surmised that afternoon. As one hemisphere pushed, the other reacted, causing his right arm and leg to move uncontrollably. He was neurologically reacting to what can only be termed a hostile takeover.

I reached for Bob's hand as we stared silently at the screen— locked on the white mass and its ugly destructive face (for surely, something so large and destructive must have a face and a personality). For hours now, as we went through tests with Chase and met with new doctor after new doctor, I found myself whispering a subconscious prayer, "Please, God, not surgery," but now, as I stared at the image before us, although my lips did not move, I could feel a silent scream forming in my own brain. In panic, I wished that they could take him into surgery right then, even wished that they'd already done it days ago. Something this large was beyond too big for such a small boy to carry without great damage. Suddenly, invasive, terrifying surgery seemed like the only salvation. I just wanted that awful white ball out of Chase and as far away from him as possible.

Bob took a picture of it with his phone, and we absorbed the reality that it was inside Chase. As our minds filled with questions, we began something like a word guessing game with the man before us, hoping for hints we knew he could not give us.

"Can you tell us what they think it is? Or even what it resembles?"

The resident's look was apologetic. "I'm so sorry. There's no way to know that until they have a pathology report on the tumor itself."

"Okay, I get that. But can you tell us . . . are there any things they see in this tumor that even point to whether it's benign or malignant?"

His face grew sad as he kept quietly, kindly saying, "I can't say. We won't know," again and again.

In our hearts, we knew he couldn't answer us, and yet the questions came out just because they had to. His expression conveyed how much he wanted to help but that he didn't know the answers, and even if he did, he really wasn't allowed to say anything. We needed to talk to Dr. Alden, and even with his expertise, the truest answers would only come when they opened Chase's skull.

As the resident was about to turn off the computer and leave, he hesitated for just a second. "The most I can do . . . and you can't hold anyone to this . . . this is me speculating, do you understand?" He paused, his look incredibly serious.

We nodded solemnly, thankful for any hope he could give us, even fleetingly.

"I can point out here," he said, gesturing to an area of the tumor on the screen, "that there appears to be a fluid or cyst-like component to this tumor. And I can tell you these characteristics often go, not always, but *often*, go hand in hand with benign tumors. That is all I can say."

We looked at the images, at each other, at the sleeping two-year-old whose head enclosed the most insane time bomb, and we all hoped and prayed that this resident was right.

As he left, I turned to Bob, my voice lowered to a hoarse whisper in the hope of not waking Chase. "That thing is in his head! How is that even possible?"

Bob nodded, reaching for my hand. "I know."

"Is it wrong to say that I wish they could have put him into surgery, like, yesterday? Bobby, it's too big, too much . . . how is his head not exploding?"

"I honestly don't know. We just have to trust their timing."

Hospital protocol suggested that only one parent should sleep in the ICU with the patient, but with nowhere else to go, and having no desire to leave Chase, Bob and I both stayed, taking turns sleeping in shifts, one on the narrow couch, while the other sat in the armchair next to the hospital bed. Every hour, all through the night, a nurse woke Chase to check his numbers and his eye movement. Sometimes he screamed as the small light held in gloved fingers interrupted his sleep, and other times he barely woke, but somehow that first hospital night passed quickly into the next day. And in the morning, shortly after the shift changed, he managed to score a penlight from the new nurse and mimicked his nurses, using it to look into his stuffed elephant's glassy eyes.

The following afternoon, Dr. Alden and his team, including the resident, came to look at the pictures in more detail with us and present their surgical plan. Whether or not Chase really needed surgery was no longer a pressing question. His current neurological condition was traumatic, to say the least, and the operation was scheduled for the next day.

Dr. Alden scrolled through the images just as the resident had done, and he told us all the same things in much of the same cadence—pointing things out, explaining what he saw without ever indicating what it might mean. Indeed, surgery would make what we were dealing with much clearer, but the idea of standing in a room, needing to make decisions while feeling like we held only part of a picture or story in our hands was terrifying. Knowledge was needed for surgery, but complete knowledge would only come *with* surgery. And all the decisions were up to Bob and me, two individuals who must agree in order to move forward—two individuals who, up until yesterday, had never even heard of "continuous EEG monitoring."

But then Dr. Alden scrolled past the pictures of Chase's brain and moved on to pictures of his spine. Using a pen as a pointer, he gestured to multiple areas along the curvature of the column. "Do you see here? These shadow areas?" We nodded, waiting.

"It's possible that these were here previously and it is just shading on the image, but I'll be honest with you. I'm a little concerned about them, and we will be watching them. There are some tumor diagnoses where a metastasis like this is not uncommon, if that's what we're actually seeing. And if that's the case, it's something we may need to talk about at some point, but I don't think we're there just yet."

His implication was clear: Irregular cells might not be confined to the tumor. "We will keep you updated about tomorrow, but expect that it'll probably be pretty early."

After the neurosurgery team left, Bob and I sat and talked for a minute while Chase played with what was fast becoming a collection of stuffed animals on the bed. In low tones, I spoke to Bob, gesturing in Chase's direction.

"We need to tell him."

"Okay, but what? What are we going to say?"

"I don't know, but we have to at least give him some idea."

"Okay, fine, let's do it." Bob wasted no time. He got up, and the two of us went over to the bed, totally unprepared to break down these adult worries into something our son could even begin to grasp.

"Chay, Daddy and Mommy need to talk to you for a minute." Bob turned expectantly. It was on me now.

"So you know how you had that seizure and we rode on the ambulance?"

He nodded. "Sure, that was cool!"

I hesitated, searching for words to inform, but not scare. "The thing is . . . the seizure and your being a little sick in the hospital, all of it is because there's a ball in your head."

He looked up, excited. "A ball?! Really?!"

"Yes, a ball, but not a good kind. Not like the kind you play with at Grammie's house."

He interrupted me. "How big is it? Is it a big ball?"

Bob and I glanced at each other over his head for just a second, and Bob took point. "Well, it's pretty big. I'd say it's probably about the size of a peach."

Chase parroted the word, his lips exaggerating the sound as he pondered it. "A peach? *P-p-e-e-e-ach*? What's that?"

"Okay, forget the peach," Bob said. "It's about the size of a baseball. How 'bout that?"

Chase smiled. That analogy worked for him. "Yeah, a baseball!"

I was quick to interject. "Okay, Chase, I know baseballs are cool, but this one is bad. It's what's making you sick. And Dr. Alden . . ." he looked at me blankly as I quickly regrouped. "Okay, remember the doctor who said, 'Chase, can you touch your nose?' Remember him?"

He nodded.

"Dr. Alden is going to help you. He's going to get the baseball out so it can't hurt you anymore because it's a bad baseball."

He thought for a moment, his head tilting to one side as he repeated the words. "Bad baseball?"

Mugging an exaggerated frown and crossing my eyes, I repeated, "Bad baseball."

Bob nodded and did the same, making Chase giggle. "That's funny!" But he sobered quickly. "Hey, Mommy, Daddy. Is it going to hurt me?"

Oh my word. How do we even . . . Once again, Bob and I exchanged glances over Chase's head.

"Oh, sweet boy, hey, listen to this. It's going to be okay. They're going to give you some medicine that will make you sleep, and when you wake up, it'll be all done."

Chase thought for a minute and nodded his head slowly. "Okay, deal. Like magic?"

My throat tightened as I looked at Bob. "Yep. Like magic."

And there it was in those moments. Belief. The resident who trusted that the tumor was benign despite medical knowledge, the parents who trusted he was right even as we were forced to hold his words with open hands. The tiny boy in the bed who trusted that the bad baseball would come out like magic, believing the words we laid out for him. How like the love of God to manifest itself here. We believed the best of each other and held on to belief for each other because that's what God does for us. It's His love that believes all things, endures all things, and never fails—in this we were and are secure.

8

We Were Never Created for Separation

It was Wednesday evening, August 1, and it had been close to forty-eight hours since we'd left the house and our three other children behind. Because we were in the ICU, the kids could not visit us, but Bob and I were grateful that our church family had surrounded them. I'd been getting texts from various friends with pictures attached of Karsten crawling, Darcy playing, and Aidan eating a meal—the types of things Bob and I would see on a normal day. Even though my parents were there to oversee their care, people had gathered in the kids' suddenly parentless state, keeping them busy and happy. The pictures sent throughout the day were tiny visual gifts, helping us be close to them even when we felt worlds apart.

Because there had not been time to pack when everything first happened, we made do with the little we had on hand. I washed my hair with a hospital baby shampoo sample and tried not to think about my other babies, especially my Karsten, who was still a

nursing eight-month-old. It hurt my heart and my body. The decision to stop nursing had been ripped from my control the minute I
climbed onto that gurney with Chase. Bob and I missed the other
children terribly and wondered what they thought and how they
felt with their world turned upside down.

By this time, Darcy and Aidan knew as much as Chase did—
that the bad ball had to be removed. That was why the ambulance
had come for their brother. But there had been no face-to-face time
where we could see their expressions and answer their questions.
Out of necessity, we had instructed their grandparents to tell them
about Chase's condition quickly before they were inundated with it.
For both the grandparents and children, those hours and days were
such a commotion that nobody remembers how that conversation
happened or what was said. What everyone did know was that it
felt torturous to be separated. *If we could only hold them in our arms
right now.*

Chase's surgery had been scheduled for early Thursday morning,
so late that Wednesday night the staff brought us papers.

Sign here for consent to perform surgery.

Sign here stating that you understand the risks of surgery.

Sign here to confirm that you understand he may not make it
out of surgery.

Sign here to say that we can bill you for this horror.

And on and on it went. Because the hospital had just built
this new facility bearing a new name and insignia, there was a
crazy moment that seemed like something Radar O'Reilly from
*M*A*S*H* would request: We had to sign and initial papers stating
that we understood that the papers we'd just signed were on letter-
head with the old name and insignia.

Finally, they brought us the brain tumor study papers again—
another copy of the same papers I'd been given by the doctor on the
first day. The study would not hurt Chase or take anything from

him unnecessarily, and if Chase's case could assist the doctors in helping others, how could we not?

That night the nursing staff continued to monitor Chase hourly, and our sleep was fitful, often interrupted with the quiet comings and goings of staff checking in. At 3:00 a.m., I awoke and could not go back to sleep. I sat cross-legged on the faux leather couch against the window and took in everything in the room. Bob dozed in the recliner with a light blanket thrown over him, and in the bed, Chase lay spread-eagle with cords on almost every appendage, machines clicking and purring softly all around him. I could hear quiet voices and footsteps in the halls that never slept.

In just a few hours, they'd open my son's head and cut into his brain. They'd open the head that I birthed and cradled—and cut into him to try to save his life. And should he survive the terrible, ferocious war to wrestle his brain from the clutches of this life-eating pariah, they had informed us when we signed the papers that they might have to remove healthy parts of the brain to kill the sick parts and how that removal might change who Chase is—mentally and emotionally. In other words, even if he survived, there was a chance that the personality of the child we knew and loved would in some way cease to exist on the operating table that day.

For a moment, I hugged my knees to my chest. I'd read about people who went into that posture when they were shocked or grieving, and I found myself doing it now. It was the one way my body could emulate my heart with its desire to curl in on itself, to somehow shield itself from this day. Finally relaxing, I pulled out my iPad and started writing a good-bye. I didn't know if I'd see Chase again or if he'd still be my Chase. The brain is extremely delicate, and its reaction to trauma is often so inexplicable that nobody could tell us the most likely outcome.

The confession of how badly I wanted to find a "normal" in all of this poured out of me onto the page. "There is no normal. There is only Christ. I'll see you on the other side, Chasey Bear." I typed the final words in deep, silent sobs as I watched him sleep. Surgery day was here.

A few hours later, as the sun rose over the lake, the calm atmosphere in the room became energized. Nurses moved quickly around Chase's bed and room: typing things into the computer, unwrapping his head, removing tubes and cords, trying to remove all the residual adhesive on his skin with warm washcloths. We were going forward into a great unknown, and it produced a raw feeling of powerlessness in the pit of my stomach that only seemed relieved by movement. I wonder if this is why people pace when they're nervous.

Bob and I worked together with Chase—distracting him from his hunger pangs, playing with him, talking to him—but we hardly spoke to each other, saying little more than "How are you doing?" answered by "Fine." We were in agreement on the course of action and our love for Chase, and that was all that we had the capacity to handle. The days in which we'd be able to articulate our feelings and grieve over the moments we were living were still weeks away. Right now we focused on breathing. Somehow the preparation for this surgery felt like preparing for death.

We were escorted from the ICU to the surgical floor. In the pre-surgical area, people in mint and powder-blue scrubs came in one after another and introduced themselves while they watched Chase and compared him to their notes and charts, asking questions we all already knew the answers to.

The biggest question of the morning was whether Chase would need a mild sedative to calm him and help him forget that he was being separated from us. Two-year-olds rarely go with people they don't know, and Chase was no exception. It was a rule that we had taught all of our children to heed. How would he react? We would not be allowed to follow him into the operating room, not even to make him comfortable.

At that moment, a short, larger-than-life personality burst in, his strawberry-blond hair with just a hint of gray sticking out from under a surgical cap. His name tag said he was "Dr. Roth," and his loud, jovial voice greeted us, or more specifically, Chase. Dr. Roth's eyes stayed on Chase as he introduced himself as the anesthesiologist, and when Chase backed away, he bent down so his burly elbows rested on the edge of the bed.

"Hey, Chase," he said, his eyes twinkling. "Would you like to hear about the time I put a gorilla to sleep? A real, live gorilla! It's true!" Suddenly, we were all transported to a zoo by his words. The small room we were in disappeared as we were pulled into the story of this anesthesiologist, his encounter with a large primate, and the crazy hope that the "sleeping medicine" would keep the gorilla from waking up. "After all, a gorilla can be very cranky when it wakes up in a strange place."

Reaching into his lab coat, Dr. Roth pulled out an anesthesia mask and said to Chase, "Do you like strawberries?" He casually tossed the mask onto the bed next to Chase.

"Go ahead," he said, "play with it. Doesn't it smell like strawberries? Have fun. I'll be back shortly."

Chase only had a few cords attached to him at that moment so we sat on the bed enjoying the opportunity to hug and be close to him. I kissed his head despite the goo from the electrodes that hadn't been totally washed off and touched his cheeks that were still too rosy from all the steroids. We played with the mask and giggled together because we were still thinking about the zoo and not about surgery. Chase held the mask up, sniffed it, made a face, and then passed it to me. Sliding my glasses onto my head, I put the mask to my face as Chase, with thumb in his mouth, giggled and Bob grabbed his phone for a picture.

That was the final moment captured before we said good-bye. What do you say to someone in that moment when nobody knows what will be coming next? I don't know. I've stood there, breathed there, and I still don't know. We talked about the sleep that was coming and taking out the big, bad ball and other little things you say just to fill time. Only one thing remains excruciatingly clear to me from those moments: I don't think anyone is ever fully ready to say good-bye. Separation is painful, even if the person lived a full, long life; I don't believe we were ever created for separation.

The red-haired doctor was back. This time he spoke to us over Chase's head and said that he had something to induce sleep and lessen Chase's anxiety about leaving us, but he wasn't sure if Chase would need it. He told us to kiss Chase and say our words while he was still there.

Bending over, I kissed his smooth forehead, wanting to remember every second of this time. "I love you, sweet boy. I love you so much." Bob followed, kissing and hugging his son while I watched silently. There were so many things that we wanted to say, deep and important things, but we knew we had to keep it lighthearted. So Bob and I kissed him and loved on him as if we were tucking him into bed for the night. For Chase, this was nothing more than a magic nap to remove that bad baseball. I believe Dr. Roth could sense how lost we felt because as we finished, he quickly turned to Chase and invited him to kick his outstretched hand as hard as he could—the perfect distraction.

Chase, who'd spent nearly two days being told *not* to kick doctors, shrieked in glee and obliged, kicking the large hand. Dr. Roth grunted in feigned discomfort, saying, "Wow, you're so strong! Do it again!" This routine continued for a moment or two as orderlies quietly entered, unlocked the wheels on the bed, and began to move it silently forward. The orderlies looked ahead as the doctor walked backwards, one hand on the rail of the bed, one hand outstretched against Chase's foot. And that tiny boy on the bed stayed focused on the doctor's antics and continued to kick with all his might. As they passed through the doors leading to the operating theater, the anesthesiologist never looked up but continued in a singsong voice, speaking to Chase even as his words were meant for us: "We're just fine. We're going to be just fine now. And we'll be back soon."

And with that, the sound of my precious boy's laughter faded with the sound of rolling wheels down the hall, and we were left in the empty room of baseballs, gorillas, and wishing for just one more minute.

9
FEELING INADEQUATE

Absentmindedly, I watched a sunbeam come through the tall windows of the waiting room, stretching through the narrow alley that separated the children's hospital from the high-rise next door. It warmed the clinical white floor and continued up the equally white wall past a round metal clock as we started into the third hour since Chase had been taken to surgery. Bob kept himself occupied with mindless tasks on his laptop, and I sat with Emily and my two childhood friends Laura and Kathryn, who'd both made the trip downtown for the day. We talked about silly things, inane things, anything to *not* talk about, not even think about, how completely powerless we were to help or comfort Chase right now.

Just then, Wendy, the brain tumor coordinator, came to find us with an update. Her role was not unlike that of a wedding coordinator, taking all the moving pieces and fitting them together flawlessly for the big day, except the big day was more somber than joyous.

Wendy was amazing and calm, and the few times we'd spoken with her, we drank in everything she said—this morning especially, as she was our only link to Chase right now. She'd been to the operating room. Maybe she'd even seen him. I felt hungry for her words.

"Dr. Alden just wanted to let you know that things are going really well. And actually, they're preparing to close now, so it won't be too long before he comes to find you." She strongly emphasized her next words. "And you need to know that Chase is doing great."

I couldn't stop the questions racing through my mind. *After only three hours in surgery, they were preparing to close? Didn't brain surgeries always go for at least double that time? What happened?* I posed these to Wendy. She reassured us that Chase was doing well, but she couldn't answer our questions and only reiterated the promise that someone would be out to talk to us soon.

Nearly an hour passed after she left, but strangely, the minutes flew by as we waited for news. Finally, Dr. Alden entered the room, still in his surgical garb.

"Is he okay?" The words tumbled out of my mouth as he stood in front of us and everyone leaned closer for his words. He nodded and then gestured for Bob and me to follow him from the room. "Why don't we find a quiet area where we can talk?" He ushered us into a tiny conference room.

For us, that tiny room would hold life-altering words.

Dr. Alden motioned for us to sit and we did, both willing him to speak and terrified of what he'd say. As we settled into the chairs, he began to explain. "The first and most important thing you need to know is that the surgery itself went well and Chase did great." He paused and let us take it in. Chase was okay.

"The second thing you need to know is that the resection was successful. The tumor was very close to the surface of the skull; so close, in fact, that we were able to cut into the skull and start removing it almost immediately."

We stopped him with what was now the biggest question on our minds: "Were you able to take the . . . I mean, did you remove the whole . . . ?"

He nodded graciously, knowing what we were having trouble articulating. "Yes, I was able to remove the whole mass." And then he stopped short, saying no more for just a second too long. The good pieces of news had brought with them a rush of relief, but there was an unspoken caveat that hung in the air like a palpable threat. We waited for the rest.

"During surgery we were able to send a sample of the tumor to pathology." And then, it came: "According to the preliminary pathology findings, this tumor appears to be malignant. We won't know for sure until the final pathology comes back, but it holds many of the characteristics of the metastatic diagnoses I mentioned as we went over the MRI."

Numbness set in with those words, and while no tears came, a terrible lump formed in my throat. But Dr. Alden wasn't done. I could sense the heaviness of the news by the compassion in his eyes. "When we opened the skull, there was the tumor, and as I said, we were able to successfully remove it, but there were also tumor cells on the subarachnoid layer."

Bob and I glanced at each other for the briefest of seconds. Even though some of the words were distinctly foreign to us, the concept resounded like a peal of thunder. There was more. The removal of the tumor hadn't been enough. "Basically, there are tumor cells on the surface of the brain."

I drew my knees to my chest. I could feel my body shaking as Bob asked, "Were you able to remove those cells too?"

The doctor leaned forward in his chair. "I was able to look at one or two, but they were all over, too numerous to be removed safely." These words felt like death—the growths were too widespread to be successfully removed. They covered the top of Chase's brain like a fine dust. He paused again as if to let us absorb this new piece of news and then continued.

"Based on what we found today, I believe we may need to look at the areas of shading on the spine as well. It's quite possible that those are cancerous cells." This wasn't a single destructive object; it was a complete infiltration. *Oh dear God . . .*

There have been certain moments in life when I wished to cry and could not, times when the hurt was so large that crying seemed too light, and this was one such moment. The pressure of this news seemed to suck the air out of the room.

We tried to sort through the hundreds of questions, both rational and not, that flooded our minds. There were few answers other than the surgery findings. The conference room was set aside for the telling of the news. Many more doctors would plan the next steps. At one point Bob asked if we'd be allowed to see the tumor. Dr. Alden seemed surprised by the request but offered this gentle counsel: "I don't know if that would be wise. For some things, it is better to keep a slight distance."

We wrapped up the conversation, thanked Dr. Alden, and went back to the waiting room and our anxious friends, who had surmised by our long absence that the news was less than optimal. We answered their questions as best we could, and someone suggested we pray. My eyes were burning, and my throat felt fiery and constricted, and as Bob reached for my hand in prayer, I could feel his shake ever so slightly.

Sometime later, we were led back to Chase's room in the ICU. As we were escorted down the hall of the ward, I could see that the privacy curtain to the sliding glass door of Chase's room was open, and there were at least two nurses working in the room as we walked forward.

Chase was screaming and fighting them amid cords and

monitors. He wore only a diaper, and he seemed so vulnerable. Suddenly, he saw us and got up on his knees in the bed, his hands clutching the side railing, screaming: "I want my mommy! I want my daddy!"

The nurses were startled and even chuckled a little at his spirit and strength. It wasn't until many months later that we would fully understand that when the brain is cut into nobody can say how it will react when it's closed. Sometimes children are unable to talk or move for some time afterwards, if at all. The smiles on the faces of the staff stemmed from the profound relief that he was definitely talking and moving.

It took a while to get him calm. For his safety, he needed to be still, and as he lay in the bed and cried, I could see the broken trust in his eyes. Not too long ago we'd been talking about sleeping gorillas and baseballs and playing kicking games with doctors, and the next thing he knew was unspeakable pain. An ugly, puckering scar covered his head from the hairline above his left eye all the way back to the crown and down almost to his neck and ear. The stubble of his dirty-blond hair, which had been quickly shaven prior to surgery, stood out amongst the white gauze and purple blood stains of his scalp. It was terrifying to see him like this.

We looked to the staff for help; we didn't know how to comfort a child we weren't even sure we were allowed to touch. He seemed to want to run away from a pain he couldn't escape, and the confusion and agitation radiated from Chase as he squirmed on the sheet.

Someone encouraged us to come closer to him, and in a moment of great cowardice, I deferred to Bob. "You go, okay?"

He looked questioningly at me. "Are you sure?"

I was sure. I felt physically ill. As I stood by the end of the hospital bed, my son seemed broken. He was bloody and swollen and broken, and I was so weakened by how much he was altered that I didn't know how to tangibly be close to him. The bonds of comfort through which we'd always communicated were torn.

Bob silently moved to the bed, let down one of the railings, crept onto the side of the bed, and balanced his nearly six-foot frame against the very edge so that his presence was felt without touching Chase. He whispered quietly to him, things I couldn't even hear, and Chase's voice calmed to a whimper, his lips still curled in pain and confusion. Bob remained there, just so Chase would know that someone was close to him as he rested and finally slept.

Though Chase had made it through the initial surgery well, there was a potential complication developing. A small pocket of his brain was filling with blood and fluid, and the surgery and neurology teams were still worried and monitored him closely even though his head was closed. Even a small pocket could grow quickly, causing pressure and seizures, and so for the first several hours after surgery, we sat in fear that at any moment, Chase might need to go back into the operating room to drain the fluid and release the pressure on his brain.

At 5:00 p.m. that same evening, he was taken for another MRI to check the progress of the swelling. And while my brain felt nothing, my body had absorbed enough. When I felt so faint that I couldn't stand, a nurse got a wheelchair, and she and Bob took me back to Chase's room in the ICU. Everyone was gracious and understanding, but I felt deeply weak and inadequate.

How could Bob still be standing? And all the other parents in all the other rooms? Why did I have to act like a giant baby who couldn't handle anything? My internal voice was a condemning bully. The truth was that we'd been more awake than asleep for nearly four days straight.

We were instructed to lie down and rest, as there was nothing to do while Chase was in the MRI. Wendy came again and sat with me for a few minutes. "Ellie, you need to rest." She took my hand.

"It feels counterintuitive to take care of yourself when Chase is suffering, but you need to. For Chase's sake."

She gestured to Bob in the recliner with just the slightest smile, her voice gentle with nearly tangible compassion. "And you need to do this for Bob, too! The last thing you need is to pass out or get sick yourself. How do you think Bob will feel if he's splitting his time here with Chase in this hospital and then going across the street to visit you in another hospital? The best way to be strong for Chase is to use these times when you're not with him to take care of yourself. This is a marathon, not a sprint, and exhausting yourself now will not help Chase in the long run." With that, she gave me a big hug and left.

Bob, who seemed physically unfazed by the long day, promised to stay and rest with me. I curled up on the couch, my face to the wall, and within seconds it hit me: This was the first time since the surgery that it was just the two of us, the first time we'd stopped moving and talking and being talked at in three days of hospitals, and here I was on that stupid couch because my body had failed me when I needed it. I began to cry.

At first, the tears were soft and full of self-pity, but then I started thinking, and the condemnation of nearly passing out vanished in the crushing reality. *Chase. Malignant. Spreading tumor cells. No answers.* The tears became heavy, deep sobs that I couldn't muffle despite my balled fist pressed to my lips.

In an instant, Bob was next to me, and just as he'd comforted Chase, he comforted me, holding my shoulders while I sobbed, telling me it was going to be okay—that we were going to be okay. We sat like that for some time, him holding me while I cried, me repeating, "My boy . . . my sweet boy . . ." almost like a prayer. And after Bob prayed for us, I could not take any more or cry anymore, and both of us fell asleep for a few minutes.

And then the most needed reprieve came: A sleeping Chase was wheeled back into the room. His condition was stable, the swelling had subsided, and Chase was actually doing well enough to be moved out of the ICU the following day. There would be no more surgery that night.

What was unfolding with Chase—the surgery, the scans, the days on end of stress and decisions—all of it carried so many moments of me feeling woefully insufficient. On some level, this trial he was enduring was holding a mirror up to me, displaying how weak I was, how much I fell short when he needed me most.

As a parent, I had relied on expressing my love through physicality: a pat on the head or back, a kiss on Chase's chubby cheek, holding his tiny hand in mine—and suddenly, all of that changed drastically. His head was wrapped and attached to cords and machines, his hand was barely visible under an IV needle and tubes, and his back was covered in a third set of cords attached to a computer, which monitored his heart, pulse, and oxygen. Three of the four sides of his bed were blocked or covered in medical impediments; the only way to even attempt to stay close to him was to crawl into the one open side of the bed, leaving a few inches between him and me. It wasn't comfortable for either of us. All the cords made Chase nervous; he'd cry out at any movement, fearing someone might inadvertently pull or tear at something.

Relational bonds and physical bodies felt broken, and in facing the knowledge that Bob and I had little left when this battle was barely getting started, we were confronted again with our own weakness. There was nothing left in us to face a malignant, spreading tumor. The only thing we could possibly do was turn to heaven and, like David, say, "My refuge and my fortress, my God, in whom I trust" (Psalm 91:2, ESV). Our ability to keep surviving would have to come from a source far greater than our powerless selves.

10

LEARNING TO LIVE IN GRACE

On Chase's surgery day, family and friends from our church had been dropping in to be with us, and when Chase was back in the room and sleeping, Bob and I took turns sitting and talking with them in the waiting room. A few friends left the hospital to walk down the street to the Disney store, returning with small gifts for Chase. There was shared pizza and needed support. It was disarming and amazing to feel so connected to other people in such an isolating, difficult moment. When the hospital security guard came by to say the visiting hours had ended, despite the shadow of malignancy and so much still unknown, it was with full hearts that we said our good-byes until the next day.

Just then, our senior pastor and his wife arrived, having cut short their summer vacation since I'd first called after Chase's seizure. Clergy are not bound to restricted visiting times in hospitals, an inexplicable acknowledgment to the One who knows no such limitations either.

The four of us—Daryle, Jean, Bob, and I—stood in the dark around Chase's bed in near silence. Chase had finally fallen asleep, his face and head turning more puffy and discolored with each hour as fluid rushed to the place where his head had been opened. Earlier, when Chase had realized he couldn't hold his "La La"—a small security blanket—next to his face like he normally did at bedtime, we folded two of his favorite "La La" blankets, each about a foot in length, on both sides of his face, so that he could feel them against his cheeks. Despite his pain, he had finally slipped into a drugged sleep, completely unaware of our movements in the room.

Finally, Daryle broke the silence. "Ellie, as we were driving in, God kept bringing something to my mind, and I think it needs to be said." He gestured to the bed where Chase lay and hesitated for only a moment. "*This* has nothing to do with decisions you made."

I caught my breath and wished I could see Bob's expression across the dark room. I knew exactly what Daryle meant. Somewhere, in the back of my mind, I had questioned whether the decisions he referenced were in any way connected to why we were here, going through all this.

Some seven years earlier, before I'd known Bob, I'd found out I was pregnant. The man who would have been a father had urged me to terminate the pregnancy, and when God graciously stopped me from even considering it and drew me to His side with the most incredible love, the man had washed his hands of our relationship and walked away. I never heard from him again.

I was picked up and protected by my family and church as the Lord grew closer and changed me, all while a tiny girl grew and changed in my womb. And less than a year after my beautiful daughter of grace was placed in my arms, Bob came into my life, saying words that reflected God's great redemptive love, a healing balm for my pain and scars. Bob fully accepted my past, coming to love Darcy before he knew he loved me.

Within another year we were married, and Bob adopted Darcy, almost like a fairy tale. But here, going through this with Chase, from the moment we first heard, "There's a large mass," terrible, self-destructive thoughts had whispered vengefully around the edges of my consciousness.

I have a beautiful daughter and an amazing husband, but maybe this is the moment of reckoning for past sins. The moment where I'm paying, we're all paying, for what happened. Maybe Chase is sick because of those decisions I made and all the ways I messed up.

It sounds strange, and as I write the words down, it seems illogical and implausible to listen to such thoughts, but I had been listening and hadn't even realized it until the moment Daryle spoke. No amount of medical reassurances erase the "*What if?*"

"Chase's tumor isn't a sentence for wrongs that have been done," Daryle said. "It is a statement that we are all fallen, we are all broken, and have been since Adam and Eve. What is happening to Chase, this tumor and its diagnosis, is part of a sovereign, gracious plan that far exceeds what we know and understand at this time."

Standing around the bed, we began to fit our thoughts and feelings into the only grid that would make sense in the days to come. First, there was no condemnation, because Jesus covers our sins with love, and this cancer wasn't recrimination of any sort. Second, His love takes us down paths we would never dream of entering by our own volition as part of His sovereign plan for our lives. Once again, we were known. I didn't have to listen to my secret thoughts; everything was laid out in the open and then covered by grace.

We talked about the surgery and the day in general, and when words seemed about to run out, and in truth, when we were about to run out because we were coming to the end of our strength and ourselves, Bob posed the best and most pressing questions. "How do we do this? How *can* we do this?"

Daryle's answer came with great clarity and has shaped everything since. It was so dark in the room, save the eerie glow of monitors, that we couldn't see the expression on his face, but his voice—this quiet, calm voice that spoke the Word on Sundays, the voice that had spoken to us in marriage, adoption, and a hundred other things since Bob and I first met—filled the room with gentleness and confidence.

"There is only one thing you can do," he said. "The only choice you have today and in the days ahead is to live in a moment-by-moment dependence on the grace of God to see you through." Steadily living in this dependence would be the only way to survive.

He unpacked the idea into practical terms for us. "How will this look? Exactly like it sounds. Ellie, Chase will cry, and all you have to do in that moment is pick him up. Bob, the doctor will come in, and all you'll have to do in that moment is speak to him and answer his questions. You can't think about tomorrow, where you'll be next week, or what the next year will bring. All you can do is take this, by the grace of God, moment by moment." Every inhale and exhale was its own moment of grace with no expectations for the next breath.

It sounded too simple, this breathing in moment-by-moment grace, but sometimes when the wind is knocked from our lungs and we become filled with condemnation, doubt, and grief, we forget what it takes, or we remember, but it feels painful and impossible to act on it. For the first time, we considered the blessing of broken-ness in its ability to pour us out weak and worn, if we would let it, at the very feet of Jesus—the only place we should ever really need to be. If we could stay there forever at His feet, despite all that was yet to come with Chase, we'd do more than survive—we'd thrive.

Our need to live life in moment-by-moment grace never ceases. More than once, I have been ashamed to admit that standing in an ICU room over the bed of my son wasn't enough to forever embed in me the lesson of living in total dependence on God. The truth is that selling a house, putting kids in a new school, stretching finances to the limit, keeping up with the endless amount of dishes—all of these things and many more—still open me up to the same stress and fear of the unknown, not unlike a large brain mass had done.

We will never find a circumstance in which moment-by-moment grace is not both desperately needed and graciously, abundantly given by the One who knows us best. No matter what your hard thing is in this moment, inhale and exhale and trust that the most beautiful grace will meet you there.

11

WHEN LIFE STOPS BUT WE KEEP BREATHING

A normal two-year-old boy is active, but a two-year-old boy on steroids is a sight to behold. Someone had to stand or sit next to Chase's bed at all times to make sure he didn't fall overboard in a fit of slightly off-balance energy. Only four days after his brain surgery, Chase's pain was being managed with just the slightest medication, the areas of fluid continued to recede in his brain, and continuous monitoring indicated that not a single seizure occurred. By this point we had been informed that more intervention against the remaining cells would be needed, and while we felt deeply blessed by what could only be termed a miraculous recovery, we anxiously awaited our discharge and the upcoming meetings to learn what would come next.

Chase did get an occasional reprieve from staying in bed. If someone carried him and sat right next to him, Chase was allowed to make brief trips across the room to sit by the windowsill overlooking the lake. He and his favorite neurosurgery nurse, Amy, would do just that. As we waited for Chase to recover and counted down the days until his next steps, Amy was waiting and counting down the days until her boyfriend, a US Marine helicopter pilot deployed overseas, returned. One day, Amy brought Chase a toy replica of the AH-1W Cobra Attack helicopter that her loved one piloted far away, and the two of them sat on the windowsill and "flew" it over the lake.

On the fourth post-surgery day, Bob had to return to work, so Darcy, Aidan, and Karsten all stayed with various friends from church while my parents joined me and Chase at the hospital. The *Cars* movie played on a near-constant loop, despite Dr. Alden teasing Chase by saying that he had removed the "*Cars* part of the brain," so Chase should really find a new movie to watch. Chase sat cross-legged on the bed, one arm wrapped in an IV stabilizer lying across his lap and the other pushing toy cars over the hills and valleys of sheets and pillows with Bapa by his side.

As my mom and I watched the antics, the tall doctor who had dropped off papers with me on the first day came in with a woman whom he introduced as a research fellow.

"We were wondering if you might have a moment to talk."

"Of course," I said.

"Actually, is there someone who could watch Chase?" he asked.

The point was unspoken but could not have been clearer: They didn't want Chase to hear their words. The moment suddenly felt very big, and I felt very small. *If only Bob were here.* The doctors paused at the door.

"Since Dad isn't here . . ." (Before they learned our names, all the hospital staff referred to us as Dad and Mom) "is there someone you'd like to come with you?" My mom silently raised her hand.

I took Chase's hand. "Chase, I have to go talk to these doctors for a few minutes, okay? I'll be right back. You get to stay here with

Bapa!" Chase, who'd had more than enough separations and terrible surprises, had recently been clinging to my arm in fear whenever a doctor arrived.

"But Mommy, will you come back to me?"

"Of course, sweet boy. We're just talking. No needles or anything, and Bapa will stay with you the whole time, okay?"

"No more nap with the doctor?"

"None whatsoever, my sweet boy. Just watch Bapa and make sure he behaves, okay?" I winked at my dad, forcing an atmosphere of gaiety that nobody but Chase actually felt. Relinquishing my hand, he giggled and sank back onto the bed.

Mom and I accompanied the doctors down the hall into yet another small conference room. This time, I knew why we were here. These doctors were going to tell us about Chase's tumor.

"So as I mentioned already, I'm Dr. Rishi Lulla, and this is my colleague, Dr. Rebecca Loret de Mola." We took a seat, my mom and I on one side, the doctors on the other, and as I took out my tablet to take notes for Bob, Dr. Lulla laid his hand on the table to stop me. His voice was gentle. "Don't worry about taking notes. Just listen. I'm going to write down everything that gets said here today." And then, in bold black ink, with surprisingly legible script, he began to sketch and write as he talked, and with his voice came the sound of the other shoe dropping.

He explained who they were and that the two of them were heading up Chase's neuro-oncology team. *Neuro*—relating to the nervous system, in this case the brain and spine. *Oncology*—a branch of medicine that specializes in the diagnosis and treatment of cancer. He was the doctor tasked with trying to eradicate the cancer from my son. *Cancer*. It wasn't just a tumor. Chase had cancer.

My eyes darted around the room, afraid to make contact with anyone. And it wasn't just any cancer—it was the one they had most

hoped it wasn't when everyone saw the first MRI. Atypical teratoid/
rhabdoid tumor or AT/RT. As he said the name aloud, all I could
think was that it was a strange name for a cancer, and it sounded
more like some kind of angry dinosaur. *Atypical* . . . as if there were
such a thing as a brain tumor that was typical.

As Dr. Lulla began to lay out some of the specifics of the cancer,
I only half listened. There was only one thing that I cared about.
Just tell me if Chase is going to live.

I heard frightening words: The cancer was vicious, malignant;
it was spreading and was often characterized by sudden recurrence.
The doctors alternated speaking as Dr. Lulla continued to write
down brief descriptions on the sheet in front of him. I felt like they
were holding back—not hiding facts, but giving me simple details,
only as much as I could mentally or emotionally handle—similar
to how Bob and I had been protecting Chase when we told him
about his tumor.

This cancer made its home in the central nervous system, attack-
ing the brain and sometimes the spine, too, but in some cases, particularly ones in which there was a genetic component, it attacked
the kidneys as well. Chase would need to have his kidneys checked
immediately, and pending those results, our other children might
have to be tested as well.

This might not stop with Chase. Dear God.

There was to be a whole team overseeing Chase's care, multiple
teams, in fact, and we'd have a designated nurse who would set up
all our appointments and next steps.

Dr. Lulla reached across the table to reassure me. "The most
important thing to remember is that you will never be alone in this.
Think of us as your safety net. We'll be there every step of the way
for anything you need."

Once again, the terrible lump sat in my throat. I have no recollection of it now, but my mom told me afterward that I drew my

knees in to my chest and was visibly shaking. All I remember is wanting desperately to keep from crying because this conversation was too important to disrupt. And dear God, how I desperately wanted to know his chances for survival.

"The thing with AT/RT is that it's still a relatively new diagnosis. So there are really only two options available to us right now." Dr. Lulla drew a line down the middle of the paper. "The first is a recently published chemotherapy protocol led by doctors in Boston, though I think we could definitely do it here. They're actually seeing some success with it, but it's involved and intense." His words struck on something I'd never even considered: We might have to leave our home and even our state for treatment. *Could we actually do this?*

He paused. "The second option is a clinical trial . . . but it's still new enough that they aren't to the point of knowing results. In reviewing this case with the brain tumor board here, we really feel that the first option is the best one for Chase. But I can't stress this enough—it needs to be what you and Dad feel most comfortable with because you know Chase best." He paused again. "Do you have any questions for us?"

I finally worked up the courage. "If I can ask . . . If you can tell me . . . What is the percentage of survival?"

There was the slightest hesitation as they looked at each other, possibly questioning whether it was wise for me to know. Dr. Lulla nodded to Dr. Loret de Mola, and she leaned across the table and spoke the truth. "Given the placement of the tumor and how far it had already spread before it was discovered, we would probably place the survival rate at 20 percent." *Inhale, exhale . . . 20 percent.*

"I honestly . . . I just . . . wow, 20 percent?" I found myself both crushed and oddly encouraged because the number I'd been imagining as they'd described the cancer was significantly lower than that figure.

Dr. Loret de Mola's eyes were full of sympathy, and then she threw a lifeline into the sea of terrible words. "I know this is hard to even consider, and I know that statistically it's '20 percent,' but all that matters is that he's here with us now. So the better way to think about numbers is this: Chase is either 100 percent with us or he isn't. Right now he's 100 percent here, and that's all that matters." I felt a slight release to the lump in my throat. No matter what came, Chase was still here now. Somehow, I needed to try to remember that truth.

Since we were on the subject of difficult questions, I went for broke. "This protocol out of Boston—the better option—may I ask, if you had a child in a situation like Chase's, would you do it?" They both said yes, and I believed them.

Dr. Lulla continued. "The protocol is hard. It requires a lot, and there is also Chase's quality of life to consider, but we need you to know that we would not be suggesting this if we didn't think it was right for Chase. I . . . *we* really feel that this is Chase's best shot."

He put up a hand to wave off my immediate response. "Don't answer us now. Talk it over with your husband, and we'll meet again in a few days because we don't have a lot of time. AT/RT is definitely something to start addressing right away. And in regard to quality of life . . ." He paused again, as if searching for the best way to state his next words, his posture changing slightly as he emphasized a crucial point.

"Like you, we only want what's best for Chase. Whichever option you choose comes with difficulties and risks, but I want you to know that our goal as his team is to do things for him. The moment any intervention turns into us just doing things *to* him and not *for* him, it's time for us to have a different conversation."

As we talked further, I learned that they wished to send Chase's tumor to Philadelphia to be studied by a geneticist and his records to premiere facilities in New York and other cities for more opinions and other possible options. Within a week, all would report back with their recommendations for the first option from Boston—the hardest road through treatment—which would be completed in Chicago. So we sat in that conference room, which had become a war room, and talked and planned while "ground zero" was down the hall playing cars with his grandfather.

I remember wanting them to know Chase as I knew him and wanting them to understand what a stubborn fighter he was. I opted not to share how he'd stared down a truck, but I told them about the time Chase tried to jump off a couch over Karsten's head, and we laughed a little.

I removed my glasses and passed a shaky hand over my eyes. "I'm so sorry. I shouldn't be laughing when we're talking about cancer. I think this is just how I'm coping."

But both doctors smiled. "You know, I'm glad you're bringing that up because this is something we wanted to talk to you about anyway," Dr. Lulla said. "One of the things we love most about our patients is their incredible resilience, and at times, you may see us laughing or playing with Chase or other kids because they're alive and we're celebrating it. I just don't ever want you to mistake our joy expressed with the children as a callous attitude toward the cancer or treatment. We will always take the cancer seriously."

We were a team now. After promising to be in touch very soon, the doctors left, and I stood in the hall next to my mom. I couldn't go back into Chase's room—not yet. Having spoken about chances of survival and quality of life left me feeling permanently altered, and I knew my face would give me away if I saw my precious boy right then. The thought of going into the room and looking at him with his clear, trusting brown eyes—knowing all the while in my heart that I might need to say good-bye to him soon—was too much.

When I finally reentered the room, Chase was still sitting up on the bed. His skin was puckered and swollen around the stitches, but already it looked so much better than at first, and with his swelling-induced black eye, he looked up and smiled. "Mom! You came back to me! Come look at this bridge we built!"

His totally unaltered attitude encouraged me to be still and find joy in that moment, and somehow I smiled back and kept breathing. The gravity of the situation would come and go like waves for weeks, but in this moment, the greatest problem in front of me was where to park the tiny cars on the sterile white bedsheet. We were going to survive.

That afternoon we were discharged from the hospital, and because Chase could barely stand on his own, we decided it would be best for our family to stay with my parents for a few weeks so that we could have help. That night, after everyone was tucked in under the same roof, Bob and I sat at the dining room table of my childhood, and all the words from the meeting were repeated. All the scary words and diagrams and notes the doctors had written came pouring out, making my heart feel old and worn.

Ever the calm one in a serious crisis, Bob was quiet, only stopping me a few times to ask a question.

"What do you think? What do you want to do?" I finally asked.

He didn't answer immediately; I knew he was collecting his thoughts. "I feel like . . . it's just that as long as Chase is doing well, we should do everything we can for him. Even if it's the harder way. Don't you think so?"

"I'm terrified of what it's going to mean for Chase and our family, but I'm with you. As long as Chase is alive." I had to stop for just a moment to catch my voice and breath. "As long as Chase is alive, let's do everything we can. And if he . . . if it doesn't work, there will be no regrets. We will have done everything there was to do."

Bob leaned forward. "Okay, let's pray about it overnight and just let it sink in. I still need to talk to Dr. Lulla, but we're agreed—this is the direction we're leaning, right? We're doing this?"

I nodded. "Oh, dear God, give us wisdom."

Bob pushed back from the table to get some water. "Okay, so now we need to let people know what's going on. How much do we actually want to tell them about the diagnosis? Should we say the name?"

I shook my head. "If we do, people are going to look it up online; do we want that? I know this sounds mean, but I don't want people projecting things we haven't been told yet, and I really don't want people coming up and crying around Chase and the other kids. I really, really feel that the best way to deal with his life right now is to make the most of it. We absolutely can't bury him while he's still alive."

As I talked, I realized that Bob was at the computer. "Bob, are you looking? They told us not to look . . ."

"I know."

As we stared at the screen, unable to pull our eyes away, we saw the gist of what I'd been told earlier in the day, and we also saw some of the outliers and speculative words they'd tried to keep us from when they'd reminded us that Chase was still here and that was all that mattered.

This was a rare cancer with only about thirty new cases a year. The phrase "long-term survival" was used to describe living sixty to seventy-two months with the disease—five to six years. That was considered "surviving." The numbers were someplace between abysmal and terrifying. The percentages of survival were seemingly linked to and lowered through a specific series of markers—based on the tumor placement in the skull; if the cancer had spread beyond the skull; if the child was under the age of three. Looking at what the Internet had to offer us, even though we logically knew that not everything could possibly be true or true of Chase, it felt like the most awful gut-punch all the same. And with the words on the screen came terrible doubt: *How could he not die?* Statistically speaking, everything was against him.

"Oh my word. Should we tell people all this stuff? Should we actually lay this out for them?"

Bob sighed. "You know what? No, I don't think so. We can say the name, and people can look it up if they want to, but Chase is here. That's all any of us need to think about right now. Let's put in a link to Wikipedia or something, but let's not . . ." He searched for words.

"I don't want to sweep it under the rug, but this isn't something that anyone needs to deal with right now because we honestly don't know what's going to happen. If it comes to it, we'll deal with it then. Let's just focus on Chase tonight."

Late into the night, we sat together at the computer, trying to put the diagnosis and its implications into conversational words, and occasionally, when our hearts grew faint, we'd bring up pictures of Chase—a happy Chase with no swollen scar arcing his head. Bob's friend sent him an e-mail with a song attached: Matt Papa's "I Will Trust In You My God (Hymn In A)." We listened to the words, drinking them in, these words that reminded us that God's plans are not the same as ours and that He's with us through every moment.

In that moment when faced with an impossible treatment decision, when neither option seemed plausible, the hardest thing was to let God be God. From our earliest days as human beings, we are bombarded with rhetoric that encourages us to fight anything we don't understand. It is strength to never give up and never give in; it is strength that remains unbending under greatest duress.

Surrendering to something—anything—is most often considered failure. It signifies that the force has won and we are weak.

We intended to fight the cancer and fight it with all we had. I'm not talking about submitting to the disease itself, but rather fighting the presence of it in our lives. We surrendered Chase's life to God, not to the cancer. The disease was far too present to reject and too big to fully comprehend, but God was even more present than mutating cells and good beyond tumors and treatments—and it was to this that we submitted. A dear friend of mine has told me many times in rough moments, "The only way out is through." So the decision came that night to submit, walk through, and take from God's hand this that He'd allowed as part of a plan that we did not and will not ever completely understand until we see His face.

There would be no rest from the reality of the cancer, but our peace that night came from trusting that God knew things we didn't about Chase's life and made promises that He would faithfully keep, even though the keeping of them looked nothing like what we had imagined. This was the only way we'd keep breathing.

12

SEARCHING FOR SHELTER

We jumped into the cancer fight headfirst, pursuing the recommended course of treatment. The day before it was to start we were called to the hospital for meetings and exams to make sure we understood what was going to happen to Chase and to make sure that he was strong enough after his surgery to begin what lay ahead.

The hospital sits on the edge of the city and the lake, and the cafeteria is halfway up the building, beautifully designed as a tranquil place for the families who spend their days living inside the walls of the building. Two-story glass walls and ceilings create the effect of stepping into a greenhouse high above the streets. The scene felt oddly peaceful with the sun-warmed glass walls, even when the area was packed with patients and families and staff all gathering to eat. As we sat at a small yellow table, Bob and I talked while Chase picked at some food. He was distracted, both excited and nervous to be back in "his hospital."

Being parents to four active children should have taught us to pay attention, but as we talked, we completely missed that Chase wasn't sitting in the middle of his chair. Little by little, he had inched his way to the left until, suddenly, he keeled over and fell to the tile floor, hitting his head.

"Chase! Are you okay? What happened?"

Chase responded by wailing pitifully, refusing to speak.

"Chasey Bear, can you answer me? Where does it hurt?"

Under normal circumstances, a parent would pick the child up, check for any visible injury, hold him and comfort him for a few minutes, and then they both would move on. But when the parents hadn't slept well in days and the child had undergone brain surgery and wouldn't stop crying, we didn't comfort him and move on—we called the neurosurgeon.

Chase turned out to be fine, and an unexpectedly pleasant result was that our appointments got moved up a few hours because all of Chase's doctors wanted to make sure he was okay. He'd been on their radars for only about two weeks, and already he was finding his own way through hospital life and interactions. Chase's neurosurgeon, Dr. Alden, who first discussed the reality of the tumor with us, stood in a clinic room and actually laughed a little at Chase's antics. Despite being slightly unsteady on his feet, Chase bounded around the room in his little blue shoes and tried to climb the tables and chairs. It's hard not to laugh when you watch a child, who by all accounts should be lying in a hospital bed, pick himself up—scars and all—and try to run around a room. There is a pure joy of life that comes in those moments. And so it was, in a moment of laughter, we were cleared by neurosurgery to begin treatment.

Moving to a room across the hall, we sat in the neuro-oncology clinic, seeing doctors we'd already met and meeting others who would be on Chase's team. We spent a large part of the time with Chase's new nurse-practitioner, Kristi. Bob walked a now-restless

Chase up and down the halls of the clinic as I sat with Kristi in the room and went over the plan for his first chemotherapy and the drugs he'd need to take. She already had a large binder put together with the plan, and in a patient voice she laid out what I absolutely needed to know.

All told, there would be about ten different chemotherapies that Chase would need; sometimes, as many as five would be given on a single admission. She had a fact sheet for each one and placed them in front of me to go over. On the sheet was an explanation and pronunciation of the drug, along with a list of side effects divided into likely, less likely, and rare—rare often being terminal.

Under the list of likely effects for Chase were things like hair loss, hearing loss, possibly permanent loss of feeling in his fingers and toes, skin sensitivities, nausea, vomiting, and fevers, to name just a few. Effects that were less likely included neurological complications and damage to organs. I could hardly bring myself to think about the list of things that rarely happen. Kristi went through the explanations as slowly and graciously as possible, given the information.

"We will also need to schedule an EKG for Chase—to get a baseline on his heart. As long as he's on this one," she pointed to the paper describing a particularly nasty drug, "we'll check his heart every six months."

I excused myself to find a bathroom, and when I found one down the hall, I locked myself in it and stood against the wall in the silent little room. I felt like I couldn't breathe, and I started having chest pain. I could hear Bob and Chase in the hall, but I needed a minute. How was this possible? We were living in a time when I could fit my entire life into a flat little phone that lay easily in the palm of one hand, but here we stood, hearing nearly barbaric side effects of experimental treatments and being told that this was the best possible choice. It wasn't the fault of the doctors here—we'd talked to multiple specialists at premiere facilities across the country. *I shouldn't have to decide. I shouldn't have to decide between saving his life and damaging it irreparably.*

The information we'd read about AT/RT was still fresh in our minds, and life had started to feel like a free fall with no ground beneath. There was a terribly long string of revelations constantly coming at us, and it had begun to feel like situational vertigo. After a while, it was nearly impossible to tell which way was up and which was down. And the crazy part of these days was that Bob and I felt both clear and yet tormented in our decisions. We knew what we needed to do for Chase, but we dreaded doing it.

Two weeks after the brain surgery, after all the teams had cleared Chase, chemotherapy began. As we'd learn more fully in the months ahead, when the brain is home to such an aggressive cancer, there is rarely full recuperation. Waiting to treat it any longer than absolutely necessary gives the destructive disease an aggressive advantage. We'd declared all-out war on the battlefield of Chase, and so two weeks to the day of his surgery, stitches still puckering the surface of his head, we went back in for more.

The morning was one of those late summer days when the sun rises early and the sky is clear and the heat has yet to come. We packed Chase into the backseat of the car with our suitcases. We'd been home for only about a week and now we'd be gone again.

As Bob got the car ready, I hugged Darcy and Aidan closely. Aidan was happy to be at Grammie's house again, but Darcy was old enough to start questioning.

"What are they going to do to Chase? When will you be home? Can I call you if I need to talk to you?"

I held her close. "Of course you can call me anytime, Sister! Look, they have to give Chase some medicine to try to kill the cancer in his body, so this is going to be hard, but it's also good because everyone is working to help Chase." I paused over the hardest question yet. "I don't know when we'll be home, but I'll let you know as soon as I find out. Be good for Grammie, okay? Be her helper . . . I love you."

All the drugs that Chase required would be far more than what an IV in his hand could withstand, so the team had set up another surgery to insert an intravenous central line. They'd cut into his chest and attach an IV deep into a vein close to his heart. He'd keep that central line for the duration of his yearlong treatment. Surgery was scheduled for the morning, and that same afternoon they would start chemo. No recovery necessary, no time wasted. He'd be fine after the anesthesia wore off, and he'd be carefully watched, so there was no point in waiting. While he was under anesthesia, they would do a spinal tap to confirm the presence of cancer cells and then they would inject the first chemotherapy—directly into his spine.

Many times when a person is forced to do something terrifying in his or her life more than once, when the scary thing is faced again it somehow loses its hold because it becomes familiar. You find that the thing you dreaded wasn't so terrible after all. Not so when you are sending a child to surgery. We've hated it and feared it every time, and while, on some level, it becomes more physically simple as we know the routines of the surgical floor and staff, it seems more mentally and emotionally daunting to leave our child yet another time.

That first day of chemo as we prepared for Chase's routine surgery for the central line, it wasn't just us standing in the room, but also the ghosts of us from two weeks prior, saying good-bye before the brain surgery. Those memories should have held no power over us, and yet they were so strong and carried so much emotion that the simple act of being back in those pre-op rooms was enough to bring both of us to tears.

Chase accepted his "nap with the doctors" as a normal part of his life; the only indication that anything had changed was when he grew very quiet. In order to help with any pain or separation anxiety, the staff requested that a parent carry Chase back to the operating area, which Bob was more than willing to do. A surgical nurse ordered Bob to "suit up" in a surgical mask, a hairnet, and a funny yellow jumper that covered his clothing. Pretending that he could barely move, Bob marched stiffly around the tiny pre-op room, and Chase burst into fits of giggles as he watched—the perfect way to go into surgery if you must.

"Be brave, sweet boy." I kissed his head as he nodded, acknowledging my words, and then Bob swung Chase up into his arms and they were gone.

Beginning Chase's cancer treatment required total immersion, not unlike arriving in another country without knowing the language. When Chase was released from post-op, his chest was wrapped in tape and gauze and had a funny-looking white tube that split into two parts with blue caps on the ends. His chest looked scary with all of the medical paraphernalia protruding from it, and once again, just like we had experienced after his brain surgery, we weren't sure how to safely relate physically to him when these nonflesh things became a part of his person. We were taken to the oncology floor and shown into a beautiful room overlooking the lake, and a few minutes later a tall woman with blonde hair and a beautiful smile came in.

There is a way nurses enter rooms that communicates they know what you are going through and they understand, and this knowledge radiated from her. There was another girl training with her who quietly shadowed her every move. Together, Jenny and Megan went through the room introducing us to the space and telling us what we'd need to know next. The surgery had gone well, Chase's blood pressure and pulse looked good, and his chest was nice and clean.

Jenny put one pink bucket for vomit at the end of the bed, say-ing, "He'll need this," and then she dropped another one on the floor, pushing it with the toe of her shoe into the corner under the television.

"I'm going to need you to save his diapers. Just put them in there." Seeing our questioning looks, she continued, "We will need to weigh them to make sure his kidneys and bladder don't slow down too much."

Pausing, she let us take in those words and then moved on. "Also, when you change him," she gestured to an area by the door where various boxes of gloves hung in dispensers. "You're going to need to wear gloves . . . *every time*. But don't wear the blue ones. You'll need these," she said, pointing to the highest box that was filled with purple gloves. "These are special gloves that will protect your skin from toxicity as you change him."

Bob stopped her. "What happens if his kidneys or bladder *do* slow down?"

"Don't worry. We are going to run fluids to hydrate him until his output reaches a certain level before we even hang the chemo bag, and then we'll continue to monitor his output every hour over the eight hours the chemo will be running. And . . . if . . . *if*" she stressed the word as if to communicate the lack of probability, "his bladder was to slow, there's another medication we can give him to counter the effects."

This was a new level of shock and horror: to realize that the very remnants of the chemotherapy that would be given to Chase could potentially slow or shut down his organs and was so toxic that it could accidentally harm us if we came in contact with it. Jenny saw the looks on our faces and stopped, the first time she'd been still since she entered the room. Her voice lowered a little and her eyes softened as she looked at us, *really* looked at us, and said, "It's going to be okay. It feels like it won't, but it will be. I promise."

Two nurses were present when they hung the first bag of chemo. Chemotherapy has so many serious implications that it required constant accountability. Over the next few days, we'd learn that there must always be at least two nurses in the room, that the purple gloves must always be worn, and that some of the bags are even carried into the room in light-sensitive coverings because sunlight would compromise the fluid inside. The nurses would hang the covered bag from the IV pole and then hook it to the tube in Chase's chest. One nurse cross-checked the other aloud as they read the information on the chemo bag, Chase's bracelet, and the computer.

"Name? Date of birth? Patient number?"

Finally, the nurse called out the name of the drug to be injected and the exact dose to be given. It was a strange chant that echoed in the room, and we'd hear it so many times that we could say it with them. As I write these words and remember those days, I can hear the sound of their voices still.

It only took a few hours for Chase to figure out that the nurses on the oncology floor loved the kids and that he had to expend little effort to be a giant flirt. And so with Bob's help, that first afternoon and the next morning, Chase began to roam the halls of this new home (as leaving the ward was not allowed) in nothing but a diaper, a pastel hospital gown, and bright yellow socks with puffy grippers on the bottom. He held Bob's hand, and Bob held the IV pole, keeping Chase's cords slack and away from his feet. It didn't take long for the two of them to find their rhythm.

The nurses at their station would watch to catch his eye. "Hey, Chase!"

He'd look away quickly, despite a glint in his eye. "Nope!"

"What? You don't want to say hi to us?"

His eyes would sparkle, and then there would be a full-blown cheeky grin as he'd continue to ignore them. "Nope!"

But he wasn't fooling anyone; everyone knew how much he

enjoyed this because he'd pass the station again and again, just for the pleasure of telling them no.

The effects of the chemo quickly caught up with Chase, and in less than twenty-four hours, it began to hit him so hard that he stopped walking the halls. He, my child who had never been still, suddenly didn't want to leave the room, and when he would move it was with a restlessness that signaled his growing discomfort. He wanted to be held as much as possible and would spend long periods of time in Bob's arms, his scarred head resting on his father's broad shoulder; his eyes, though open, were unseeing and weary, holding just the slightest look of confusion. It was heartbreaking to see.

Nearly every day Dr. Lulla would stop by for a few minutes to check in with us, offering counsel and letting us know what to expect. Yes, Chase was getting weak, but that was completely normal for what he was being given. He was on track, given the course. And while Dr. Lulla tried again and again to connect with his patient, Chase remained in a serious state of angst toward doctors. Most visits generally ran something like this: Dr. Lulla would enter the room and greet Chase. Chase would scream. Dr. Lulla would call him "dude" or "Dr. Ewoldt." Chase would scream. Dr. Lulla would ask him what he was doing/playing with/watching. Chase would scream. Dr. Lulla would leave the room. Then Chase would giggle and say, "I like Dr. Lulla. He says 'Dr. Ewoldt,' but I'm not a doctor . . . but he's my friend!"

Nearly as soon as the chemo started, Chase's appetite waned, and after only three days, despite medication to help combat nausea and vomiting, meetings with a dietician, and constant coaxing to eat something, Chase stopped eating and drinking altogether. Painful sores covered the inside of his mouth and throat—one of the first of the side effects. By the time we were discharged, after multiple discussions with his team, it was determined that Chase needed to have a prescription for IV nutrition. He would be hooked up to the nutrition IV bags for twelve hours of every day. We didn't know this at the time, but it would be sixteen whole months before he'd be able to sustain his own body with regular food. For now, everything centered on keeping him as alive as possible.

Our hearts longed to be home with our other children, and we eagerly counted the days until we would be discharged. On the morning of the fifth day in the hospital, we pulled Chase out of the large cupboard by the picture window in his room that he'd grown fond of climbing into and put him on the bed to finish his fifth and final chemo drug for this round. Jenny was on duty, and as she finished the chemo and detached Chase from some of his cords, she pulled back his hospital gown to check the dressing around his central line, as each nurse did routinely throughout his or her shift. Today it seemed that she looked closer than usual, and then, with quick, deft movements, she began to feel the area around the port despite Chase's protests. As she lightly pressed around the tube in his chest, a bright fluid oozed out and discolored the gauze. She immediately felt Chase's forehead for fever.

What would unfold in the next few hours was intense and rare and only added to our feeling of free-falling. As doctors and surgeons with worried looks came in and out of the room, we learned that Chase's central line had become infected and would have to be removed and replaced immediately.

To this day, nobody knows if the infection was caused by a contaminant or whether Chase's body was reacting to foreign materials. All we knew is that this had the potential to get extremely terrifying with an infection being introduced to his body while his immunity had dropped from the chemo. What was happening to him was not common. *Chase, common? Ha!* As the day continued, the prevailing sentiment was that we had every right to be upset at this complication. Chase had gone through enough, and this was one thing too many.

There was a beauty and security in watching the staff around us—our new extended family—react protectively to Chase and this newest obstacle, and yet, it felt nearly comical to start being upset with a faulty central line and a third surgery in two weeks. This latest setback felt like the cherry on top of a tall confection, piled high with things that we had the right to be distressed about. And so, on Tuesday, August 21, only days since his last surgery and the beginning of what would be months of chemotherapies, Chase went back into surgery to replace the central line. When the line was removed, Chase's chest was stitched up tight, and another smaller line was sewn into the underside of his arm, slightly above his elbow. Within hours of the surgery, we were finally allowed to go home.

There had been no respite for us since we'd learned Chase's diagnosis, and for a minute, all the craziness was suspended as we felt the joy of being reunited with our family. We were free for two days before we had to go back to the clinic to see the doctors and get another brief chemo injection. The team had arranged for all the supplies we'd need at home to be delivered to the house before we arrived. They'd also promised us there would be a home health nurse who would walk us through Chase's at-home needs.

I knew I'd like this nurse almost as soon as we met. Her name was Phyllis, and she had a deep faith and a complete understanding of home health care. She knew crazy things off the top of her head, like how to stuff a clean baseball sock with uncooked rice and turn it into a heating pad by warming it in the microwave. She also not only put up with, but laughed at the well-worn jokes my dad told, and that endeared her to our family right away.

Preparing an IV bag had a strange rhythm to it, not unlike the hospital nurses verifying chemo protocols, and Phyllis's teaching style was strong and matter-of-fact as she stood at the dining room table stacked high with various supplies. She washed and gloved her hands and began to go through the motions of preparing the IV bag, all the while speaking evenly and calmly while I watched.

I looked at Bob, who was standing on the back porch, watching the kids playing in the yard. "Bobby, do you want to come and do this?"

He turned, and for a second I saw the faintest hint of the same impish smile I'd first seen when we were dating. "Nope. You've got it. I took Chase into the OR, so why don't you do this . . . and then you can teach me how."

Mentally cursing his cleverness in slipping out of the tutorial, I turned back to the table and the sound of Phyllis's voice.

"Now, you'll need to time this because you'll take the injection port—the white plastic cap at the base of the bag—and you're going to swab for fifteen seconds, dry for fifteen seconds, inject, mix, and you'll need to repeat that for as many times as you have something to add to the bag." I furiously started taking notes.

"And then when everything is added and mixed just so, you'll need to get all your supplies to a place where he'll be able to sit quietly and you can lay things out. And it needs to be clean. You must never do this in a bathroom or kitchen." She looked around the room.

"Like that couch over there. That'll work. You'll need all your supplies—alcohol wipes, saline flushes, and heparin—and you also need to make sure you change your gloves. You should not be wearing the same pair you used to mix the bag." I felt the tightness in my chest again.

"If anything touches skin, the ground, or anything other than the end of his central line, you need to throw the syringe away and get a fresh one. Everything must remain uncontaminated."

She lifted the bag and walked it over to the couch, preparing to attach it to Chase. "Now, here's how you remember the order: S-A-S-H. It goes saline, attach, and then when you take the bag off, saline, heparin. SASH. Just remember that in between each thing you attach, you need to remember to swab for fifteen seconds and dry for fifteen seconds. This will help cut the risk of infection."

Most of the words she said were foreign to me, but I repeated the order until I memorized the pattern that would become my lifeline. It was too difficult to wrap my head around the fact that I was actually pushing something into Chase's body and pushing back the blood in a vein. The responsibility in my carefully gloved hands left me feeling slightly sick.

"Oh my word, Phyllis, I don't think I can do this."

She chuckled quietly, an oddly comforting sound. "Tomorrow night, you'll prepare the bag while I watch and help, and two nights from now, you'll be doing this by yourself, and I won't even need to be here."

Although it sounded crazy, she was right. Within two nights, working as a team, Bob and I attached our first solo bag, and in the next months, we'd do it so many times that I still have dreams about doing it now. I'm pretty sure there's still a box of old saline flushes lying around this house today.

For all my years as a mother, I would often go to the back porch door to call children in for dinner, but on this evening, I went to the door to call a child in for his IV bag. The normal-but-not-normalness of it all bordered on the surreal. But then I spotted Chase. He was running slowly around the backyard, trying to keep up with his siblings, wearing a dark-green washcloth on his head and carrying a kitchen spatula in his hand.

Smothering a nearly hysterical laugh, I called out into the yard. "Chase, you need to come in now! Miss Phyllis is ready to put on your bag." He ran toward me.

"Also . . . where did you get that spatula, and why do you have a washcloth on your head?"

He refused to give away his source for the kitchen utensil, which almost positively meant my dad was involved, but Chase looked up at me with the clearest of expressions and said, "I gotted the wash-claf for my baseball." He pointed to his head. "It itches."

Of course it does. Of course you did. Why not? The logic of a two-year-old is surprisingly difficult to refute.

After the bag was safely attached and Phyllis left, I wanted to sit up late reviewing the papers and understanding the pump and the IV and how to help Chase, but I knew I needed to rest. Aidan was undergoing his own little surgery at our local hospital early the next morning. I had scheduled a tonsillectomy for him back in the spring, long before we knew anything would happen to Chase. And so we went from one hospital, one surgery, and one son to another hospital, another surgery, and another son in less than twenty-four hours.

Aidan wasn't excited, but he was oddly expectant. At only three years of age, he'd watched the events unfolding with his brother and perhaps been a little envious of the attention and gifts, and so he welcomed the early morning run into his own operating room because he'd be a little like Chase. We were fast becoming a family with some serious hospital bragging rights. It was getting to the point where the person with the most ID bracelets won.

The next morning as Aid was wheeled out of his own pre-op bay for his procedure, both Bob and I felt so ready to be done with surgeries. It felt like it had been weeks and weeks where we'd been looking for a break, some relief, anything . . . and all that came at us were more complications and more of the proverbial deep ends into which we kept being thrown.

A short time later, a nurse called me back into post-op, and I lay on the bed next to Aidan as he slept off the anesthesia. When he finally woke, the nurse came over to check on him, and he uttered a single hoarse word through the pain and swelling in his throat: "Stickers." Aidan has always known how to get the best deal in a situation, and you better bet that little boy got a whole bunch of stickers.

We brought Aid home to rest, and before we cut off all the hospital identification bracelets, Aidan and Chase began to compare "war stories" and who had the most Band-Aids covering IV punctures.

"Chase, look. I got a needle in my arm like you."

At this revelation, Chase gasped. "Aidan, do you have cancers like me?"

Aidan was quick to shake his head vehemently, and both boys sighed in relief. Chase's sigh held just a hint of pride, even though his perceived advantage was actually a terrible thing. Aidan decided that his lack of cancer meant he was still beating his younger brother at something.

"But did you have surgery like me too, Aidy?" Chase's words sounded excited as he examined the brightly colored Band-Aid on his brother's arm. "Were you brave like me?"

It took a moment to realize that Chase equated the small adhesive on Aidan's arm with the surgery itself. But their conversation was too precious to be interrupted with adult truths in this moment.

"Yes!" Aidan exclaimed hoarsely. "And I got a blue-white-red Popsicle *and* stickers!"

For one moment, Aidan won and Chase stomped off to find Bob and demand why he hadn't been given stickers as well. Aidan decided to take his victory and run with it.

"Mom? Um, since I just had surgery like Chase, can I lie on the couch and watch movies all day?"

Early the next morning, Bob, Chase, and I left the recovering Aidan and the rest of the family to go back to Chase's hospital for more chemo and meetings. During this visit, as he had done on a couple of other occasions, Dr. Lulla mentioned something called the "nadir." He explained that it was the deepest point of each chemo cycle, the moment when the drug is working strongest, and the numbers of blood cells are the lowest. The nadir is often highlighted by fevers, and Dr. Lulla assured us that based on the particular drugs Chase had already received, the nadir could be pinpointed to a window of ten to fourteen days from the time the chemo had been given. These words were spoken on the eighth day.

Feeling rather skeptical, I raised a question. "What if Chase isn't prone to fevers? In fact, I don't think he's ever had one. Will there be other signs to watch for, in case he never gets a fever?"

"Well, each child is a little different, but usually you see a significant drop in their energy, and most children do get fevers." Dr. Lulla absolutely knew what he was talking about, but in our complete ignorance, we assumed that since Chase had never had fevers when he was sick, he was unlikely to begin now. So we dismissed the doctor's words of caution, not flippantly, but definitely thinking we probably knew best. And we returned home that Thursday, excited to enjoy the whole six days before we had to come back for more chemo.

On Friday Bob's parents flew in from Portland and my sister Carrie came up from Tulsa. For the first time all week, nobody had to be in any hospital, and it was amazing.

That morning, Carrie, a teacher at heart, gathered the older kids for a project. She took them out into the backyard, covered their hands in acrylic finger paint, and had them make handprints on sheets of crisp white paper. Carrie had the kids press the heels of their hands together, splaying their fingers so that the final result resembled wings. In truth, Darcy's looked like still wings, Aidan's looked like blurred wings, and Chase's handprints hardly resembled wings at all because he had no patience for such things.

The kids spent some time drawing in the bodies of butterflies, and then, as the paint dried and the artists ran through the yard screaming and giggling with their paint-covered palms, my sister knelt by the papers and wrote phrases from "Beautiful Things," a song by Gungor that would remind us that we weren't facing any of this alone: "All this pain . . . I wonder if I'll ever find my way . . . you make beautiful things out of us."[3]

I stood over the prints and snapped a picture. I wanted to remember it forever. When we can't find shelter and the pain in life hurts and we fight it hard, there come the moments when we realize we can only find true shelter in a Loving Hand. And even as He lovingly cradles us close, God allows the hard things to shave away the layers of sin and self until we will be, like the apostle James said, perfect and lacking in nothing, complete . . . *beautiful*.

As I turned I saw Chase—wobbly, unsteady Chase—who'd grown tired of all the artwork and decided to attempt feats of daring instead. He had come into the living room, stripped his shirt after painting, stacked a small plastic chair on top of the soft couch cushion, and climbed on top. And there he sat, rocking on the unsteady chair perched too far above the hardwood floors, laughing at something on the TV.

"Chase!"

"What? I'm being careful!"

"Chay, what would Dr. Lulla say if he could see you?"

The impish look he threw me was his way of saying it would be strange for him to be anywhere other than teetering on the brink of another disaster.

"He'd freak out."

This is Chase. He will always push the boundaries of safety and sanity just a little bit. I think he would find life terribly boring if he didn't.

The next morning was Saturday, and while Carrie went running, my sister Meg came to visit. Chase played for a bit, but we could tell that the chemo was slowing him down. It was as if a switch had been flipped, and the energy was suddenly draining from his body. He dragged his IV bag—zipped into a portable black satchel with its pump—across the room with him, and just walking the length from the kitchen back to the couch, a distance of maybe twelve feet, was enough to wind him.

This was day ten. The reminder about the chemo nadir came back like a shadow, and we found ourselves watching and waiting. When we had talked through the protocol with our medical team, Kristi had urged me to watch Chase but not stalk him with a thermometer. Her words had seemed odd at the time but now snapped into clarity as I fought the urge to check him every few minutes.

By midmorning, Chase was lying on the couch, and within a short time, his cheeks warmed with the first fever. I cracked open my binder filled with instructions and numbers. The hospital had given extremely specific instructions on what to do in case of fevers, details pinpointing fractions of a degree of temperature. A fever itself wasn't terribly dangerous, but for a compromised child such as Chase, who had a tube protruding from his arm and recent surgery wounds on his head and chest, a fever could be a sign of an infection. Because the chemo had killed his white blood cells, we were given no choice but to transport him to the emergency room if he reached a certain point. Infections move fast and fevers spike; time was of the essence.

Chase's temperature rose from 99 to 101 as we threw clothes and toiletries into bags. The oncologist on call had confirmed what we'd been prepared to hear, but I wasn't prepared for the additional warning: We were to drive Chase to the city as long as he was stable, but if for any reason Chase's condition became less stable, we were to pull over immediately and call 911. This was serious.

While we packed, Meg kept watch over Chase. When she had first received word of Chase's diagnosis, even before he started chemo, she'd bravely shaved her dark, curly hair for Chase so that someone he knew would be bald like he would eventually become. She was secretly thankful for what she termed a "low-maintenance hairstyle," and she and her husband both waved off our words of gratitude for this selfless act. Her sacrifice was a beautiful gift to us, a tangible way to join our suffering and identify so closely with Chase's. When her head was cold, she knew her Chasey Bear's head would be cold too.

Meg and Chase were buddies, and she sat on the floor next to the couch while he tossed and began to whimper. The whole house grew quiet as the next few minutes unfolded, and she stroked his back and called him "Pinky," one of her pet names for him. By the time we carried his limp and sweating body out of the house that August day, his fever had climbed to over 102. Chase had hit the nadir with a vengeance.

The first fever would reach nearly 104, and after a few hours in the emergency room and immediately starting him on antibiotics to protect his weakened body, we'd be admitted to the oncology floor for a stay that would turn into eleven days in isolation to protect Chase from people and people from Chase. The only ones allowed through the doors were medical staff and Bob and me. Everyone who entered the room had to be covered in a yellow smock and wear medical gloves and a mask, rendering them unrecognizable to Chase who, half out of his mind with fever, screamed at anyone who entered.

The fevers would range as high as 105 and would only be broken by medical intervention for the first five days as he lay in the bed and shrieked if people touched him because every part of his body hurt. It was terrifying to witness him in the grip of this thing—a fever, not the cancer, but a fever—as we prayed for a reprieve. The next round of chemo was indefinitely postponed.

As Bob worked from the hospital, I'd sit with my tablet and rest on the couch overlooking the lake, listening to music, as it became both the comfort and prayer that I otherwise could not articulate as Chase grew increasingly weak. I listened to songs that spoke the words of God and encouragement, and sometimes, leaving the couch, I'd sit on the end of the hospital bed and play the songs quietly for Chase.

He was unresponsive in his fevered sleep, but I believed his heart and spirit could drink the music in beyond what his body could show. The words we listened to again and again rang like a cry in all of our hearts: "Whatever may pass and whatever lies before me, let me be singing when the evening comes."[4]

It wasn't until the fifth day in the hospital when our friend Judi was with us that Chase seemed to really wake up in the evening and see us, asking to be held. The nurses helped move him, carrying him to me almost like the nurses had when I gave birth to him. Still attached to all his tubes and monitors, Chase sighed and rested against my chest as I sat on the couch.

He was so weak that he could barely open his eyes and he could not lift his head. But he was alive and his body had finally broken a fever on its own, and after five days of not even being able to touch him or comfort him in his pain, Bob sat next to me, stroking Chase's arm. We wept in relief, knowing that when we'd almost run out of hope, finally the corner had come and we'd turned it.

Whether it was standing over Chase's first chemo bed, his head still cross-stitched with the signs of a major brain trauma, calling him in to dinner when "dinner" was an IV bag, or sitting at the end of a fever bed, praying for him to wake up again, anger felt pointless. From faulty central lines to multiple hospitals on a daily basis and spiking temperatures, everything felt totally out of our control. Every time I had been tempted to think that I had the right to be upset or distressed, to demand shelter and reprieve as things continued to push at us and unravel us, I remembered God's words to Job: "Will you discredit my justice and condemn me just to prove you are right? Are you as strong as God?" (Job 40:8-9). The challenge, though stinging, reminded me that God doesn't answer to me for the things He places in my path. As hard as it is to admit when I'm hurting, my very breath is a ridiculously generous gift from Him.

When life throws hospitals, infections, and complications of any kind; when days pass and we have no direction or sense of time and we don't even know where to turn for shelter, there is a promise that remains unmoving, a promised place of rest. "God is our refuge and strength, always ready to help in times of trouble. So we will not fear when earthquakes come and the mountains crumble into the sea. . . . Be still, and know that I am God!" (Psalm 46:1-2, 10). He wraps us in His never-failing love and asks us only to be still and acknowledge Him as our shelter when everything else falls apart.

And if we're honest, it's never actually a question of *if* we will fall apart, but when. It will happen in one way or another as surely as we have breath because the world is broken and so are we. But which way do we fall? Will we stubbornly cling to our rights and the things we place around us for comfort and happiness, or will we surrender everything to Him who understands our unfolding life far beyond our wildest imaginations? He alone is our shelter.

13

PREPARING FOR LOSS

It's a strange blessing how terrible things can become normal and hard things become routine. A part of our brains struggles to accept this new reality, and yet we fall into its rhythm because we are creatures of habit, and if we do something often enough, the familiarity of it often seems reassuring.

It only took two rounds of chemo for us to begin settling into a familiar pattern with Chase's treatment life. We would have four or five days of chemo, be home for two or three days, go back for a quick clinic visit, then be home for forty-eight hours at most before going back to the hospital because Chase had a fever, a sign that his immune system had crashed again. Our connection to our other kids was primarily through video chats, as Chase often remained in isolation. The most toxic chemotherapy drugs were given to Chase during the first few rounds and were the most intense on his little body. The hospital admissions would stretch on . . . eleven days, twelve days, thirteen days.

At one point during his thirteen-day admission, we sat with Dr. Lulla and Dr. Loret de Mola and listened to their concerns. While Chase wasn't actively getting worse, he also wasn't actively getting better, almost reaching a crucial moment where, if he didn't start to turn around by the next day, we "may have to have a different conversation." Bob and I sensed they were looking for Chase to turn the corner as much, if not more so, than we were. But the next day, miraculously, his white cell count began to regenerate, and his fever broke on its own. No further conversations were needed at that moment; however, it would not be the only time he narrowly missed being transferred to intensive care.

During those long fever days, Chase's hair began to fall out; his pillowcases were changed often as the crisp, white fabric became covered with it again and again. At one point, I took a picture of his head when he was sleeping just to remind me how small and frail we all are. Not even our hair is our own.

Two days into one admission, Chase's lab results were so poor that the nurse informed us that Chase was going to need not only a blood transfusion that day but probably a platelet transfusion as well.

By midafternoon, they delivered the blood in a small bag, and it ran through the IV for more than two hours. Bob and I watched Chase sleep, having been informed that if a person has a bad reaction, it often happens with the initial transfusion from another donor. The nurses had instructed us to page them immediately if anything even slightly changed, so of course, we were hovering.

Chase lay in the bed and began to turn bright pink, suddenly waking as this liquid energy poured into his body. We speak of life being in the blood, and we sing about the power in the blood of Jesus, but I have never before witnessed the amazing work of this life source play out as clearly as I did with Chase that day.

With the blood transfusion being a success, the platelets were readied, and Bob and I sat back in our seats, relaxing. But about a third of the way into the platelet transfusion, Bob suddenly sat up in his chair, and the noise made me jump. He nearly threw down his laptop as he quickly moved to the other side of Chase's bed to find the call button.

"His temple is swelling. Chase's temple is actually swelling. El, come here and look at this. Call the nurse. Call her *now!*"

Entering at a run, the nurse deftly paused the pump, while examining Chase's entire body, checking his vitals, and paging a doctor. After a few minutes, everybody calmed down, and even though a swollen temple is not a common allergic reaction, the consensus was that it had been exactly that. Chase was given an antihistamine and subsequently completed the transfusion. When the crisis was over, the room was quiet again. Chase was sleeping, and Bob and I had a minute to process what had happened.

"How are you doing?" Bob asked.

Raising an eyebrow, I stared at him in disbelief. "That was insanity!"

"Yeah."

"I struggle with . . . I just can't even . . . all of that drama was over a platelet transfusion! It wasn't even the cancer that caused it."

"I know, but it's a necessary part of the protocol. We can't forget—this is Chase's best chance."

I nodded. "I know, I know. I just feel like the entire thing is this crazy exercise in allowing short-term pain for long-term benefit. I know in my heart that it's right. I have peace, but days like today just completely wear me out. Insanity."

Bob sighed. "Me too . . . and now I've got to get back to work."

And that was it. Thirty minutes ago we'd been in panic mode, but now it was back to the grind.

Nearly every week, Chase had to have chemo injected into his spine. Because lying still for an injection and a spinal tap was impossible (little boys aren't known for being still, are they?), he'd be put under anesthesia, and every week that we went through the motions of this, it felt like we were reliving the brain surgery again. Often Chase was given a mild sedative to make separating from us easier.

As the sedative began to take effect, "Mellow Chase" emerged.

"Can I give you a kiss? You're the best Mommy ever."

"Of course you can give me a kiss, sweet boy." I stifled a laugh as I leaned over and he planted a sloppy kiss on my cheek.

"BEEP!"

One of his little fingers pressed into the end of my nose, and he giggled. "I just beeped your nose! Daddy, can I beep your nose too?"

Easily distracted, Chase turned his attention back to me. "Hey, Mommy, am I going to have a nap with the doctor?"

"Yes, sweet boy."

"Will it be magic?"

"Of course."

"No needles?"

"Nope. Magic, remember?"

"Okay, I'll be brave."

"You're *so* brave!"

He nodded. "Yes! I *am* so brave!"

He thought for a minute. "Hey! You go take a nap in the chairs while you wait for me, and then we'll both take naps, okay?"

I thought it was a brilliant suggestion.

The IV tube in his arm was surgically replaced with tubes in his chest again, and by this time, Chase had gotten somewhat used to them. He was terribly protective of them but also a little proud. We wound an ACE wrap around his chest to cover the other bandages and to keep the tubes from pulling, tucking their ends into the wrap so they didn't hang out under his shirt. Occasionally, when Chase was sure there wasn't a medical person for miles, he'd pull up his shirt and ask us, "Do you want to see my tubies?"

So the tubes were "tubies," and we called the ACE wrap a "taco" because it turned his chest into what looked like a giant burrito. More than one nurse became momentarily confused while changing his bandage when Chase sat in the bed with his arms in the air, screaming "Taco! Taco!" until his chest was rewrapped.

For their own protection, chemo patients rarely leave their floor, so when Chase was feeling better, we'd often walk around the three halls that made up the ward. Chase loved to engage the staff, and he'd stomp around shirtless with his "taco" around his chest, his IV pole trailing behind, and playfully growling, "Hey, no smiling in the hospital!" to anyone who even dared to look at him.

Sometimes we'd walk to the small playroom, and he'd sit and play with other children, while I'd sit with their parents. There were language barriers and grief barriers, so when we spoke to each other at all, the adults exchanged diagnosis stories. It is a sight like no other to watch a handful of children, weak and too thin, their skin translucent white, sitting around a small table and playing "Ants in the Pants." Chemo took their strength, their hair, sometimes even their skin colors, and so many other aspects of their unique identities. There in that ward the playing field was level, their differences gone—there were just sick babies, sad hearts, and shared experiences. And sometimes these little kids, attached to their IV poles and pumps, would sneak glances at one another as if to shyly communicate "You look like me. You know what this is like."

One day, as the sun streamed in through the huge picture windows of the south-facing playroom, I sat with Chase at the craft table when Dr. Lulla came in. It was the day after one of Chase's spinal taps when a doctor from Chase's team would routinely update us on the results. Dr. Lulla greeted Chase, who ignored him in favor of finger paint, and then motioned me into the hall to talk. Leaving Chase with a hospital volunteer, I stepped away from the table, and we stood in the doorway.

"The CSF [cerebral spinal fluid] results are back—the fluid is still positive for abnormal cells."

I could tell by the look on Dr. Lulla's face that he wasn't happy about this, but knowing we'd signed Chase up for a lengthy protocol, I didn't comprehend why the presence of cancer cells after only eight weeks of chemo was bothering him.

"Okay," I replied hesitantly.

"Here's the thing," Dr. Lulla said quietly. "The chemo should force an almost immediate remission of cancer cells. Typically, with AT/RT, you want to see this right away."

And then it struck me. This cancer that we'd assumed we had several months to eradicate needed to disappear nearly as soon as the chemo touched it. I looked away and focused on Chase in the playroom.

How could he look so healthy and be so sick?

This news came hot on the heels of the six-week MRI results, which showed that while the lurking cancer wasn't growing, neither was it disappearing.

Folding his arms, Dr. Lulla leaned against the doorway as we talked, and the dreaded words came. "I know . . ." he hesitated, "when we first laid all of this out, we talked about trying to postpone the radiation until the end of treatment, but I don't think we can postpone it any longer."

"Okay. What are we talking about if we do it now? Like, what does this mean for Chase long term?"

"Statistically, the younger a child is, the more likely there are to be neurological and developmental repercussions. Ideally, we don't like to radiate children under age eight, and I'd been hoping to at least get Chase to age three, but this . . ."

He paused again, weighing his words and their implication. "My recommendation is that we don't wait any longer. The spinal fluid isn't clearing with the chemo alone. I'll take this to the tumor board, and we'll see what the recommendation is, and we'll go from there. Let me know if you have any questions, okay? And the same thing goes for Bob. Just have a nurse page me if he wants to talk."

He hesitated for only a moment, as if again looking for the right words to say. "As always, the decision is ultimately for you and Bob, but if this is something we're going to do, we'll need to move fairly quickly."

I nodded and thanked him, and he moved down the hall and out of the ward. Suddenly it felt like there wasn't enough oxygen in the hall. For the first time, I began to wonder what would happen if Chase's treatment didn't work, if the tumor started to take over his brain. Once again, I just couldn't bring my mind to equate his seemingly strong exterior with a weak interior that was slowly but surely succumbing to a terrible disease. In the few times I'd let the terminal shadow creep into conscious thought and potential scenarios, it left me sobbing until I was too weak to stand—so harsh and barren are the thoughts that come with even the prospect of loss.

I couldn't help but remember a season of my college days when I spent a summer working at a retirement home. I was on second shift, splitting my time between the main floor and the area where the Alzheimer's patients lived. Locked behind big doors for their own safety, the men and women would wander the floor as they wandered through their own minds—their lives slowly deteriorating, their memories slipping farther away. Some grew angry as a result of the disease while others became happy. But there was one woman whom I could never forget.

Her name was Louise and she knew and feared her illness. She'd sit in a wheelchair in the middle of her bedroom, white stringy hair hanging around her face, and behind her thick, smudged glasses, tears would roll down her cheeks. When I'd come into the room, she'd grab my arm and say, "I'm not crazy. I'm really not. You have to believe me." She had felt the neurological changes coming, and they had become her waking nightmare. She knew her brain was essentially killing her, and there was nothing she could do.

And suddenly, when I thought of the end stages of brain cancer, I pictured Louise. I pictured her going mad with worry and sadness, and I imagined the same scenario happening to Chase. In my mind, I could see the cancer eating away at his mind while he slowly went crazy from the pain and the degeneration of the disease. I could picture Chase begging me to believe that he wasn't crazy. It was awful.

On some level, I wanted to cry, but tears felt too light and easy. A guttural scream seemed more appropriate for the emotions that bombarded me, but I was standing outside the door of a playroom filled with children and parents facing their own nightmare scenarios. So I took a deep breath and rejoined Chase as he painted pictures. It was the only thing I could do.

That afternoon, as Chase had more chemo and napped in his bed, Bob worked in the chair next to him, and I sat on the couch mulling over my thoughts. When Dr. Loret de Mola, our Dr. Becca, as we had started calling her, came in to make sure we'd heard the results from the spinal tap, I found the courage to ask what came next if treatment failed.

"Becca, honestly, I'm terrified, but nothing can possibly be worse than what I'm picturing in my mind. I need to know."

Her eyes filled with compassion and her words were measured, watching me closely for my reaction, ready to stop at any moment. "We would do everything we could to make him comfortable. As the tumor grew, Chase would sleep more, and then one day," she paused for a moment, "he'd stop waking up, and then one day, he'd simply stop breathing."

I had needed to hear her words, but the feelings they evoked were too much, and as we continued to talk, I finally started crying. Bob, wearing earbuds, stayed in the chair next to Chase and continued to work at his computer. But I could tell he'd heard every word because his face was shuttered—he was processing it. Dr. Becca's description was much easier to accept than what I'd envisioned, and yet, in my heart, I knew the reality would be far worse should we have to live it.

This day was turning into a "cancer day," our code phrase for a day when the awfulness of the disease was even heavier on our hearts than other days. Sometimes these days seemed to happen for no reason, and other times they were triggered by bad news or stress. Invariably, they hung like a cloud of sadness over us, and we couldn't escape their unshakable heaviness even though we knew that we had so much to be thankful for despite the cancer, and that we could and should trust God. Hearing about the spinal fluid and then talking about the need for radiation had been the one-two punch to bring on a raging cancer day, and this last discussion was the final blow. I was down for the count, and after Dr. Becca left the room, knowing Bob was with Chase, I went to the elevator, hit the button for the first floor, and then walked out of the hospital.

I hardly ever left the hospital; the air was humid, cool, and refreshing. It was the kind of Chicago day where the temperatures still climb but the change of season is felt in the air. As I walked, the sun was blotted out by dark clouds, and farther ahead, I could see the lake reacting to the wind in choppy waves tinged with white. Surrounded by tall, gray and dark buildings, the scene seemed to echo my heart. Crossing Lake Shore Drive, I found a quiet place to sit on cement pilings by the shore, and while I took in the vastness of the lake, the wind whipped at me.

There were moments when the heaviness crossed into despair, and it felt like how I imagine drowning must feel. What did it look like to surrender to the heaviness? I didn't know, and I was too afraid to find out. The weight of it all was pulling me in, and I was honestly afraid to go down lest I not come back up.

I remembered a friend encouraging me to go to the book of Psalms when I got discouraged, so I pulled out my phone, opened the Bible app, and began scrolling through Psalms. I needed something—anything—that would remind me of truth greater than the tragedy that was unfolding in front of me. Something that would drench the fire of heartache, or at the very least, reduce it to a mere smolder instead of this raging feeling that threatened to consume me.

Over the soundtrack of the lake, I silently read several psalms. As my eyes glanced over the words, I felt almost panicked about finding something to comfort my soul. I hated the feeling of despair. Watching gulls land on a buoy nearby, I took in my surroundings and then turned to another psalm, realizing that I was frightened. The grief and loss that hovered and the feelings they provoked were so much bigger than me. And then I read these words.

> Yet I am confident I will see the LORD's goodness
>   while I am here in the land of the living.
>
> Wait patiently for the LORD.
>   Be brave and courageous.
>   Yes, wait patiently for the LORD.
>
> PSALM 27:13-14

I read it again and again. These were the words I needed on this cancer day.

As I sat by the lake and Bob sat by Chase, and we had no idea how long Chase would live or what the next few weeks would look like as radiation began, this verse spoke comfort. God's goodness would come to us, even here, even now, even in the cancer. We had only to wait patiently.

14

SEARCHING FOR PURPOSE

As Chase recovered from his fevers, his doctors met to decide the direction of his treatment. By the time we were discharged a few days later, the recommendation was official. Chemo alone wouldn't be enough to hold the cancer at bay. Radiation appeared to be a looming necessity. We were tasked with deciding whether or not to accept the recommendation while Dr. Lulla and Chase's team worked on coordinating the radiation and treatment together.

The first night back in my parents' house, Bob and I sat up long after the kids were asleep, the sound of Chase's IV pump floating quietly down the hall. It was time to make treatment decisions again. Bob grabbed a pad of paper and a pen. "Should we make a list?"

I shook my head. "I don't know. I mean, what do we know about radiation so far? It can cause developmental delays . . ."

Bob interjected, "Don't forget the spine thing. If they have to radiate his spine, it won't grow as well or as long. He'll always look like he has really long arms and legs. What did the radiation doctor say about cognitive function?"

I mentally rewound to a meeting a few days earlier. "His words were, 'There is no glass ceiling, but Chase will always be behind other children his age.' It will take him longer to learn things, and it will be much more difficult for him to retain concepts."

My stomach cramped as I spoke these words, and I threw my hands up in frustration. "Bob, how can we do this? How can we honestly even consider doing this to Chase?"

He raised his hand, palm up. "Slow down, slow down. Let's go back to what we know. Chase's body and mind are both doing really well right now, but the scans don't lie: The chemo isn't working by itself, and if we don't do something, the cancer is going to start taking over again. That's what we know, right? I think we should consider radiation. Remember what we've always said? If he doesn't live, we will have done everything we can for him. And right now, he's doing so well, I feel like we owe it to him to try."

I sighed. He was right. And then the rationale of it all dawned. "Bobby! Flip the argument." He looked at me like I'd lost my mind, and I wasn't sure that I hadn't.

"I mean, if you flip it and ask yourself if we are honestly not going to give him this chance because he might struggle in school if he survives, the question kind of answers itself. I don't want to give up on him when he's handling treatment so well. Not even for complications."

Bob slapped the table with his palm in agreement. "And we're still doing things *for* him, not *to* him."

"Okay."

"Okay." The heaviness of the decision, even in its sudden clarity, still robbed us of speech.

My mind was already racing forward with thoughts and plans. "I hope Chase can do proton radiation. Not only is the center much closer to us, but I read something that made it sound like it would burn away less healthy tissue. Anything we can do to minimize the damage to Chase would be awesome."

"Yes," Bob said, "but that also means that his radiation would need to be postponed on the days when he's already admitted at the hospital downtown. Or he'd need to be transported by ambulance to the suburbs on those days. That's kind of a big deal."

Having an ambulance transport would definitely be a big deal, but we shared a smile as we both thought the same thing at the same time. Chase would probably love the bragging rights of riding around in an ambulance.

And then the next part of the decision and its implications hit me. "Bob, I'm not ready to talk about the side effects with other people. I'm okay with family and the people who are closest, but I'm not ready to explain or defend our decision. Is that okay?"

He nodded. "Honestly, there's no need to talk about it right now. If this doesn't work . . . there's no need to. . . . Don't worry about it for right now. Just tell people the chemo isn't working and he's having radiation, and leave it at that."

Two weeks later, the preparation began. As we'd hoped, Chase had been approved for the proton radiation at the center close by. While Bob stayed close to us and worked from the lobby, Chase and I stepped through a dark staging area with computers and machines into a huge white chamber—the radiation room. With curved walls and glowing lights along the sides of the room, it reminded me of a giant MRI tube or a planetarium auditorium. Huge metal plates hung from cables on the side of one wall; behind a window at the back of the room was a control booth; and in the center, under the apex of the circle, there was a table. *The* table. This would be where Chase would be taken, five days a week, for the next six weeks.

As I took in this space for the first time, Chase stirred and whimpered in my arms. Hugging my neck a little more tightly, he voiced his thoughts. "I don't like it." Oh, how I wanted to agree. The radiation beam would only be activated for minutes, but each procedure would take hours to line up his body perfectly so the beam went exactly where it must and nowhere else.

Today Chase would be put under anesthesia in order for the staff to begin measuring and lining up his body for the eventual radiation. While he slept, a plaster mold of his face would be made, serving as a model for a rigid mesh mask that would go over his face and head and be screwed to the table to hold him in place during his treatments. He would also have tiny black spots permanently tattooed in several places on his torso as visual guides for the beams. To this very day you can still see the tiny marks stamped into his white skin. I was thankful that he would be sleeping through it all.

Chase whimpered again. "I'm scared."

As I held him closer and cradled his head, trying to make it better, I reassured him. "It's okay, buddy. It's going to be okay. Look, Chase, there's nothing to be afraid of in here. It's like a big spaceship!"

He managed a hesitant smile and lifted his head to look at the ceiling. "A spaceship?"

I nodded. "Of course, can't you see it? You'll be on this table, and you'll fly to the moon! And spaceships are fun and go fast. You'll have to tell me what it looks like on the moon, okay?"

He still looked a little worried but nodded as he took in his surroundings. It's a little more difficult to be really scared in a room that's actually a cool spaceship.

The two most common types of patients coming to the radiation center were brain tumor patients like Chase and men with prostate cancer. The men would sit in large groups beside the floor-to-ceiling windows in the waiting area, drinking their required hydration amount and talking, while the one or two other families with children would stay close to either the playroom or the beautiful fireplace that took up nearly one entire wall.

On his first treatment day, Chase decided he wanted to run the length of the room, no small feat with an IV attached. I slung the black vinyl case over my shoulder, gave his IV tubing enough slack so that he could run without tripping, and power walked behind him as he raced from one end of the room to the other, smiling an impish grin as he ignored the people who called out to him. He ran by the staff, and they cheered for him while the men in their groups looked up and chuckled. Chase pulled against the IV, and for just a moment, I found myself wishing we'd named him something that meant "sits still for hours."

When it was Chase's turn for his appointment, Bob once again stayed close to us but had to continue working from the lobby. As Chase's name was called, he stopped mid-run, wheeled around on a heel, and yelled, "Bye, Dad! Don't worry for me, okay? I'll be right back!"

We were ushered back to a small room with sliding doors, just like the pre-op bays in the hospital. A young nurse entered the room. "Hi, Chase, I'm Shena, and every day when you come here, I'm going to be your nurse!" Her winning smile had its desired effect; despite Chase's fear of this new environment and her white medical coat, Chase didn't scream. He was clearly intrigued.

Shena went to a cabinet and took out a large orange poster board. "Somebody said that you like the *Cars* movie. Is that true?" she asked, hoping to make Chase relax.

She flipped the board over to show us what was on the other side. "Chase, this is a special chart. Every day that you come to see me and get your radiation . . ." She stopped when she saw his blank stare.

"Your spaceship, Chase," I interjected. "Every time you see Miss Shena and go for a ride in your spaceship."

Nodding, Shena continued, "Yes! Every time you do that, you're going to get to pick a really cool sticker from the sticker bucket until each one of these white squares is filled, and then you'll be done in your spaceship! Are you ready?"

Chase nodded enthusiastically. "Yes! Where are my stickers?"

After we were introduced to Shena and all of Chase's vitals were logged, we met with the anesthesiologist on duty, and then the nurses came for him. For all the world, it felt just like he was going into a real surgery. One or two nurses from the radiation room came to the preprocedure bay, walking alongside the bed with Shena and me to push it down the hall—a hall that suddenly seemed way too long and too short at the same time.

Every child undergoing daily radiation had his or her own unique routine, and the nurses were more than happy to comply, offering support and encouragement. Some children wear favorite pajamas each time, others have on a favorite sports jersey, and some carry a personal security blanket with them. I remember one darling girl who loved the song "Moves Like Jagger," and we'd know whenever she was headed in because we'd hear Adam Levine's voice down the hall as she sang along and danced in the bed. And there were even rare days when I caught a glimpse of her nurse dancing with her as they pushed the bed to the edge of the radiation room.

Shena and the other nurses encouraged me to bring things that made Chase comfortable and keep those items close to him as he began this new and scary routine. So I wrapped him in his favorite blanket as I carried him the few steps from where the bed was parked in the hallway to the radiation table.

"Mommy, can I listen to my song on your phone?"

"Of course you can, sweet boy. Which one is your song?"

"You know, the one from the hospital."

"Buddy, we listen to music in the hospital all the time. Do you remember any of the words? What are the words to your special song?"

At first his humming was nearly unintelligible, but suddenly the sounds separated and I understood—they were the very same words he'd whispered after the first fevers in the hospital.

"Oh my soul, oh my soul, worship His holy name."[5]

With words of praise on his lips, we entered the spaceship.

I could feel Chase's body tense, the music now ignored.

"It's okay, baby, it's okay. I'm here with you. Remember, it's just going to be a little nap while you fly around the moon for just a minute."

Chase was wearing just a diaper, with his favorite blanket tucked around him. He whimpered again.

"No needles?"

"No needles. Magic, remember? You have your tubies; everything can go in there. They're just going to shine a magic light to help you get better."

"Are they going to shine a light at my baseball?" He pointed to his bald head.

"Yes, they have to, but it's okay. They'll do it while you're sleeping. You're so brave, my sweet boy. Are you going to be so brave for me?"

He nodded even as he clung to me, his eyes wide and anxious as he continued to look around. "I'm so brave." He said it tentatively, as if to convince himself.

The whole time we talked, the nurses were directing us to stand by the table while the anesthesiologist prepared the syringe that would be attached to Chase's line. The nurses silently signaled, and I adjusted Chase in my arms, promising to hold him until he slept. The doctor took the tube hanging from Chase's chest and inserted the milky liquid that would put Chase to sleep. As the medicine went up the tube and coursed into his small frame, I felt his body begin to go limp as he whispered repeatedly, "I'm so brave, I'm so brave. . . ." Finally, his eyes rolled back in his head, and he sighed into unconsciousness.

The moment he was unconscious, the entire staff seemed to jump into action. Chase was laid on the table, and I was ushered from the room. I was not permitted to stay or watch. They needed to go to work, and although I understood completely, it wasn't enough to stop the tears as I walked down the hall. Shena would stay by Chase's side, and the nurse escorting me kindly offered me a box of Kleenex. Holding your child as he slips into unconsciousness is something both sad and raw. In those moments, the weight of his body felt like the weight of the decisions we'd made on his behalf.

In the waiting room, Bob was hard at work on his laptop. He looked up when he saw me, his eyes softening. I sat down next to him, and he squeezed my hand in his as I recounted the story of Chase's bravery.

"He said that? Are you serious?"

"He completely did. I couldn't even believe it. He's such an old soul."

We didn't say much more as we settled in for the wait. I was too anxious to focus on reading, so I wandered the room, got a cup of tea at the beverage station in the corner, and absentmindedly picked up a few scattered pieces of the jigsaw puzzle lying on a big table by the window. Meanwhile right down the hall, an unconscious Chase was bound to a table, while doctors tried to burn the cancer cells out of his body. I felt almost crazed with how badly I wanted to protect him from this, and I moved restlessly, the silicone bracelet I wore on my right wrist brushing against my skin.

Glancing down, I stared at the bracelet closely, as if I were seeing it for the first time. It had been a gift from a girl in our church. She, like so many others, had wanted to do something for our family, so she had the bracelets made and sold them to raise money for us and Chase's treatments. A soft gray color, chosen to represent the brain, it was stamped with three words. They shouted at me in this overwhelming moment. Those three little words were why we stood in this building and why we willingly submitted our son and ourselves to face whatever came next. CHASE AWAY CANCER.

The first radiation treatment went well, and in less than two hours, a nurse came out to the lobby and called me back to the preradiation area. Shena stood over a still-sleeping Chase and motioned me to join her. Her voice was just above a whisper.

"He did really well!"

I breathed a sigh of relief. "Okay, what's next?"

"Well, I want to take his vitals one more time, and then you can take him home." She turned around from the computer screen as if remembering something important. "I put lotion on his head and back, and you'll want to do that probably twice a day, like maybe after treatment and then again at night, before he goes to bed. It'll help minimize the burns."

The left side of Chase's skull, the entire area under the surgery scar, was bright red and hot to the touch. Doubt washed over me again. *Dear God, what have we done?*

Even though the treatments themselves went as well as could be expected, Chase's body deteriorated under the combined weight of radiation and chemo, and we couldn't help feeling an impending sense of loss—loss of health, freedom, and choice, even the potential for loss of life. As the weeks went by and Bob had to go back to the office, I was so exhausted from not being able to sleep at night that someone from our church had to drive Chase and me to the radiation center each day. Life felt fragile and unraveled. Everything felt wrong and against any kind of plan, especially a good one.

Early on, when Bob and I were discussing radiation as an option for Chase, I started thinking about Psalm 139, which describes how God forms each one of us and knows everything about us before we ever take a breath; that He knows even the exact number of days we will live. Each of us is "fearfully and wonderfully made," (verse 14, ESV), a verse that was spoken over all of my children when they were born, including Chase.

The words *fearfully and wonderfully made* kept coming back to me in the days we had to decide Chase's treatment. If God knew Chase's life before time itself and proclaimed that Chase has been fearfully and wonderfully made, then Chase with cancer, with radiation, with short-numbered days—this Chase with all his visible and invisible scars—was more perfect and right than Chase before the diagnosis. This is how God saw our son being most beautiful and most wonderfully made on this earth for His glory. No decision we made could lose him a day or even a minute, as it all was already known and planned.

Such beautiful grace. The thought that God can take something broken and damaged and know before the creation of anything that this fallen thing would weave into beauty He described as fearful and wonderful is breathtaking to me. We had spent weeks and weeks wishing for normal and mourning losses, and yet, in this one psalm, the promise and reality screamed, not just for Chase, but for all of us: This was part of God's perfect plan for our most beautiful selves, the selves that would bring Him the most glory in this life.

To hold life with open hands and seek the good in the hard things is a fight. To seek these things knowing that we may not ever see the good this side of heaven and yet go on seeking is a continuous battle. But I believe with all my heart that the plans laid out for us are for our good, our future, and our hope. The trials that come both test our strength and develop our endurance should we let them. As Scripture states "when [our] endurance is fully developed, [we] will be perfect and complete, needing nothing" (James 1:4).

These thoughts and verses are written around my house and have at times been taped to my kitchen cabinets and doors because I've needed to see the words and be reminded of them every time I turn around. When all that could have been washes over me afresh, when Chase's weak voice whispering, "I'm so brave, I'm so brave," echoes in my mind, I need to know that there is a purpose far greater than I can imagine. This is what brings hope and even joy in loss. *Hold on.* The beautiful life plan is still unfolding.

15

When There is No Relief

With the first radiation treatment in the books, Chase slept for most of Monday after we left the center, and he seemed out of sorts, not even fighting Phyllis and his weekly central-line dressing change the way he normally would have. In the back of my mind, I felt something near panic as I watched him lie with Bob on the couch that night and fuss halfheartedly. A listless Chase was never a good sign.

"Bob, do you think he's okay? Do you think I should call somebody?" I stood over the couch, wishing there would be some sign to let me know if this was normal postradiation behavior or not.

Bob shook his head slightly, trying not to disturb Chase. "Let's just see what happens. Right now, we don't have anything to really tell them. He's tired? He's crabby?"

I smiled. "That's not exactly news."

Smiling back, he angled his head to try to see Chase's face. "Let's just see how the night goes. We've never done this before. This might just be how it looks."

I prayed he was right.

When we arrived at the radiation center the next morning, Chase picked a Spider-Man sticker to mark day two on his chart, and Shena took his vitals. All his numbers were good, but Chase was not quite himself. A few minutes later, our anesthesiologist for the day entered the room. It was Dr. Roth, the gorilla doctor! Even though it had been months since we'd seen him, we picked up where we'd left off on the gorilla story. As he continued the crazy true story, I watched him watch Chase. As he examined him, he sighed.

I was immediately alert. "Is Chase going to be okay? Are you sure it is okay to put him under again?"

Dr. Roth nodded but hesitated. "To be honest, these are the decisions I hate. It's quite possible that he's starting to fight a small virus."

He shrugged. "It could be one of several things, and going under every day is not ideal, but his vitals and lungs are perfect and he has no fever. Only time will tell, but giving him more time between treatments isn't helpful because this cancer isn't something you wait on. I'm going to take him in there today, but I'm going to be watching him like a hawk."

So into the "spaceship" everyone went. Chase, too tired to protest the procedure, held an iPod that was quietly playing his special song, "10,000 Reasons." I kissed him and whispered, "Be brave, sweet boy," to which he responded, "I'm so brave." I joined Bob in the waiting room as I had the day before, armed with my box of tissues but trying not to cry. Two days down, only about thirty more to go.

By the time the second radiation session was done, it had become clear that Chase was, indeed, struggling. After being called back into the small room where Chase slept, I was joined by Shena, Dr. Roth, and Dr. Hartsell, Chase's radiation oncologist. Chase had needed to be intubated while he slept. He had a low-grade temperature and had begun shivering under the blankets, a sign that his temperature was likely to start climbing. Arrangements were made for us to immediately see Dr. Goldman, one of the hospital's neuro-oncologists who had office hours in a building next to the radiation center. Chase was too weak to stand, and it was a long way to carry him, so we got in the car and drove across the parking lot.

Dr. Goldman is to oncology what the idea of Santa is to the holiday season. Wherever he goes, toys, candy, and jovial banter follow, and all the children love him. You can hear him coming—in fact, many times, you hear him singing in the halls long before you see him. On a floor full of children enduring terrible, grown-up things like chemo and radiation, a larger-than-life personality like his is medicine of the most wonderful kind.

This day, though, even Dr. Goldman had to work hard to coax a smile out of Chase. Not even the green dinosaur mallet that he pulled out of his lab coat pocket to check reflexes brought a giggle. Chase was sick, and he needed to be treated, but everyone was hesitant to send us all the way downtown, especially when we needed to stay close to the radiation center. After a conference call with Dr. Lulla and a quick bribery trip to the toy closet with Dr. Goldman and Chase's nurse, Monica, it was determined that we should stay local for as long as possible.

We'd gotten used to certain procedures at our downtown hospital, where most of the staff knew Chase's story. Had we been in an airport, we would definitely have been labeled "frequent flyers." But here in the local hospital, even though everyone was wonderful, it was unfamiliar. Nobody knew us, except my mom and her friend, also named Monica, who joined Bob and me, bringing us the two things we needed most—prayer and iced coffee drinks. After we'd spent a couple of hours in the emergency room, Chase's fever started to rise, and when his lab results were in, he was admitted as a patient.

Despite medical intervention, Chase's fever continued to rise and his heart rate wouldn't come down. The doctors came and went, talking to us and then stepping out in the hall to phone Chase's other doctors and make plans. Chase himself was in fairly good spirits as he'd been given stickers and a comfortable, soft pair of yellow hospital pants, but monitors don't lie. His heart rate was staying way too high while the fever hovered around 104.

After repeated sessions of consulting with us and stepping into the hallway to get on the phone with Dr. Lulla and Chase's team, all the white coats concurred: Chase needed to "go home." For the second time in my life, I stood in the middle of a room while a doctor apologized that the case was beyond the resources of the facility. The team from Chase's hospital was coming for us again.

My mom, who hadn't been with us for the first transport after his July seizure, stood near Chase's bed, her eyes wide and teary. She quietly exclaimed, "Oh my," every few minutes. Watching her being shaken by this made it even harder. She'd always been strong for me. And just like that, my stomach dropped and my hands were shaking. I wasn't afraid for Chase, but waiting for the transport took me back to that initial diagnosis moment. How I hated this feeling of weakness. "God is good, God is faithful, and He is in control. He is my rest and my strength." Over and over, the words became my mantra as we waited on the transport. *God, make my heart believe those words.*

"Chasey Bear, how are you doing?"

"Good, but I just have some fevers, Mommy. Can I watch a movie here? I like my yellow pants!"

"Hey, Chasey, I don't think we're going to watch a movie right now. Dr. Lulla misses hanging out with you, and he's worried about your fever, so he's sending an ambulance to come get you, okay?"

"Okay. Can I watch a movie when I get to *my* hospital?"

"Of course, sweet boy."

The team arrived in what seemed like only a few minutes, and among the group of blue shirts that day was a transport nurse named Craig. We'd met Craig when Chase was first diagnosed. We learned we had mutual friends, and he'd stopped by a few times to check on Chase and encourage us in those early days. Though I was deeply thankful for a familiar face, his presence also spoke volumes since I knew he often accompanied more serious cases. If he had come for Chase, they must have been worried.

After Chase kissed his grandmother and father good-bye, the team wheeled him out of the room and down the hall. Hurriedly slinging bags over my shoulder, I worked to catch up to their quick steps, turning to look back for just a moment. Bob and my mom stood in the middle of the hallway.

"You'll be right behind us?" I asked Bob.

Nodding, he said, "I'm leaving now. Go, before you lose them."

His words came just as Chase's gurney turned a corner. The tears in my mom's eyes were the last thing I saw as I headed quickly to the emergency vehicle bay.

On Chase's discharge papers, it stated that his fever was 104.5, but even that temperature raging through his little body was not enough to keep him from feeling terribly important about being back on an ambulance. He was smiling as he was loaded onto the back of the rig, and I was directed into the cab as the sirens began to sound.

From my front-row seat, I saw the town disappear behind us as we got on the ramp leading to the freeway, bypassing lane after lane of slowed cars in the heaviest part of rush-hour traffic. Finally, the cityscape came into view.

Almost there. Dear Lord, bring us safely home.

Craig leaned forward, his voice carrying into the cab, "Ellie, he's doing great back here."

As we crossed the river, buildings that soared upward hemmed us in, and the roads became more narrow and congested. My seatbelt tightened as the ambulance slowed suddenly in an intersection. Attempting to clear a path with the siren blaring and lights flashing, the rig crawled forward into a small opening.

The driver at my side competently handled the full rig like a small car, weaving in and around vehicles pulled as far to the sides of the road as possible. Above the wail of the siren, there was another lower sound. It was both unusual and yet familiar, a sound you don't forget but can't always place—the sound of metal against metal. It was so brief that I thought I'd imagined it, and within seconds we were free of the gridlock and at the intersection closest to the hospital.

"Did you hear that?"

A voice from next to Chase's gurney floated forward. "I think you just scraped that cab as you passed." Face set, the driver slid both hands to the top of the steering wheel and leaned into the final turn taking us to the emergency entrance.

"I know, but I have a child on board. I can't stop."

Quickly disappearing in my side mirror, the cab driver stood in the center of the narrow, two-lane street, waving his arms and gesturing angrily. As I looked forward again, we were pulling up to the doors of the ambulance bay.

When we arrived at the fourth medical facility in twelve hours, there was a room waiting for us. We were home. We were safe. After a while, Bob arrived too. What felt like a forty-hour day was finally over. Or so I thought.

Much later, as the night-shift nurses crept into the room, giving medicine and checking on Chase, the usually familiar, comforting sounds changed. The nurses' movements became more urgent, and then through a sleep-induced fog, I heard the snap of a switch and light flooded the room. I saw our nurse holding Chase's chest tube

in her gloved hand. Still disoriented, it took me a minute to realize that the white tube was bloody, and it was no longer surgically
attached inside Chase's chest! Chase woke up from the commotion
and started screaming. He wasn't in pain, but the medical staff had
started to answer pages and gather by his bed, and that was enough
to push him over the edge.

The last vestiges of sleep vanished in the adrenaline rush when the
paged resident in charge arrived and began to give orders. "Okay, we
need to keep him completely flat. Mom, Dad, can you help with that?
He needs to remain completely flat. Try to keep him still, please."

Nobody was sure how the tube had been pulled out and whether
something had been in the tube when it became detached. If something had been infusing, it was quite possible that fluid had pooled
around Chase's muscles and heart and not gone into the vein. For
this reason, Chase had to lie perfectly still to prevent the risk of an
embolism—a clot threatening his heart.

Maybe it was because it was deep in the hours of the night,
but the whole scene seemed to have a dreamlike quality. Bob and
I looked at each other over Chase's prone body, and we wished it
actually were. *This can't be happening.*

After nearly constant monitoring for half an hour, Chase promised
he could lie still without our assistance, and everyone began to relax
as Chase stayed stable with no signs of heart issues. And somehow
the night passed with little to no sleep before the next wave hit us.

"Chase is stable, and he's going to be okay, but he needs fluids and
medication. Are you sure he doesn't take anything PO—by mouth?"

We were sure.

The resident sighed. "Okay, then we're going to have to place a
peripheral IV, because he's going to need these things. Let me page
vascular access and see what we can do. We'll keep you updated."

We turned to Chase as the room cleared. "Chase, how are you
doing?"

"The doctors held me down." He gave a dramatic, injured sniff, indicating he was clearly exhausted. "Why did they wake me up? Mommy, I didn't mess with my tubie. I didn't pull it out, I promise."

Sitting on the edge of his bed, I stroked his bald head as he yawned. "I know, sweet boy, I know. You just had a super tricky tubie that decided to sneak out of you while you were sleeping. Dr. Lulla will make sure it all gets fixed in the morning, but for now, they need to keep you hydrated, and so they're going to have to put a tubie in your hand, okay?"

His body went rigid in the bed. "Needle?" he whimpered.

"Yes, needle."

He screamed. "Noooo! I don't want a needle!"

"*Ssshh, sssh*, it's okay, sweet boy, it's okay . . . no needle right now. Don't worry about it now. Daddy and I will tell you when it's time. For now, everything is okay."

Bob looked at me and frowned slightly. He wouldn't have divulged anything to Chase until they were ready to put the needle in.

I mouthed the word *sorry* as he crossed the room to the bed.

"Hey, Chase, I have a great idea! Since you don't have any tubes right now, I'll climb in here and we can snuggle together and go back to sleep. Deal?"

Chase giggled. "Deal!" For now, the needles were forgotten.

With the sunrise came decisions. After only two days, radiation had to be postponed. Not only was Chase too sick to be radiated, but now the central line issue had taken top billing for the biggest problem of the day. Midway through the morning, and far into the biggest coffee to be found, a nurse performed a routine check on the IV in Chase's hand. As she went to adjust it, Chase moved, and in the perfect storm of his movement, her timing, and Bob and I being too far across the room to lend an extra set of hands, the line in Chase's small hand collapsed, rendering it useless.

This had been one of the last places they could find on his body to place an IV because chemotherapy weakens the veins, and now it was gone. There was blood on the sheets and Chase was completely beside himself, having gone from screams of anger to genuine tears rolling down his cheeks in exhaustion and fear as he begged people not to touch him anymore.

We had all grown profoundly exhausted of people gathering around the bed and trying to figure out what to do. There'd been no relief, no break in the action for nearly twenty-four hours straight, and the ridiculous part was that, once again, it had nothing to do with the cancer itself—all of this was side effects and complications from treatment, not the disease.

As the sun rose high in the sky, I sat on the windowsill above the city holding a venti Americano in one hand and a tired and limp Chase in the other. He rested in my arms while they changed the bloody sheets, and Bob took a picture of us because I wanted to remember that moment.

If you saw that picture today, yes, we look tired, but for all the world, we look like we're having a good day, sitting and sipping coffee and cuddling in front of an incredible view. For me, as a person who understands safety through both peace and control, spinning out of control from place to place in a constant bombardment of events made me feel a helpless, lashing-out sort of anger. The kind of anger that wants things to stop so I can pin them in place, alphabetize, and organize them because if everything is in order, then everything has a purpose and will have no choice but to make complete sense. But that isn't how life works, is it? The good comes with the bad and the stress with the peaceful, and it's all mixed together in ways that can't always be separated, much as I wish they could be.

It comes down to finding our rest and relief not in the circumstances, but in the One. The One who promises rest for the weary and strength to the weak because even crazy days are ordained ones.

16

PRACTICING THANKFULNESS

After the central line fell out that crazy night, Chase went back into surgery within a few days to insert a new one. He wasn't discharged until after October 31, so despite an IV cord in his leg and bandages everywhere, we managed to get at least his arms into a Spider-Man costume for trick-or-treating. His siblings, dressed in their costumes, surprised him with a visit. They waved to Chase through the window of his room and brought candy for the nurses. Darcy, ever the princess, donned a medical mask to go into the isolation room for a brief moment and take Chase some candy. Aidan, a fellow superhero, just wanted to play in the playroom, and Karsten, dressed as a clown fish, hated the idea of being dressed up at all. He sat and sulked as only a one-year-old can, refusing to respond to anyone who spoke to him. As stressful as these recent days had been, it was so wonderful to have our whole family together for a minute—even in the hospital.

After we returned home, radiation continued and the late fall days slipped into a somewhat comforting routine as Chase visited his spaceship every day. He greeted the nurses and Miss Shena, picked a special sticker for his chart, had us count the stickers and the days, waited for the staff to call us back to the spaceship, listened to "10,000 Reasons"—his song—sometimes even asking the nurses and doctors to listen with him. He grew far more comfortable with the room, but every day we went through the ritual all the same.

"Mommy, I'm scared. I don't want to take a nap in the spaceship today."

"I know, my sweet boy, I know. But I need you to be brave for me, okay? Only a few more days." I think I was reassuring myself as much as him.

"Okay. I'm so brave, I'm so brave . . ." And his voice would drift off as the anesthesia took effect.

Most days held radiation treatments. Some days were radiation and then down to the hospital for chemo or blood transfusions, while other very special days started at the hospital, and then Chase would be transported to the radiation center in an ambulance. These were days when he was well enough to proceed with treatment but was too weak to be discharged from the care of a medical team. The medics and nurses would ride with us in the ambulance, and Chase thought he was a king with a really flashy entourage. When our white "limo" would pull up to the glass doors of the radiation center, people would crane their necks to catch a glimpse of who was arriving on a rig that day. Tiny Chase would be wrapped in blankets and belted to the gurney, and he'd nod and smile to those around him as if to say, "Oh, this old thing? Yes, it's my ambulance, and it makes me the coolest person here today. Ha." Like all patients who come by ambulance, Chase was taken to a special waiting area—he really did think he was a VIP.

Despite his resilient attitude, Chase's body was breaking down. The cancer was being held in check, but the treatment was wearing him out. Any hair left untouched by the chemo was completely taken by the radiation. He was so white that his skin had taken on an ethereal glow, and in some areas it had actually started to break down. Despite frequent transfusions, it was flaking like paper, and the slightest bump would bruise him. Any open scratches on his body were covered in antibiotic creams to try to keep infection away, and Chase grew frightfully skeletal, his eyes sunken and bruised with scabbed lids. The tape used to keep his eyes closed during radiation had begun to rip the delicate skin off, no matter how careful the staff was in removing it.

Chase's hearing was also deteriorating, which affected his speech. He couldn't hear his own voice pitch, so he was forced to speak louder. To add insult to injury, he was now badly sunburned from his sessions in the spaceship, and all the lotions and creams in the world didn't seem to help the sore, blistering skin. One large red patch on the side of his head where they'd removed the tumor and a long scorched stripe stretching from his neck to the base of his spine were the worst. His back looked like an inverted skunk—a red stripe on white skin—and required frequent care.

Each time we had to treat the skin, we were forced to undo the ACE wrap—Chase's safety "taco"—that covered the central line in his chest, and the vulnerability of the exposed line terrified him. He would dissolve into tears and fits of hysterical screaming, and any touch, even from Bob or me, seemed to hurt him. Applying the heavy lotion we used at least twice a day to soothe the burns—and now his raw eyelids—had suddenly become a two-person job: one person to hold a screeching, flailing Chase, the other to actually apply the lotion and rewrap his chest. Each new day of this increasing struggle washed over us with a guilty sadness. The smallest aspects of his care were becoming a minute-by-minute fight. *Dear God, let this be worth it, please.*

The week of Thanksgiving, his little body gave in to the low white blood cell counts, and we were hospitalized once again with fevers. We had missed so much daily life with our other children, and even though we'd spent our anniversary in the oncology ward, Bob and I had yet to miss a birthday or a major holiday. But barring a miracle, we knew we were suddenly looking at Thanksgiving in the hospital. Chase wouldn't recover in time.

I could forgive God for allowing the cancer, but forgive the cancer for keeping us from our family on a special day? That felt different somehow, and I could feel my heart harden against the thought. Whether the feeling was disappointment or bitterness, I do not know, but I wanted out. I had been "handling" the big cancer moments, but when they threatened my small normal moments, I balked.

My mind gravitated to various memories. Every Thanksgiving my father places five kernels of colorful dry corn next to my grandmother's china at each place setting. The little piles look out of place next to the shine and glitter of family heirloom serving pieces piled high with sumptuous foods, but he does it anyway. And when we are all fed, he calls our attention to the five kernels and tells the story. His voice low and serious, he takes us back not to the first Thanksgiving, but to the second winter when more Pilgrims came. More people than those who had already settled in the new land had food for. The rations got so lean that they were down to five kernels of corn per day—not per meal, but per day—and yet, the Lord spared their lives.

Dad's words, spoken at the height of blessing, surrounded by family, friends, and good things, have always challenged us to be thankful at the possibility of it all being stripped away, the possibility of just praying to survive another day. Goodness knows that I had plenty of actual food at my disposal in the cancer days with Chase, but emotionally and mentally, I often felt down to five kernels.

Life often pushes us to a place of emotional starvation. We get pushed and pushed again, and suddenly there doesn't seem to be the resources to cope with all the craziness around us. And therein lies a great danger. If I don't deal with the hard things, if I just keep tamping them down, willing myself to just survive the situation, the stress becomes a rock in my heart. The hardness sets in, cutting me off from effective communication with the ones I love and the One who loves me.

A few weeks before this hospital admission, closer to the start of radiation, Chase was sitting on the kitchen floor, playing with pots and pans, and as I crouched down close to him, he asked, "Mommy, can we pray?"

"Of course. Do you want me to pray?"

"No, me!" He opened his mouth and said, "Dear Jesus, thank You for my cancer! In Your name I pray. *AMEN*!" The sentences were short, excited bursts, and the amen was shouted loudly. And when he was finished, he turned to me with the most joyous expression and yelled, "Mom! I prayed for my cancers!"

Chase gave thanks with a simplicity I felt I no longer possessed, and then he was released into a joy I could hardly believe in—for "my cancers." Jesus wasn't kidding when He talked about the faith of children.

I share Chase's prayer for this reason: I had prayed for healing, strength, peace, acceptance, joy, submission, and more strength in regard to Chase's cancer and the treating of it, but never once had I prayed *for the cancer*. Yes, I had prayed that God would use Chase's cancer, definitely, that it would not be wasted. Absolutely. But to actually be thankful for the cancer and what it had brought about in our lives? I had not prayed for that, and I wasn't sure I could.

Especially not when it took me from those I loved not only on the holidays but on the every days. I couldn't pray for something that threatened to take the ones I loved from me. And so I sat in a hospital room, mentally glaring at hard thoughts with a rock in my chest and a lump in my throat.

Late on Wednesday afternoon, as we faced the reality of a holiday admission, Dr. Goldman stopped by our room to check in. Chase hadn't had a fever for a day, but his morning labs showed that his white blood cell levels were still decimated by the chemo, and until the numbers improved, he needed to stay in the hospital. The timing of his discharge was ultimately up to the doctors.

Dr. Goldman played with Chase as he talked to us, and he saw what we felt: Chase was weak, but we all wanted to be home. "Go!" he said, "and I know you will, but I need to tell you anyway. If he gets another fever, bring him right back, okay? But for now, you guys pack up and get out of here. Be with your family, and have a happy Thanksgiving! And Chase? The next time you get on the ambulance, you tell them to put on the sirens for you! They don't like to, but I used to ride on an ambulance, and I know there's a secret button on the dashboard, so you tell them I said that they should do that for you, okay?"

As Dr. Goldman backed out of the room, waving his arms over his head like revolving emergency lights and emitting a high-pitched wail that was supposed to be a siren, Chase doubled over in giggles in his hospital bed. We were going home for Thanksgiving.

Somehow, despite traffic, we made it back in time to attend the evening Thanksgiving service at our church, and Bob insisted he'd stay with Chase while I went. I sat in between my mom and Darcy in the sanctuary of the church, surrounded by people who'd been bringing our family meals, folding our laundry, and doing a hundred other little things to keep us on our feet. We listened to people share what they were thankful for and the ways God had been working in their hearts, and I found myself deeply grateful to be in the room. But I was still mired in the confusion and heaviness of heart that stemmed from carrying a thankless thing in a thankful season. I still struggled to reconcile cancer to thankfulness, and it hurt me that I couldn't.

I spent much of that day praying and thinking, and it was the end of the day before I realized that I'd been pushing God for answers. Like Jacob I wrestled, but in doing so, I was putting myself face-to-face with the One who loved and made me. And I realized that I might never get the deliverance I sought, but the cancer was the impetus that pushed me deeper and deeper into grace and the seeking of God's heart as I wrestled through the doubts and fears that come with a loved one having a terrible illness.

"I sought the Lord, and he answered me and delivered me from all my fears" (Psalm 34:4, esv). This was the answer. The cancer kept me seeking, and God gave me grace to look for Him in it, grace to be delivered, and more grace just because He is good and faithful. It was all a gift, and even though it came wrapped in hospital rooms and cancer treatments, it was precious because it was gracious and ultimately tailored perfectly for my needs.

If I was truly, deeply honest, I would need to tell you that I love comfort, and that's one of the biggest reasons for both my wrestling with fear and my thankfulness—cancer destroyed my comfort forever. Comfort is a security trigger for me. Comfort blunts the chaos, which gives me a sense of control, and that feeling of control translates into further security. It's all a little mashed up and circular and bent in my brain, but it's true.

When I'm comfortable and feel like everything is under control, it's alarmingly simple to feel that I lack for nothing—that I'm secure. Cancer exposed my inability to create my own security and highlighted my need for the only One who can banish fears and bring me true safety. It's only when I have no answers and I have become an emotional wreck, sitting huddled in this disease that shreds the layers of my false security, that I can see the real and important things in my life around me. Pain and heartache are inevitable because we aren't to the final chapter yet, but even in the brokenness, there is a light and even a beauty that I would have missed if my comfortable cocoon had stayed in place. I can be thankful in, and thankful for the brokenness because despite its horror, it leads to unbelievable places where I can see the goodness of God.

17

CELEBRATING IN ALL CIRCUMSTANCES

It was Wednesday, December 12, 2012—12/12/12—the final radiation day. After six grueling weeks, Chase was finally "graduating." It was an extraordinary moment, as it also marked something nobody thought we would see: Chase's third birthday.

"Mom, this is the last day for the *wray-dee-ay-shun*!" His lips curled around the difficult word in an exaggerated slur.

"This is it, Chasey Bear! You did it!"

"Are my friends going to be there?"

"Of course!"

"Did Auntie Meg really get a cake?"

"You betcha!"

He parroted the words as he giggled, kicking his feet against the car seat. "You betcha!"

Early that Wednesday morning, I wrote Chase a letter about how precious this day was to all of us, and as I composed it, I kept thinking of the day in the conference room when we first talked about what treatment would look like for Chase. On that day, when I had asked how long he would live, Dr. Becca had encouraged us to take it "moment by moment."

"First, let's just try and get him to age three, and then hopefully, we'll get him to age four, and then age five, and then maybe, kindergarten . . ."

The sentence had hung in the air, unfinished, and with good reason. Nobody knew how far Chase would go, but we all hoped. And now, here we were, at the first of the named milestones: *age three.*

As Chase entered the center, Ginny, the lady who was always at the front desk, got out of her chair so she could see him over her desk. "Chase! Your last day! Are you ready for this?"

He nodded, barely even looking at her. "Yep. Miss Ginny, can I go into the playroom, please?"

Within a few minutes, Shena called us back for the last session in the pre-procedure bay, and Chase was ready to celebrate. "Miss Shena, Miss Shena, it's my last day!"

She laughed. "I know it is, Chase, and I have a present for you."

As Chase entered the bay, he gasped in delight. For there, lovingly placed in the center of the bed, was a Lightning McQueen ride-on push car with a bow on top. "Oh, Miss Shena!"

She bent over to hug him. "Congratulations, Chase. You deserve a special something. Now let's get you ready! We're doing something extra special this morning. You get to put your handprint on the wall!"

When each child finished radiation, he or she put a handprint and a date on the wall of the recovery rooms. The walls were bright and beautiful, a picture of encouragement to each new child coming in that there had been many other children before them. For Chase that day, doing a handprint would be far more traumatic than whole brain and spine radiation. The chemo had caused Chase's skin to be so sensitive that even finger paint on his little hands made him scream in overstimulated terror. He pulled half his fingers off the wall at the last minute, rendering a silly, smudged three-fingered print. Luckily, all it took were a few warm wipes to his hand to restore his faith in humanity. And we all laughed afterward about Chase's handprint and the legendary stories that would be told in years to come about the three-fingered child who had left it.

Bob took a picture as I wrote Chase's name and the date under his artwork, and after the picture was taken, one of the nurses said, "You know what? You should really write 'Happy Birthday' by his name too. This is a big day for him!"

Chase put a final sticker on his daily chart, and when he found a pink plastic ring in the bottom of the sticker bucket, he turned to Shena as she took his blood pressure. "Miss Shena, will you marry me?" So Chase proposed while I finished writing on the wall, and then someone came to say that the room was ready. It was time.

Nearly every doctor had heard "Chase's song," and all the nurses had been shown the music video at one time or another. Even the hospital music therapists had downloaded the guitar chords because they knew if they went into Chase's room, he'd request it. Today, "his song" played one last time in the halls of the radiation building as we made the final walk down the hall and into "the spaceship."

The words about God's love and kindness and goodness echoed in the chamber as I carried him inside, and he held my phone in his hand. As the anesthesiologist injected the medicine into the line on his chest, I watched Chase take a deep breath. The blood rushed to his head, turning his cheeks rosy and bright. His eyes closed, and he sighed as he leaned his face against mine. This was it. The last radiation day.

"I'm so proud of you, my sweet boy. You did it. Take your nap, and I'll see you in just a minute. We'll celebrate with cake."

"With cake." He yawned.

"Yes, with cake."

He smiled contentedly, the fear of this place forever gone. "I'm so brave, I'm so brave . . ." And just like I had since the first day of his life, I wrapped my arms around him because he was beautiful and perfect even in his deeply broken state, and I lifted him with hardly more effort than I had on the day he was born, so wasted away was he.

As Chase lost consciousness against my forehead, for just a moment we stood head to head, noses nearly touching in an embrace, and then I laid him on the table in the center of the machine and he was in the capable hands of the staff. The cancer threatened to take him away from us, and as of this day, this moment, everything we knew to do had been done.

In my heart, I felt the bittersweet aspect of this celebration. We'd reached the end of a difficult season, but we'd also reached the end of our options. With radiation results not available for four weeks, it was quite possible that Chase's third birthday would also be his last.

While he slept in the spaceship, friends and family gathered in the lobby, all wearing special gold "Chase" shirts with the words of Joshua 1:9 printed on them: "Have I not commanded you? Be strong and courageous. Do not be frightened and do not be dismayed, for the LORD your God is with you wherever you go." The radiation center always had a small ceremony as part of the graduation from treatment, so people had stopped their day and gathered to cheer him on and celebrate his life.

After he woke up, Chase insisted on making a grand entrance from the recovery room, riding his new Lightning McQueen car despite being hooked to an IV. As he rolled around the corner and into the waiting room, his lashless, blistered eyelids nearly disappeared in a huge smile as he saw the gathered crowd break into cheers at the sight of him.

Ginny presented him with a certificate and a gold challenge coin, much like the ones given to soldiers for special achievement. Stamped into this coin was Chase's patient number, 728, above a pattern of interlocking stars, a symbol that all who walk through the process of radiation are interlocked and supported together in love. And as I stood in the circle—family mixing with friends, church members, and the staff who had become new family—all gathered in a sort of unanimous joy around a single person and accomplishment, I couldn't help but wonder if this is what heaven will be like.

When we get to heaven, will we stand together and cheer for those crossing the finish line faithfully, united in love and never-ending worship? I know we won't understand exactly what it looks like until we get there, but I hope it will be a little like that morning at the radiation center. Radiation should have been complete hell, and on some days it was; yet at the end, there was this small snapshot of heaven that was so beautiful.

To this day, the conversations in the halls and around the fireplace in the radiation center are some of my most treasured memories. The friends who accompanied us and the staff who spent their days with us saw some of our most vulnerable, awful moments laid bare, but they continued to pour out love and help us see glimpses of really great things in the middle of our hardest season. This day we celebrated Chase's life not because it was guaranteed to be long, but because he was still here. We had survived another moment.

And down the long hall of preprocedure rooms, on the north wall of the first room, is a strange three-fingered red handprint and words that read: "Chase Ewoldt, 12.12.12, Happy Birthday."

18

LOVE CAN'T STOP DEATH

Our family loves music. In our home, the children cut their teeth on music of all sorts, and every year the church Christmas concert is a significant highlight. In fact, so important is this musical celebration to our family that I very nearly gave birth to Aidan at the event. Bob had spent weeks preparing for the concert in a dual role as a conductor and a soloist, and though I could feel the pain of my contractions intensifying, I unknowingly assumed that there were long hours of labor still ahead. So I dressed up in the nicest clothes that still fit around my swollen body and went to the church that night. *Why not?* I can honestly say that I've never been so thankful to hear the triumphant finale—Handel's "Hallelujah Chorus"—in my life.

Bob still maintains that I didn't tell him our son was coming until the very end, but I think he forgave me the moment he ushered me into the ward and the labor nurses all swooned a little because he was still in his tuxedo, and they thought he looked dreamy. Aidan came about thirty minutes after we left the church, just one of many memorable moments tied to this annual event.

This concert was a part of my growing-up experience. I would look forward to hearing "O Holy Night" sung, the tenor soloist's voice echoing in the vaulted space. One year was especially significant because I was in the choir, Bob was helping direct, and he asked me for our first date during concert rehearsals. I had to see him nearly every night that week for rehearsals and could hardly have said no if I'd wanted to, which he knew and still smiles about when I tell the story. Each year had become filled with precious memories, and there was only one year I had to miss this prelude to Jesus' birth.

It was 2009, and it was less than twenty-four hours after I gave birth to Chase.

Earlier that week, knowing I was likely to miss the actual concert, and not wanting to repeat Aidan's birth story, I had decided to go to the final rehearsal. As I sat on the floor of the sanctuary with one-year-old Aidan and three-year-old Darcy at my side, I couldn't hold back my tears. *What would it have been like to be Mary, heavy with child, on the road to Bethlehem?* As I thought of what she endured that night, I drank in Bob's soaring voice: "Comfort ye, comfort ye my people . . ."

The year Chase was diagnosed, the concert date was the weekend after his radiation ended. Knowing he was still far too weak and immune suppressed to be in public with a large crowd, Bob and I decided that Chase and I would accompany him to rehearsal so that Chase could experience some of the music he loved so dearly. As we sat on the floor in the aisle, my back resting against the base of a pew, I could feel Chase's radiation-burned head lean against my chest in the dark. The house lights were down and the stage was flooded with light as the orchestra warmed up. Chase was struggling with the yellow surgical mask that covered his face to protect him from germs, but I reminded him that he needed to keep it on if he wanted to stay.

At the podium, Aaron, the director, was making announcements to the participants and then, turning slightly to face us, said, "We have a special guest with us tonight. Chase is here to watch the rehearsal, so everybody do your best."

I felt Chase sit up a little straighter against me as he heard his name and the applause that went with it. His ears were so filled with fluid that we had begun to wonder if he could hear much at all. Tonight, as he sat wrapped in the sound and echo of the large choir and orchestra that reverberated off the walls around him, his eyes shone in wonder and he hummed along. In this acoustically perfect environment, he could hear and feel the music.

I could tell he was tired and that nausea was beginning to hit him. The type of radiation treatment he'd sustained either makes the brain more wakeful than normal or less so—for Chase, it was less. He would fall into a deep sleep and be gone for long hours, something he hadn't done since he was diagnosed. But now he wanted to sit and wait for the choir to sing Michael W. Smith's iconic "Gloria,"[6] as he knew every word by heart.

When I was young, at the beginning of December, several women would get together to decorate the inside of our church and make it beautiful for the holidays. There's something so precious and special about this act. All of the drab and old becomes something elegant and festive in the lights of the tall evergreen trees.

There was one tree I loved the most, and every December, decades later, it still graces the foyer in our church. The first time I saw it, the transformed tree took my breath away. Against the red and gold ribbon reflecting the white lights, there were small parchment scrolls. On each piece of paper, in beautiful calligraphy, were written the Hebrew names of God. *Elohim*: the Creator; *El Shaddai*: Almighty; *Adonai*: Lord. The names covered the whole tree proclaiming a God who loves and cares and fights for His people more than I could ever understand. And yet this year there was one name that stood out among the rest . . .

As Chase and I stood next to this tree, never having made it to the point of hearing "Gloria," him clutching his IV bag and me reminding him to put his mask back on, all before he doubled over and vomited from all the treatment, there was one name I loved more than all because it meant more to me than it ever had before. *Jehovah Rapha*: the God who heals. Looking at that piece of paper, God felt even more personal to me. He called Himself the healer knowing just how desperately we would need healing.

In this time frame after radiation, Chase had been given a reprieve from all treatment and all clinic visits for a few weeks. This was to be a season to let his body recover after intense fighting, and we weren't required to go to the hospital at all unless there was a problem or need. It would be our longest absence from the hospital since he'd been diagnosed. But the season of rest was also a season of waiting. At his last scans, the very ones that had forced the time line for radiation, we knew that the cancer had still been in his spine, and there was no guarantee radiation had worked.

The next scheduled scan was only a few weeks away on January 17, but it felt like a lifetime. We had no choice but to wait out the days, and so, once again, we prepared for a bittersweet celebration. This Christmas was miraculous because Chase was still with us . . . and it could be our last one with him on this earth.

It's hard to describe the crushing weight of this knowledge. Yes, we are all mortal beings who live knowing that anything we do or experience could be our last, but somehow the kind of knowing we felt with Chase was different.

The statistics we'd first read were branded in our brains, and those thoughts were double-edged: We wanted to push them as far away as possible so our moments together with Chase would not be clouded with sadness, but we also needed to let the urgency sink in to use the time we were given genuinely and joyfully. But at times, the urgency was wrapped in a whisper of guilt: *You should make this extra special because it could be the last. You should make this extraordinarily memorable because it could be the last. Is this how you want him to remember it? Is this how you want to remember him?*

Making the most of our time, we decorated the family Christmas tree in the front window of my parents' house, adorned with all my parents' ornaments I remembered from my own youth: the matching reindeer made out of clothespins and felt, along with the dough baby Jesus in a manger made of Popsicle sticks. Each had a date and sometimes a few carved words explaining who had given the ornament to them, often long before I was born. Treasured symbols of friends and family through the years. We put them all on the tree and told the kids stories from long ago when Grammie would spend hours trying to untangle all the lights and how sometimes Bapa would invent crazy games to keep us out of the room as we waited, because the lights took all of Grammie's energy. The kids giggled at the thought of their gray-haired grandmother as a young red-haired mom tussling with knotted-up Christmas bulbs, the last of her patience waning. There was also the story of their Aunt Meg's "Baby's First Christmas" cradle ornament that she and I would move from place to place on the tree until we got caught. And my own children were in awe that Auntie Meg and I had ever been small and in trouble.

This was also the time of year when both Aidan and Chase loved hearing their birth stories and would beg me to repeat them over and over again. Especially Chase—especially this year.

"Tell me how you held me again. Tell me how when I cried, you told me it was going to be okay because you were there."

Chase loved his birth story this year more than any other because there were pictures of him and me in the hospital together. In one picture, I lay in the hospital bed with an IV needle taped to my hand, holding Chase. He often asked to see this picture and would then say, "Aw, Mommy, I'm a little baby and I'm crying, but you have a needle and you're being brave like me."

Just seeing someone else in his family in a hospital with an IV brought him a much-needed sense of connectedness. So we sat in the old wingback chair under the grandfather clock decorated with evergreen boughs, and he asked to hear the story yet again, my younger December boy.

"When you were born, the doctor caught you, and he said, 'It's a boy! Did you know it was going to be a boy?' And I said that I did know." I could feel Chase snuggle into my lap, as he loved this part.

"And then the doctor said you were holding your head up by yourself! He said you were so strong!"

He looked up. "But Mommy, don't forget that you holded me when I cried, and you said it's going to be okay."

I nodded. "Of course. The nurse put you in my arms, and I said, 'It's okay, sweet boy, it's okay. Mommy's here now.'"

Chase reached up and put a hand on my cheek. "Aw, Mommy . . ."

But I could see that he was hearing the story differently this time. He was barely three, skeletally weak, and lay cradled in my arms not unlike his infant self, and after I told him again how he cried and I held him, he curled into me as if hiding from something.

"Will you keep holding me?"

"Of course, sweet boy!" I stroked his smooth head as he continued.

"No, Mom, will you hold me so the death won't get me and take me away?"

Oh, dear God, Jehovah Rapha, please not this. Not now.

When the big brown eyes of your tiny three-year-old look into your own, and he asks urgently and honestly to hold him against death, there are a hundred directions the brain goes over the sound of your heart breaking for the horror of the moment you find yourself sitting in. Bob and I had never given Chase the burden of a terminal diagnosis to carry. He knew he was sick and that it was very serious, but we'd determined to leave the terminal implications for the time when he needed to know, and he hadn't needed to know yet.

Just as I would never ask a small child to carry a package several times his own weight, neither would we ask him to carry this heaviness that was much too great for him—unless it was absolutely necessary. We continued to hope for the January results, showing that the treatment may have worked. Yet even in our guarded conversations with him and our care for choosing the right words, Chase knew. That day, as I sat holding him, I wondered what God was preparing him for, that Chase would know and articulate these words. *What was on his heart?*

Then came the hardest moment: the one where I could not lie, and I've never felt quite so powerless. It took me forever to answer him. I wanted to say, "Yes, of course I will, baby!" One of the greatest joys of parenting is speaking comfort and security into the lives of my children. Even the monsters under the bed fear the mama. However, as choked up as I was even to think of these words, I had to speak the truth as I hugged him close.

"Oh, my sweet boy, I can't. I will hold you forever in this life. My arms will be the last thing you remember, but if Jesus wants to take you away from the cancer, it's okay to go with Him."

He whimpered. "I don't want to."

Fighting tears, I went on. "I know, sweet boy, and that's okay for now. But hey, Chasey, did you like the concert when we listened to the music?" He nodded.

"Okay, well, heaven is like that, only . . ." my voice broke. "Only much, much more beautiful and wonderful. And in heaven, there won't be any more cancer. Your baseball will be beautiful, and your body won't hurt, and you'll get to have music and singing with Jesus forever."

He paused to consider it. "No needles?"

"No needles."

"Will we sing 'O My Soul'?"

"I promise."

"Will it be a long time?"

"No. You know how Daddy is about to come home from work right now?"

He nodded. "In just a minute, he'll come into this house, and being in heaven will be like that. I'll hold you here with the cancer when . . ."

I could hardly bring myself to say the words to him. "When death comes, and then you'll see Jesus—He'll be so excited to see you—and just a minute later, Daddy and I will come through the door to be with you again. It'll only be a minute, and Jesus will be with you, okay? Just like He is when you go into surgeries."

I will never cease to be amazed at a small child's ability to take huge, mind-bending concepts at nearly complete face value. With his questions out and being contented with the answers, Chase relaxed into my arms and popped his thumb back into his mouth, smiling. And in typical Chase fashion, he never once said he'd miss us—only that everyone would miss him.

This conversation by the Christmas tree in the frosty dusk, the kind of night when the lights reflect everything, this conversation pierced my heart, and I can feel it still. There are some conversations that don't dim with time. In my heart, I always pictured these sorts of conversations happening when I was old and gray and Chase was tall, strong, and looked like his father—and he would be sitting next to *my* bed. It seemed to be happening about fifty years too early, and there was a bitter taste that stuck in my throat from the words that had been spoken at his request.

Think about it for a moment. Christmas is light and love and family and joy and putting aside the things that usually worry and bother us in order to focus on the things that we often daily ignore—the things that truly matter. It's a time to stop running around and remember who we are and why we're here, and yet, for all the joy, it's bookended by an awful lot of terminal. It's because we are terminal in our sin that Jesus came as an infant. It's because there was no way to make it right between us and the Father that Jesus died in our place, offering ultimate healing—to be made whole in Him. It's because we live in a world where mothers hold their children close and pray that death will not come for them yet. All of this is what makes God our Jehovah Rapha. He came for each of us to be healed. As I held Chase close under the holiday decorations, I gripped the eternal promise that brought the only hope possible: My love could not stop death, but His love conquered it forever.

19

When Joy is Confusing

The day of an MRI is as if you are standing in front of two doors. One door opens to a continuation of the life you have known and made your peace with, while the other door opens to scary changes and heartbreak. You never know which door will be opened to walk through until you hear the results of the scan. There was a strange suspension of reality while Bob and I waited for the phone call from the doctor, which usually doesn't happen for hours or sometimes even days. It's terrifying to stand in front of the two doors. And a part of me always searched for a third door. *Why isn't there a third door that holds neither cancer nor complications?*

Christmas had come and gone. My parents' small house that had been stuffed to the rafters with four daughters, their spouses, and the grandchildren had grown quiet again. It had been a wonderful time full of games and laughter. Now Darcy was back in school, the windows were covered in January frost, and it was time to start chemo again.

About a week into the new year, Chase spent time in the hospital getting chemo, came home for a few days, and was then readmitted for inexplicably high fevers. Before we had time to think, it was January 17: MRI day. The moment of reckoning was finally upon us.

Chase was scheduled to undergo anesthesia, be scanned, and while he was still unconscious, the staff would transfer him from the imaging floor to another area to take samples of his spinal fluid. These tests would tell the doctors if the radiation had worked. The results of this day would determine the course of our future.

As Bob and I waited out the MRI, we had the same trivial conversation we'd had many times over the past few weeks.

"Are you doing okay?"

"Yeah, I'm fine." Bob's voice was resigned.

"What do you think? Do you have a feeling about which way this is going to go?"

"Honestly, no. I have no idea."

"Me neither." We kept kicking around these snatches of dialogue, lobbing them back and forth to each other because the real things, the deep things—knowing that we were both terrified of the doors in front of us—those things were too hard to put into words right then.

After Chase awoke in recovery, he was transferred to the neuro-oncology floor for blood and platelet transfusions, where we joined him. Chase was still groggy, and so we dimmed the lights in the hospital room as he lay on the daybed. Dana, a friend from church, had been working downtown and stopped by with treats and encouragement as we waited.

As we sat in the little room, we talked about mundane things. Rather suddenly, both Dr. Lulla and Dr. Becca were in the doorway.

"Hey, gang! How's everybody doing?" Dr. Lulla motioned toward the bed where Chase was sleeping. "How'd he do with the MRI?"

"Just fine. I think it was all pretty standard. Any word on the results?"

There was just a hint of an exchanged glance between the doctors, and then they looked at us. "Do you have a second to come with us? Can your friend stay with Chase for just a minute?"

Bob and I turned to Dana and she nodded, smiling and assuring us that they'd be fine and she could always page a nurse if Chase needed anything.

We left the small room and went down the hall to a large conference room. There was a big oval table in the center and desks and phones all around the border of the room. A large screen was mounted on the southern wall, and there were computers everywhere. This was where oncology teams gathered on clinic days. Many times we had walked by this room and seen a large group of Chase's nurses and doctors gathered, deep in conversation. Our presence here today meant one thing: They already had the results.

Dr. Lulla ushered us in, offering us seats opposite the screen so that we would see the projected images. I could feel the tenseness emanating from Bob, who sat beside me; my ears were ringing, and I fought dizziness. It was as if every fiber of our beings leaned in for this one pivotal moment.

Dr. Becca sat next to us as Dr. Lulla began scrolling through MRI images on the wall in front of us.

"Are you guys ready for this?" He paused to look at both of us. The seconds felt like years.

"The scan is clear."

This momentous news was delivered in a positive but reserved tone.

Bob reached over and took my hand. "Clear! Are you serious?"

Dr. Lulla nodded. "I am completely serious." He began to flip through the images, stopping for side-by-side comparisons with previous images. "See? This one on the left is the original MRI." As a grayscale image, the tumor was white and it looked gigantic on the screen.

"And then this . . ." Dr. Lulla kept scrolling, knowing exactly what he was looking for. "This is the MRI we did in October, right before we radiated. Becca, do you know where the thing is?" He paused while they both looked for a laser pointer.

Pointer in hand, he continued. "Okay, so, here we go. October. You can still see the cancer cells here and here," indicating areas of white shading. "And this on the right is today. Look at the difference." He pointed to the image of our son's head, an image that was seemingly free of any white shadows.

I felt like I was in and out of consciousness. Sometimes I heard what was being said, and sometimes I didn't. I was in shock. And the shock was quickly overtaken by what felt suspiciously like guilt. I didn't feel as happy as I thought I would. Quickly silencing the strange thought, I tuned back in to hear Bob ask a question.

"So does this mean he's cancer free? Is he in remission?"

Dr. Lulla visibly cringed. "I wouldn't use those words. In truth, we really try not to use the word *remission* in this context. What I would say is this . . ." He hesitated as he searched for the right response, giving us neither false hope nor discouragement.

"Chase is exactly where I'd want him to be at this point in his treatment. There is no evidence of disease." Then he paused again.

"Does this mean that there are no cancer cells left in his body? It looks that way, but it's hard to tell by these pictures. I really think that time will tell, but the best way to describe where we currently are in this is 'no evidence of disease.' He's exactly where we would want him to be right now."

Bob leaned back in his chair, as if digesting all that we'd just been told. "Then let me just ask you this. Is it necessary to continue with the treatment if Chase is doing this well?"

Dr. Lulla's response was quick and sure. "Absolutely. There is induction chemotherapy—the frequent and high dose chemo that Chase has been going through—and then there is maintenance chemotherapy. Chase has completed the induction, but I think it would be in Chase's best interest to continue his treatment. There are several moving parts to this: the surgery when Dr. Alden removed as much as he could, and the chemo, which has done exactly what we wanted it to do by forcing a remission of the growing cells. It has taken away what we can see on a scan. But that doesn't necessarily mean that there are no atypical cells still present in his body. This is why the rest of his protocol is still so important. Does that make sense?"

We nodded. It hadn't been enough to pull the weeds out of the garden. Now we had to make the soil such that no weeds would ever grow again.

We talked for a few more minutes and then went back to Dana and Chase. Chase had woken up from choking on his vomit, and poor Dana had to keep her promise to page a nurse. They were cleaning Chase up as we came in, and as the nurse left, Dana looked up and raised an eyebrow. "Well?"

Bob and I looked at each other and then looked at her. "It's clear. His scan was clear."

She sighed. "Praise God."

I walked Dana to the elevators, staying out in the lobby to make some phone calls. And all the calls seemed to blend together with the same questions.

How did we feel? *Great.*

Weren't we so happy? *Thrilled.*

What did Chase think? *He doesn't know yet.*

Is this remission? *No, it's "no evidence of disease." Please stop saying remission.*

If his cancer is gone, why are you going to keep doing chemo? *Because.*

The transfusions ended sometime around 7:00 p.m., and as we drove home in the January darkness, Chase played with an iPad in the backseat while I continued with phone calls and texts. This was big news, and there were a lot of people to contact, but Bob and I didn't really talk to each other.

That night, as we attached Chase's IV bag, we gathered the kids around us and told them that Chase's MRI was awesome. They were happy, but since there had been no pressing need to tell them that Chase's cancer was terminal, learning that he'd been granted a reprieve did not hold the same significance for them that it did for us.

Finally, at the end of all the important words, Aidan raised his hand. This was it, now came the questions—were we prepared for these moments of weighty discussion?

Bob signaled him with a nod. "Yes, Aidan, what is it?"

Aidan fidgeted on the edge of the couch. "Um, well, Daddy, this is kind of boring. Can we go to bed now?"

Bob gave him and the other kids permission to leave, as nobody had any more questions, but Darcy lingered, putting her head against my arm as I worked on Chase's bag. Her voice was soft. "I'm so glad Chase is okay. Does this mean he isn't going to . . ." she stopped short, as if she realized she shouldn't say "die" in front of him. My eyes remained focused on the central line in front of me.

"It's great news, Sister. Don't worry about the other thing right now, okay? I promise that I'll tell you if you need to worry." She nodded and left to get ready for bed.

I finished attaching the IV cord and started the pump. Stripping off the latex gloves, I picked up the satchel and Chase, and carried them both to the crib he slept in. Chase had just crossed the threshold of twenty-eight pounds, but he still felt too light as I carried him.

"Mom, I was so brave for my MRI."

"You *so* were, sweet boy."

"Will you sing me my song before I go to bed?"

"Sure." So I sat in the dark and sang "10,000 Reasons" as he lay in the bed, and tucking Chase in, I came back out to the living room and dropped onto the couch next to Bob with a sigh.

"Bobby, why don't I feel happy about this? It was *clear*. What is wrong with me?"

He shrugged. "I felt the same way. I'm happy, but at the same time, I'm not. I think it's because we have heard too much about this cancer to really feel safe with a single good scan. In my head, I'm just waiting for it to come back."

"I know! Me too. That's exactly what it's like. There's this giant BUT to everything from today. It's clear, but . . . it could come back at any time, and we aren't safe yet."

He sighed again. "Yeah."

"And you know what the craziest, sickest part of this is?" I debated whether I should say these words aloud.

Bob turned his head to face me. "What?"

"I'm terrified. Somehow, in my mind, I was prepared for Chase to die, but to keep on, to know this is going to keep going on, and every three months we'll do another scan and wonder if it's going to come back and Chase could have neurological damage . . . I'm the worst person in the world for not being over-the-moon-thrilled, but Bobby, I'm absolutely terrified."

He put an arm around me as I vented. "I understand. I feel the same way."

And looking up at him, I questioned, "What are we going to do? How do we even put this into words?"

Smiling ruefully, he hugged me close. "Moment by moment, remember?"

It was as if, with the news of a good scan, there was a huge direction shift. We'd been preparing for Chase to die, and without realizing it, we'd neglected to prepare ourselves for him to live. During my darkest "cancer" days, I'd envisioned our family of six as a family of five—a gaping hole in the siblings that mirrored the hole in my heart. I'd never projected a family of six, with the five of us coming around the sixth to work with the broken pieces, complications, and knowledge that our "normal" would never mirror the "normal" of those around us. My joy in the first really big, really good news we'd ever had on Chase's cancer was being hampered by my complete terror at not knowing what was to come, but knowing it was going to look like nothing for which I'd foolishly attempted to prepare.

And here is the truth of that day: I missed a lot of the elation because the situation highlighted how far out of control life would continue to be. The doctors expressed "cautious optimism," and all I could wonder was what would come next after this good news.

Both Bob and I found that we trusted God and trusted the doctors, but we didn't trust this vicious cancer and its "no-holds-barred" side effects, and so the happiest day became a terribly conflicted day.

Once again, I had been gaining my strength from my ability to cope with the situation as I thought I understood it, and when the circumstances changed, I lost what little ability I thought I had. My source of joy and peace was displaced.

It breaks my heart to write these words—that the happiest day was so hard—but I am writing them down. Read them; learn from my foolish self, standing in hospital halls, thinking I knew better, thinking I had somehow come to terms with what I saw playing out in my life. The truth is that I was wrong. I do not get to say what God will use to shape who He wants me to be, and I do not get to pinpoint and spotlight what most glorifies Him in my life. And any attempt to predict those directions, to think to myself, *Ah, this is how I am being refined . . . This is my Jim Elliot moment, my Corrie ten Boom moment. This is what will define me*—any such thoughts are silly in their attempt to understand things beyond me. God knows. I don't.

I had honestly believed for almost six months that I would be crushed and defined by the loss of a beloved child, but in that January MRI moment, it became apparent for the first time that I was to be shaped by something else—a complicated existence with a living one. And in all the pondering, the verse that kept coming to me was from Jeremiah: how God knows the plans He has for me and His plans are for my good. That led me to start thinking about all the times and places in which the Bible tells me to be thankful.

How could I possibly be thankful for His plans when I didn't trust the joy or the MRI results?

Once again, I found myself flipping through Psalms for an answer of reconciliation. Landing on Psalm 33:20-22 (ESV), I read "Our soul waits for the LORD; he is our help and our shield. For our heart is glad in him, because we trust in his holy name. Let your steadfast love, O LORD, be upon us, even as we hope in you."

Whether we would be asked to face remission, "no evidence of disease," even relapse—every label and every time frame folds into the truth that God loves us with a great and steadfast love, a love that pours out the moment-by-moment grace we need to be able to hope in Him, even when everything seems to be counterintuitive. No matter what lies ahead or when, His love is our joy.

20

Slaying Guilt

It had been six months since treatment had started, and Chase had gone from a chubby boy who ran around with a washcloth covering his "baseball" to a wispy, wan shadow of himself with healing scars crisscrossing his head and body. His eyes were narrowed in a constant squint since he had no eyelashes to protect them, and the simple act of crossing a room was often enough to wear him out.

He had become such a different person, and while we had definitely seen it unfolding, we had been too busy to process it—the whitening skin, the weight loss, the hair falling out. We had lived it all, but for the sake of our sanity and our family, we just had to absorb it as fact and keep going.

Beginning in January 2013, in the dead of a Midwest winter, Chase's treatment went through a two-month season of moderation. Chemo was every four weeks instead of every week, and for the first time, we could sit and reflect on what we'd been through.

It soon became all we could think about. Bob stayed so strong, even as I became increasingly fixated on processing the destruction.

I would flash to that sensation of getting on the ambulance and leaving our home with Chase against my chest. I could feel the moment we parted before brain surgery, the moment we sat in that first conference room and heard exactly what we were up against. In the middle of the night came visions of all the bags of blood and the hard talks we had when Chase had been lying virtually unresponsive for too long. Reliving these experiences in my mind often overwhelmed me with an inexplicable feeling of deep loss, and I would wake troubled and crying. On some level, I could hardly believe it was all real.

It seemed silly to muffle sobs into a pillow when a very much alive Chase lay sleeping across the room, but this is the strange nature of things like this. Sometimes the feelings follow the experience, and so we found ourselves processing all that had happened on a totally different level. Up until this point, we'd sought to merely survive the cancer and make sense of it enough to at least keep ourselves functioning and making the necessary decisions. Now, in a moment of stillness during treatment, we were really able to look at what had happened and how this wretched disease had destroyed so much. The delayed reaction took our breath away. How could something we already knew surprise us again?

My experience was that grief came not just with death, but with loss of any kind. For several weeks after Chase was diagnosed, as we continued to live with my parents, I struggled to go back to our house. I was fearful that I would find Chase's toys on the floor, and in my mind's eye see him without his tumor, sitting at the table and playing with trains. I knew his little shoes were still by the door, and I could picture his chubby, often dirty little feet, without the bruises from needles, shoved into those shoes, as he ran outside and played.

Most of all, I wanted to avoid the sensory feeling of the rooms, which would take me back in an instant to those first, awful moments when I saw the terror in his eyes as I held him for dear life on the gurney. The Chase I gave birth to, the Chase in my memory, was gone. His infectious laughter, which used to come easily and often from his pudgy belly, had now been frequently replaced by unearthly screams—how he hated to be touched now. Lying around on the couch or bed, being too winded to make it across the room, had replaced his energetic play. His run was now a hobble, his legs slowed by a traumatized brain trying to regain signals and his arms heavy with a portable IV bag for most of his waking hours.

The first time I entered the condo, I called Bob.

"Hey, love, how are you doing?" he asked.

"Bobby, everything is just where we left it. The movies are still lying open on the shelf from when we kept him up for the EEG." My throat closed. "It feels like somebody died in here . . . like we died in here too."

"It's okay. It's going to be okay. I'm just really glad you went over there today. Just make it through today, okay?" I nodded even though he couldn't see me. I felt so guilty. *Chase was still alive, so why did I feel this way?*

It was as if, with the clear MRI and the small break in treatment, we were able to catch the slightest glimpse of all the treatment that lay ahead. We were finally able to mourn our life before cancer and even that Chase had cancer. In the early days, we'd cried from the frustration, exhaustion, and shock, but now we were freed to feel loss on a different level. And the feeling I'd first felt when Dr. Lulla explained the scan only continued to grow: guilt. *How dare we feel so burdened when we were the ones still breathing?*

And now that we had some idea that Chase was going to live longer than six months, we began to discuss "collateral damages"— the incidental destruction that came from all our decisions to save Chase's life. We had agreed on this course of treatment, but now we sat with the damages, and we had to learn to accept them—not just on a cerebral level, but in our daily lives.

The damages unfolded over time. One day, Chase stood in the middle of the room, surrounded by his siblings, his red face lifted toward the ceiling, screaming his heart out. He clasped his portable IV bag to his chest and wailed until everyone around him was forced to stop talking. Bob walked over to him.

"Chase, you need to use your words. What's wrong?"

He stomped his foot, completely outraged. "I was trying to talk, and they wouldn't be quiet!"

This is how he'd come to deal with noise. For Chase, communication had become like a bad cellular phone connection, the kind where you can't hear the person on the other end if there's even a little static or background noise. Have you ever jumped into a pool or lake? There's the sound as your body cuts the surface of the water, and then there is the sound of the water surrounding you—a strange, fluid echo that effectively muffles noises above the surface. The audiologist said this is what it sounded like in Chase's head. His world was under water, and he could only hear one noise at a time.

His hearing had been getting worse since Christmas, and what had started as only needing to speak closely to him in crowded or noise-filled situations now became his not hearing an urgent call in a quiet house from only a few feet away. His speech was deteriorating with his hearing, and his words ran together in a slur, often leaving only one or two words recognizable in a long gibberish sentence of something very important that he wanted to communicate. When he couldn't think of the words, he would often make a humming noise in the same meter as the syllables, and he could fill an entire sentence with sound, but only ever say two or three words.

The other day, I found a brief video of Chase reciting Joshua 1:9 during this time, the verse that had sustained all of us. He did it with so much enthusiasm, but you could hardly under-stand anything that came out of his mouth (although certainly God could). "Ja-nava-hew-new-man-jee, stronan-ov-a-courage, nana-lordor-God-is-wish-oo."

To say communicating like this was frustrating for him and for us would be an understatement. It got so bad that we strongly considered keeping him under "house arrest" because taking him out into public places posed so many issues from hindrances to outright hazards. He couldn't hear when we told him to be careful, and grabbing him to pull his body out of the way of, say, a passing car, only angered him from the surprise element of our ripping into his virtually silent world. Though to be fair, pulling him out of the path of passing vehicles had angered him before his diagnosis too.

One of the chemotherapies Chase had been given in the first weeks of treatment had a side effect of hearing loss, but there was also a chance that the loss was entirely from fluid pooled deep in the ear canal, a fairly common side effect of radiation. So, with this in mind, Chase was scheduled for hearing tests. We knew there was also the possibility that he would need surgery to drain his ears and have tubes inserted, the hope being to remove as much fluid as possible and restore or at least stabilize his hearing. If the attempt was not successful, he would be evaluated for hearing aids, and eventually, he would need cochlear implants to allow him to function. Somehow, it seemed that every damage and every option would eventually lead to more surgeries.

Late that February, we arrived at the hospital for our scheduled hearing evaluation. We were ushered back to what looked like a bank vault door, and I had to duck my head as I stepped into a tiny booth, the diameter of which was only big enough to incorporate a child-sized table and chairs, some toys, and another small table filled with devices and machines to fit and know the human ear.

The tech introduced herself, telling us that she had a friend helping her on the other side of a tinted-glass window at one end of the
room. Chase was skittish when she reached for the earphones.

"Chase, it's okay. These will look so cool. They're just like the
ones Uncle Andy wears when he flies planes."

Chase tilted his head, considering this new information. "Uncle
Airplane?"

Smothering a big smile, I nodded solemnly, deciding to overlook
the sudden and new nickname for my mom's brother. "Yes. Uncle
Airplane."

"Okay." He let the tech gently place the pieces in each ear and
then clip the cords to the back of his shirt. As we waited for the test
to get started, the usual round of questions commenced as he tried
to turn gingerly and face me without disrupting anything around
him.

"No needles?"

"No needles."

"No nap?"

"No nap."

"Is it going to hurt?"

"Nope! This is just going to check your ears to make sure you
can hear me when I tell you to pick up your toys." I winked at him,
and he pulled a disgusted face. "Mo-o-o-m, do *not* say that to me!"

Moments later, the adults in the room could all hear the sound
through the earpieces, and it was hard not to hold my breath in the
stillness. Chase was doing a puzzle with the tech sitting in the room,
having been instructed to put a piece of the puzzle in place when
he heard something in the earpieces. He heard sound after sound
in varying pitches and levels, and he assembled two whole puzzles,
but then a third puzzle was set on the table.

Chase sat in the tiny plastic chair, small hand suspended with
a puzzle piece, waiting for the sound so he could place the final

piece. Even though everyone else in the room could hear the sound clear as day, Chase didn't hear anything. He looked at the technician beside him in confusion. Behind the dark glass, I could see the shadow of the tech in the booth working the soundboard so that the sound was louder in Chase's ears while the other tech made sure he understood what he was supposed to do.

"Now, Chase, remember, when you hear the sound," she emphasized each word as if it were a clue, "you take your puzzle piece and put it right here, okay?"

He nodded and listened intently but still nothing. The volume was increased two more times, and then with a gasp, Chase's eyes lit up. He threw the puzzle piece at the board. He was so excited to finally hear a sound. The results were undeniable: Chase had lost his high-frequency hearing. It was time to schedule surgery, which would take place about a month later.

The morning of the surgery, I told some friends what was going to happen to Chase, and I asked them to pray for him and us. A moment after I sent the text asking for prayer, my phone rang with a text from my friend Cindy: "He doesn't need ears to hear the voice of God."

Bob took the day off of work to be there, and a relatively short time after Chase went into surgery, the concierge in the waiting room called our names. It was already time to go to the postoperative area where Chase was recovering.

The hallway was brightly lit, but the recovery areas, each with floor-to-ceiling curtains that were pulled around the individual beds, were dim and quiet. As we entered the hallway leading to his room, I could hear Chase screaming. He had awakened and was irritated to the point of thrashing in the bed. Picking up our pace, Bob and I got to him as quickly as possible. His recovery nurse explained that the anesthesia was just starting to wear off.

"Can I hold him?"

"That would be good. See if you can get him to go back to sleep for a while."

So Chase and I settled into the high-backed rocking chair next to his bed, and I rocked him back into a gentle sleep to wait out the effects of the drugs. He settled down fairly quickly, but before he closed his eyes, he looked up at me and slurred, "You stole Daddy's comfy chair." I smiled while Bob pretended to be offended, and Chase drifted off with the slightest hint of a smile.

There was no sense of time in the small recovery areas, only the sound of other children and the soft noise of machines. When Chase finally stirred, I spoke to him gently, and as he sat against me, still wrapped in blankets and cords, he gasped. "Mom, I can hear!" With a huge grin, he stuffed his thumb in his mouth, and leaned back against my chest, content to rest and hear the sounds in the room. The tubes had relieved the fluid, and he could hear us.

The doctors smiled in somewhat incredulous encouragement, but another hearing test done that same spring would prove Chase's instincts right. There was some permanent damage, but he could indeed hear far better than before the tubes went in. And with the help of multiple therapies, he began to recover his words and pronunciation.

The damage and guilt go hand-in-hand and never really go away, no matter how much Chase thrives. When, in the summer of 2015, Chase failed the eye tests given at school three times in a row, I scheduled him for an appointment with an ophthalmologist. The day of the appointment, the doctor held the light closer to Chase's eyes, while trying to put together his medical history.

"Has he been on a lot of steroids?"

"Other than a few weeks around the removal of the tumor, no."

"But you did say that he had radiation?"

"Yes, proton radiation—about thirty treatments."

"And when was that?"

"October to December 2012. Why?"

"Usually we see this with longtime steroid use." He paused and turned to me.

"Both eyes are full of cataracts. I'd like to see if we can help his vision with glasses for now, but I'll want to see you back in six weeks. If the glasses don't help, he'll need surgery."

I could feel the guilt creeping back and got on the phone with Bob as soon as we left the office. "We did the right thing, didn't we? The radiation—all of it?"

"We did. You can't go there. Remember what we said? Flip the question: Would you be okay with Chase dying from cancer because he was going to have cataracts?"

"No, you're right, you're right. I just felt it really heavily in that exam room—all the damage. I mean, we do routine checks on his heart, all the hearing stuff, and now this, but I feel stupid for even saying this out loud. We're the ones who are still breathing."

Again Bob cautioned, "Love, you can't go there. Just take today." Then he laughed. "And send me a picture of Chase in his new glasses."

Bob was right. Ever since the clear MRI, I'd let myself get sucked into not only the grief, but the guilt, too, and when confronted with the choice, I often found excuses to stop choosing joy. Somehow, it was easier to keep walking into a place of fearful projection and lose sight of the truth that all any of us have is the day in front of us. And more so that God is greater and better than any collateral damage. Faded hearing or a cloudy eye was not a hopeless life. Realizing how beautiful God continued to be in the imperfection and brokenness was yet another step toward slaying the guilt I felt and finding peace in the cancer journey that God had given us.

21

FACING FEARS

"Four score and seven years ago . . . our fathers . . . brought forth . . . a *NEW NATION*!" Two-year-old Chase stood in the middle of the living room, rocking on the tips of his toes in blue rain boots and waving a giant plastic broadsword, a superhero cape swirling behind him as he moved.

When Darcy was memorizing the Gettysburg Address for a school presentation in the spring of 2012, the little boys had whole-heartedly joined in. For anything Darcy did, the boys wanted to do too, and as I've learned only too well in our house, if you say anything enough times in front of young children, they'll be able to repeat it on cue.

A two-year-old quoting Abraham Lincoln is a little crazy, and the colorful getup was even more crazy, but it was also a little wonderful too. When his burst of rhetoric was finished, he would celebrate like an athlete, jumping around and asking for high fives from everyone who had been listening. Occasionally, when Chase was in a really cooperative mood, he'd recite as far as "conceived in liberty and dedicated to the proposition . . ." And then he'd be done for good, midsentence. I'm profoundly thankful President Lincoln got a little further in the speech than Chase.

These words that Lincoln spoke of honor and faith in the human race and the words of God given to Joshua in Joshua 1:9 that gave courage to Israel, these would be the last words Chase's brain retained before a brain tumor ripped into it. And though Lincoln was forgotten for a season, Joshua remained, and I suppose, in a way, you could say those words became his life verse. He never left home or went into a surgical procedure without them.

For Chase, having a surgical procedure was roughly the equivalent of the average person going to their general practitioner for a bad cold—it wasn't necessarily scary or complicated, just a necessary part of life. To date, he has only ever had one major surgery—the brain surgery, but he has been under anesthesia for everything from MRIs, central line surgeries, and spinal taps to a few other random things in between. He had also needed anesthesia for every single radiation treatment, so the anesthesia team at the hospital felt like family. We knew all the doctors, and they all knew us, and the new doctors who came in had at least heard of Chase, which always made him feel a little bit legendary.

Because of his familiarity with the pre-op proceedings, he was often pretty relaxed before a procedure, only wanting to hear his song, go through his list of questions about needles and magic naps, and recite his Bible verse—it was his pregame routine, if you will. And if anything, surgeries were often used as bragging rights with siblings.

"No, Aidan, you can't come with me because I'm going to go take a nap with the doctor at *my* hospital."

And Aidan's expression would immediately crumple, his lower lip hanging out in a dejected frown. "Awww! No fair!"

But Chase would nod sagely. "Yes, it's true. Because *I* have cancers and *you* don't."

Chase's familiarity was juxtaposed by my own growing struggle. Sure, it was nice to know everybody on the anesthesia team and have them know us so personally, but somehow it never got easier to say yes to procedures. Bob and I hated saying the good-byes, parting with him, and reassuring him that we'd be there when he woke up. Going through these motions again and again felt twisted, and each parting seemed to get harder, not easier. Familiarity is supposed to breed contempt, but in this particular medical realm, it bred anxiety and weariness. Almost every time, I felt the heart sigh of "Oh please, not again" even when everything around us was stamped routine.

Because Chase had grown so comfortable, it struck me as strange that he suddenly started hating and fearing procedures. He went from being matter of fact, even bragging, to screaming at me if I even mentioned he had "a nap" coming up on the calendar.

One night, while the other kids played and my mom worked in the kitchen, Chase and I sat together on the couch.

"Chasey Bear, what's going on? Why do you scream whenever I talk about a nap with the doctor?"

At first he screamed and even growled at me. "I don't want to talk about it, Mom!" My heart beat a little faster. I knew he was really angry when he called me Mom, not Mommy.

We sat together and as I gently rubbed his back, trying to calm him, he finally told me. "The nap hurts my body, Mom—because of the doctors. They hurt me when they go like this," he mimicked pinching his cheeks together and covering his mouth and nose. "They scare me! Please don't let them do that to me!"

His words were brief and the description disjointed, but still the picture was painted in vivid detail. I could easily imagine the scenario: an anesthesia team trying to work with a struggling, probably screaming Chase on the table in the operating room and how the doctors would need to hold the mask to his face so that he could go under. Usually Chase was given a mild sedative while he was with us so that the last thing he'd remember was that moment with us. But there had been a time several weeks prior when he'd known the doctors so well and been willing to separate from us so perfectly, that we'd all decided that he could do without the forced forgetfulness of a drug.

At the time we made the decision, it seemed like such a good one—we were proceeding without drug intervention. We never considered the seconds of consciousness when Chase was taken into the room away from us and then not brought back despite his pleas. I've pictured him crying for us a thousand times, and it breaks me down every time. There, in just a few seconds of consciousness, as they held the mask to his face and he screamed for us, we weren't there.

This is why he hated the nap now. Not for the nap itself, but the mask. To him, the anesthesia mask was now a thing of force, pain, and separation. It had covered his face, covered his cries for those he loved, and for a brief second, he'd felt that he couldn't breathe. Every time I talked about the next nap, this is what he thought of, and that is why he'd scream. As he explained his fear, I could feel the tears pricking the corners of my eyes. The negative and the necessary all got mixed up together, and it hurt to hear about his fear and pain this way.

When Bob got home from work, we immediately closeted ourselves behind closed doors, and I recounted Chase's words. Bob sat on the bed, while I paced angrily.

"Bobby, this just makes me so angry! They hurt him."

"I know, but it wasn't intentional."

"I know, and I know I would have done the same thing if I'd

been in the room, but all I can think about right now is that Chase cried for us and we weren't there. I hate that!"

He sighed. "Me too."

The maternal instinct to protect my child flooded my mind, even though it was weeks after the fact. I could feel myself shaking and wanted to cancel Chase's next appointment; my irrational fear reasoning that if he never had to replicate the incident, I could keep him safe.

In truth, I think that way all the time. If I avoid the circumstances that bring a trial or difficulty into my life, I'll successfully avoid these circumstances all the time, right? I once panicked when I was driving on a certain road. It was a terribly hot day, the air-conditioning in the car was broken, all the children were crying, and I was hemmed in by traffic and couldn't make a left turn out of the large intersection I found myself in. Suddenly, I felt like I couldn't breathe. In truth, that probably had as much to do with the heat as anything, but it happened, and it terrified me to feel so vulnerable when I was actually in no danger, and so I began to avoid that intersection whenever I could. It seems silly, but that is how my brain wants to work. If it's hard, remove it. If you remove the circumstance, you remove the irritant, and then the feelings, insecurities, and fears never find you. Right?

The sight of Chase cupping his hands to his cheeks like an anesthesia mask being clasped to his face caused an all-out, punch-it-in-the-face hatred, which clouded everything in front of me. My mind was filled with a strangely futile desire for action. I wanted to do or say something, but I couldn't go back in time, and I knew in my heart, that had I been in that room, I would have soothed Chase, yes, but I probably would have helped them hold the mask to his face as his need was greater than his fear. I wanted to point a finger and couldn't as everyone had done the right thing, but my baby boy was sad and scared. This was an intersection that I couldn't drive around; I hated the cancer because of what it put us through—it truly was an I-have-to-go-walk-and-pray-it-out kind of hate. In that moment, it felt as if the disease somehow had made monsters of us all.

At Chase's next clinic, the same morning as his next procedure, we sat and talked with Dr. Lulla and Kristi, the nurse-practitioner, about his mask fear. All of Chase's teams were nothing but amazing, deciding that from this point forward, Chase would always be given the pre-medication while he was still with us. But even with all the wonderful accommodations, it didn't change that the mask and the nap scared him terribly. There would be no way around this fear for either of us. He'd have to face being put under anesthesia again, and I'd have to face leaving him under anesthesia again. Neither of us was looking forward to this time.

As Chase lay on the bed in pre-op, I sat next to him, and leaning my arms down on the bed to rest my head, we talked.

"How are you doing, kiddo?"

"No mask?"

"No mask, remember? Dr. Lulla told them they couldn't do the mask with you anymore while you're awake. In just a minute, they'll bring you some medicine, and then you'll go to sleep while we're here with you, and when you wake up, we'll be there."

He visibly relaxed for a brief moment and then tensed again and whimpered, as if the anxiety hit him in waves. I reached for his hand through the metal railing on the Stryker bed. "Hey, what do we say when it gets like this?"

Chase looked at me blankly.

"What is our verse?"

His eyes showed recognition, but he was too far in the fear to want to remember the words and say them aloud.

"Let's say it together, sweet boy. 'Have I not commanded you?

Be strong and of good courage, for the Lord our God is with you.'
Joshua 1:9."

We whispered it a couple of times to each other, and as he often
did when he felt love toward someone, Chase reached out and
brushed my cheek with his hands. "You're my favorite, Mama."

"And you're my favorite, Chase."

Then someone in scrubs came with the medicine. Chase
remained in the room with us for a few more minutes while the
drug produced the desired effect, allowing Chase not to remember
any of it.

We couldn't avoid or bypass this day—we had to stare it down
and then walk through it. Here's the crazy part of walking into
the fear: While avoidance and escape feel safe, having to step right
into the hard time and stay there is always when and how I'm most
blessed. I think this is what it means to "abide"—to accept and act
on that acceptance—to take the hard thing and walk through it.

I sat in the waiting room while Chase lay unconscious on an
operating table, but in those dark places, we were not alone. For
us that day, the presence of God was not fire or cloud, like when
Joshua was instructed to have courage, but instead peace. There
was no human, logical reason that I should have felt peace at that
separated and powerless moment, but I did. That peace guarded
my heart and mind, just as promised, because the quiet whisper of
truth was this: that neither a hurting heart nor an operating room
are out of the realm of God's power and love.

When we were finally escorted to Chase's postoperative room, we
watched him as he slept off the anesthesia. The nurses had pur-
posely called us early so that we would be the first people he saw
when he awoke, and one of his nurses gave me instructions and
encouragement.

"It's okay to talk to him. He's been sleeping for almost half an hour now." She consulted the clock on her computer and then turned back to me. "He can hear your voice, even though he's asleep."

Bob sat in the comfy rocking chair working from his laptop, while I put the side railing down and got as close as I could to Chase's ear, whispering words into his dreams.

"You're okay, sweet boy, you're okay. Mommy and Daddy are here. The nap is done, and you were so brave. You were strong and of good courage, and I'm so proud of you."

He sighed and slept a few minutes longer, and when he woke, it was with a gasp. "Is it done? Did I do it?!"

We nodded and smiled with relief. "You did it, Chase!"

He raised his hand for a high five. "Mom, Dad, I did it!"

It's hard to describe the mixture of joy and relief that comes from doing something hard and finding it was done successfully, and in the wonderful post-op moment, Chase was experiencing that very thing. And then he turned his head to really look at us. "I had a magic nap with no mask, but hey, Daddy, you stole the comfy chair again."

Bob merely smiled with no intention of deferring. "Yes, I did. But hey, Chasey Bear, were you afraid?"

He shook his head ever so slightly. "Jesus was with me."

That single sentence spoke the very words I'd prayed for—that in the moment with no parents to champion or protect, Chase would not be alone. There was a far greater father—the Abba Father—who stood watch over our son.

And that was the end of our fears. By God's grace, we faced them, we won, and we moved on. Oh, how I wish I could write those words as we walk off into a sunset while the credits roll, with our lessons learned. But life isn't like a movie. The truth is that Chase and I both still get afraid before procedures, each for our own reasons. We hate being alone, separated from each other, and totally out of control of the situation. Every single time he goes in for something new, another "nap," we have to travel back to that same dark place where fears and what ifs lurk and find ourselves in God's presence all over again.

In my tired heart, I long for the once-and-done lesson, but as my dear friend and cancer survivor, Janet, reminds me before nearly every procedure to this day, if I were given my wish for ease, what reason would I have to abide in Him? The darkness of the ongoing struggle makes the Light that much more beautiful. If it were not so continually dark, if life were only difficult once and no more, I would miss the comfort and warmth of the ever-present Light.

22

ACKNOWLEDGING ANGER

Spring finally came and with it hope. It was warm and beautiful and the kids could once again play in the yard. My mom was getting ready to leave for Maine for several weeks to be with my sister Abby, expecting her second son, and we'd rounded not only the halfway mark on chemo, but what was statistically the most difficult part. The highest doses and most terrible things, such as radiation, were far behind us now, and we'd begun thinking about a future past the next hospital visit for the first time in months. But even though life had started to feel routine, Chase's immune system was weakening under the long-term duration of the chemotherapy protocol, and he started getting more fevers.

The first fever came late in the evening, the night before Easter. It was high enough to know it was real but too low to call the hospital. Even though we felt like we knew the course inside out by now, we had to wait another hour to see what happened. The only way we could escape calling was if the fever disappeared altogether, a highly unlikely scenario. The hour came and went, and the fever was the same. It became clear that there was no way around a trip to the emergency room, but as Chase was stable and the fever wasn't spiking, the doctor on call sent us to a local emergency room.

As Bob and I stood in the hall and discussed our options, we knew that whoever went with Chase would be gone for several hours, and we both knew I was pretty sleep deprived.

"Babe, let me take him and you sleep," Bob said. "I'm not too tired, and we're just going to be fifteen minutes away. I really don't think this run is going to be a big deal."

I watched his face closely. "Are you sure?"

"Yes, I'm sure. Help us get packed, and then go straight to bed, okay?"

As I packed them up and Bob carried Chase out the front door, the small boy called instructions over his father's shoulder.

"Did you remember to pack my cars? Did you pack Baby?" He never went anywhere without his favorite blanket.

He felt well enough to consider this a grand adventure, and I could see his grin in the dark. I stood on the front porch, blowing good-bye kisses and then fell into the bed in a room strangely devoid of sound.

I never realized until that moment how I set my heart and sleep to the sound of an IV pump, how much my sense of security was tied to controlling Chase's environment, and how I was starting to find my own identity there.

Dozing in and out, I kept reaching for my phone, hoping for some news. Finally, a little after midnight, my phone lit up with a text from Bob: "On our way home." Chase had been given some antibiotics, his blood had been checked, and he could come home to sleep. We would be together for Easter after all.

We celebrated Easter morning at church as a family despite the trip to the emergency room and very little sleep. Darcy wore a flowered dress, while the boys donned sea-foam-green shirts with complementary vests and bow ties. They weren't thrilled with the ties, squirming and complaining as if I had ordered them hanged instead of dressed up, but they also knew they looked handsome and strutted accordingly. Even Karsten, who was the unhappiest one of all in his fancy clothes, stood still and managed something akin to a smile. It felt good to celebrate being together and being with family and the people we loved.

As we pulled out of the parking lot, heading to Easter lunch, I lifted my silenced phone from my purse to see more than one missed call and a voice mail, all within the last few minutes. I recognized the phone number immediately: The hospital was calling.

I knew the on-call doctor, and I could hear the urgency in his message. "Hi, I'm calling about Chase's labs. There was a bacteria found in the culture from last night. Can you call me back as soon as possible?"

Adrenaline coursing, I quickly relayed the message to Bob as I redialed the number and waited for the doctor to pick up the page. "It's Ellie, Chase's mom. I got your message."

"Yes, thanks so much for calling me right back. Like I said in the message, there appears to be a bacteria in the culture. It's present in both lines, and it appears to be growing fast. So, we're going to need you to bring Chase in as soon as possible."

"Like, how serious is this? How soon is 'as soon as possible'?" I could feel my heart pounding.

"I'm not saying you have to drop everything and run, but you should get here sooner than later. And you guys know the drill. Pack a bag. I can guarantee you'll be here at least overnight."

"Okay, we'll be there as soon as we can."

"Great, thanks. I'll let the ER know you're on your way."

What doctors had seen in the emergency room last night was good and clear, but in the early hours, as we'd tied on small bow ties and buttoned vests, something had started to grow, and it wasn't good.

Back at the house, Bob and I threw clothes into bags while my mom packed us a quick lunch and my dad kept the other kids occupied. Darcy stood next to the bed while I packed, and she rocked back and forth as she talked. "But Mom . . . why? Why are they making you go back like this?"

"Honey, I'm so sorry. There are germs in Chase's tubes, and if they don't catch the germs quickly, it'll hurt Chase."

She shook her head. "I just don't understand it."

I stopped my packing frenzy, pulling her close and kissing the top of her head. "I know, baby, I know. It's awful and I'm so sorry."

And I will never forget the look of the three children in their Easter finery whom we had to leave behind, standing in the doorway of the house with my parents, the dining room table set with good dishes and bright linens. We hurriedly kissed everyone and left—the family dinner would not happen that day. Once again, cancer and the treatment of it were pulling our family apart.

As we drove to the city, I found myself thinking, *This is a choice. This is a choice.* Putting a child into surgery is one kind of powerless, and leaving your other children is a whole other kind. More than the cancer, in that moment, I hated letting people down. Wrapping my mind around accepting this day would need to be a conscious choice.

When we reached the ER, Chase was still in his Easter outfit, and while any small boy in a bow tie and vest is cute, a small, bald chemo boy in a bow tie and vest will nearly knock you over with all the adorableness, and that's exactly what Chase proceeded to do. He made nurses swoon and tired doctors grin, because who can resist a dapper patient?

I don't quite know how, but Chase managed to charm one of his Sunday evening nurses into bringing him a new toy. What's the point of being a little boy constricted by fancy duds if you can't put them to good use? Before I could turn around, he'd been given a small golf set, comprised of two golf clubs, two matching balls, and a little plastic alligator head target with a mouth that snapped shut when the balls were hit inside.

Because of Chase's lab results and the isolation, and because of the antibiotics in his IV, he was confined to his bed, so he sat cross-legged at the head of the large hospital bed and putted the balls to the alligator mouth at the foot of the bed, creating a comical scene. The entire team of yellow-gowned, masked doctors and residents crowded around Chase's bed, reviewing notes and diagnoses as the subject of their conversation ignored them all and tried to decide whether to play another round of golf or turn the clubs into swords.

We would be discharged within forty-eight hours of coming in, and Chase would recover so quickly and well that chemo would resume only a short time later. However, just as Chase's body was weak from the duration of his protocol, his central line, which was being used at least eighteen hours every day, was getting old and fragile too.

The month of May rolled around, and as families around us finished up school and finalized their summer vacation plans, we went to the hospital again and again and again.

The chemo schedule had changed, and for a few weeks, we commuted downtown five days a week for treatment and went back home every night. Bob white-knuckled two hours of rush hour traffic both coming and going, while I sat in the passenger seat, usually facing backwards, holding a vomit bucket for Chase. He got sick on the way in from anticipation and sick on the way out from the chemo. It was terrible.

The Sunday following the first five days of chemo, I took Chase to church, but he was so tired after the chemo and struggled so much with keeping his mask on that I brought him home after only a little while. My parents hadn't left for church yet, but Chase and I decided to snuggle on the couch watching his favorite TV channel, Disney Junior. Hoping it would be a quiet day of rest, I went into the bedroom to get a blanket while Chase padded out to the kitchen for a sip of juice.

I'd only been in the bedroom for a second when I heard my mom's voice. "El! Ellie, can you come here? Quickly, please!" I ran. That urgent tone was reserved for Chase, which meant something was wrong. There, on the kitchen floor, was a trail of brightly colored spots. *Chase spilled his juice.* I exhaled in relief and looked at my mom. She looked at the floor and then at me, her eyes wide. "El, he's bleeding. That's blood."

Despite our attempt to keep our voices calm, as soon as Chase realized that he was the center of concern, he started screaming. He knew what came next—people poking, prodding, asking lots of questions, and then his being shut up in the hospital. I didn't even care that he was screaming. My first concern was for his safety. I couldn't see a cut or an abrasion, so the dripping blood could only be coming from one place: Chase's central line.

Something had happened, and instead of keeping the blood in his body, it was now functioning as a hose with a leak, allowing his life source to drain out of him. Remembering when this had happened in the fall, I started giving instructions to my parents as they hovered next to Chase. "Lay him flat! We've got to lay him flat!" I picked him up, screaming, waving arms and all, and laid him flat on the kitchen floor. My dad held his legs while my mom carefully put her hands on the sides of his head, trying to still him and protect him as he thrashed.

Lifting his shirt, I could clearly see the problem—there was a tear in the line. This was a dangerous situation. Through the same tiny hole where blood was seeping out, germ-laden air was now rushing in. I quickly retrieved the small bag we called the "crash kit" that went everywhere with Chase, sanitized my hands, and put on gloves; I wound alcohol wipes and gauze around the tear and then used a blue plastic medical clamp above the site to effectively shut the line down. I could see no swelling in Chase's chest or shoulder, so we carried him to the couch so he could lie more comfortably.

Having reached Bob within minutes, he quickly brought the other children home from church, and we left for the emergency room downtown again. After hours of consulting with various teams and experts about how to preserve the line, it was determined that the tube had ripped close to where it split into two separate tubes about halfway down his body, and a special patch kit would need to be ordered. The small area of tubing was repaired with a temporary patch, stabilizing it as much as possible, and we were told to come back on Tuesday for the repair as well as for Chase's scheduled platelet and blood transfusions.

Tuesday came and Chase and I spent the day in the clinic and the day hospital in the oncology ward with our friend Judi. The repair was completed, the timing of which turned out to be providential, as less than twenty-four hours later, Chase hit his chemo nadir, and was finally admitted to the oncology ward after being in and out of the hospital nearly every day for ten straight days.

By late Thursday afternoon, as Chase lay in his hospital bed, I saw what looked like blood smeared on his chest. "Bobby, come here! There's blood . . . am I seeing things? This was *just* repaired!"

Bob quickly got up from the couch where he was working, came over, and gingerly lifted the sheet away from Chase's chest. "Yep, that's blood. Page the nurse."

Hearing me call the nurse and knowing what he was in for again completely undid Chase, and he screamed, dissolving into tears. The worst kind, too, the kind that said "I'm so tired of this. Please don't make me do it again." And my heart broke a little because I wanted to cry right along with him, but instead, I'd have to hold his head and arms immobile so the staff could examine the line.

"Please don't let them, Mommy. I don't want anybody to touch my tubies. Please . . ."

After assessing the situation, everything was repaired again, and we were sent home on Friday . . . until Saturday night when I hooked Chase up to his IV bag and realized within minutes of the pump starting that his shirt was wet. My brain screamed even as my voice remained soft as I coaxed Chase to let me look at the tubes under his shirt. He finally agreed if I promised not to touch him. I couldn't see anything that seemed amiss, but the dressing on his chest was soaked with the fluid from the IV bag, so once again Bob and I left the other kids with my parents and we took Chase back to the hospital.

For some reason, as we sat in the ER late into that night, the staff couldn't get the line to malfunction. Nobody could see anything wrong with it, and even when something was being infused through it, there wasn't any moisture evident on the outside of his chest. It was so late at night that even the ER was quiet. I held my head in my hands, as Bob leaned forward and rested his forehead on the edge of Chase's bed, anything to try to get comfortable enough to sleep for even a second.

"You know that as soon as we leave, it's going to malfunction and we'll be back within twelve hours. I can just feel it," I said. Bob agreed, although his response was muffled in the mattress. We were feeling burned out both physically and emotionally.

At last, sometime around 1:00 a.m., the line gave out and leaked. It wasn't apparent where the source of stress was on the tube, but one thing was certain—the line was no longer viable for Chase, and it would have to be removed. Because Chase couldn't eat by mouth, he couldn't survive without it, and so at 2:30 a.m., we were readmitted to the hospital where Chase received hydration through an IV in his hand or foot until the surgery to replace the line with a port took place the next afternoon.

Even though Chase feared another surgery, he was quite willing to take his nap with the doctor if it meant that he could go back to having "magic needles" in place of the ones in his hand. We were all excited about that, actually.

The surgery was successful, and with a working port, Chase was allowed to leave the hospital. On our discharge papers were instructions about many things, including our upcoming appointments. The nurse who handed them to us jokingly said, "Now get out of here before you have to turn around and come back for chemo." For a moment, we blinked at each other: Oh, yes, Chase still had to have treatment. This spring had started to feel like we were fighting the medical accessories and side effects of the cancer rather than the disease itself.

The next round of chemo started the following Monday. The port was one week old and functioning perfectly. In the late afternoon, a few hours into the chemo, feeling tired after running the halls, spending time in the playroom, and playing hide-and-seek with his nurse Ashlee, Chase came back into his room at last. As he tried to climb back onto his bed, the chemo started to hit his system, and his strength gave out, causing him to lean against the side of the bed.

"I'm too tired, Mommy. Can you help me?"

Picking him up, I made sure he wasn't wrapped in his IV cord, but as I laid him on the bed, his back arched and he screamed in pain. It only took a moment to realize that while he hadn't been tangled in the IV cord, it had caught the edge of the pole and as soon as I lifted him the cord became taut, yanking the needle halfway out of his chest.

"Bob, page the nurse, page the nurse! Oh, Chase, I'm so sorry, I'm so sorry, sweet boy!" He was writhing on the bed, screaming as loud as he could. I willed the nurse to hurry.

The next few hours were a blur as nurses hurried, attending doctors were summoned, extra specialists were called, and Chase was watched. He lay flat on his back with ice packs applied to his chest, being monitored ever so closely. When this all happened, there had been a particularly vicious chemo cocktail infusing through the needle—the light-sensitive one, delivered to the room in a special bag to protect it. Because of its orange-red color, it has long been nicknamed "the red devil," and it came with side effects like wearing out the heart muscle. In those initial moments, nobody knew if the devil had moved from inside the vein to flooding muscle around the chest wall—an unprotected nightmare. The question remained: Had the chemo been stopped in time or was it, even as the staff watched and waited, eating away at the muscle around Chase's heart? They gave him a rescue drug, but only time would tell.

In the meantime, the port—that brand-new port—was deemed compromised and could not be used for at least two or three weeks. So Chase had to go back to needles in his hands and feet, which was not only painful, but also left him without his complete IV nutrition. Despite boosted fluids, he became more and more thin. With the daily needle pricks, his attitude deteriorated, showing a breach of trust. Prior to this, we had told him no more needles, but none of us had been able to keep that promise.

On the same night that chemo infiltrated Chase's port, I sat in the darkness of Chase's room. The darkness suited my mood and I was glad that Bob was spending the night back at home. I was angry and exhausted. I felt like the last several weeks with all the central line issues had been one long prayer of "Oh God, please not again . . ." and the answer had only been more problems and difficult situations. We'd already been informed that the following afternoon would hold yet another surgery in which a temporary line would be put in his upper arm, in a more viable location. Chase would be able to get his nutrition and even go home with the line in his arm until the port in his chest was healed and safe to use again. So there were solutions, but I was still angry.

To this day, I couldn't give you a name if you were to ask me whom my anger was directed toward. I had taken every precaution when I'd lifted Chase onto the bed, the hospital had responded and made a plan exactly as they should have, and as far as anyone could tell, the chemo hadn't done any immediate damage. But I was still mad with the powerless anger of wanting something other than what I had but knowing there was no other place to go and nothing else to do. And because this hateful moment incorporated people I loved, in truth, there was no place I would have rather been than at Chase's side, feeling as toxic as the chemo. It was all so twisted and because I couldn't figure it out and I was exhausted, I got angry and I stayed angry all that night.

As Chase slept, I read the first verses of Psalm 23 on my phone.

The LORD is my shepherd;
    I have all that I need.
He lets me rest in green meadows;
    he leads me beside peaceful streams.
    He renews my strength.
He guides me along right paths,
    bringing honor to his name.
Even when I walk
    through the darkest valley,

I will not be afraid,
> for you are close beside me.
Your rod and your staff
> protect and comfort me.

The words brought me to tears because the picture of God is so beautiful in those verses, and I longed for the peaceful stream the Shepherd promised. And even as I acknowledged His goodness, my heart was still angry that we were yet again in the hospital and Chase was going into another surgery. I desperately needed the Shepherd to restore my soul because I had nothing left.

In all the comings and goings, I'd been recharging on my own adrenaline and not the good and best Word, and so when I prayed that it would all stop and it didn't stop, in my exhaustion, I was left with nothing else to go on. It had been too long since I'd been reminded of what was real and what mattered and so I sat alone that night, wishing God had stopped this chaos when I'd asked Him to, and desperately wanting Him to carry me to still waters.

23

Accepting Weariness

The next morning came and with it the strange energy that happens right before a surgery. The normally quiet hospital room had become a revolving door of staff coming in to check on Chase and prepare him for surgery, bringing forms to be signed, and going over final instructions before someone from the transport team arrived to take us downstairs.

This would be Chase's second surgery in two weeks. Bob wasn't going to be with us for a few more hours, and when I sat on the bed and explained to Chase what needed to happen, he cried and begged for another way. The weariness and constant intensity of the last several weeks had made it difficult for even him, this child of routine medical procedures, to consider another surgery.

"Please don't make me go! I don't want another nap! No more naps! No needles!"

"I know, sweet boy, I know . . ." It seemed like those words were becoming more hollow each time I used them to comfort him.

"But Chase, remember last night when the needle pulled and hurt you?"

"Don't talk about it. Don't talk about it!" He screamed, putting a hand to his chest as if to physically protect the port from this invasion of words.

"I know, I know. In just a second, I won't talk about it ever again, but I need you to hear this." He became still, sulking angrily against his pillows.

"Dr. Lulla and the other doctors are worried about the bump under your skin—your port—and they think it needs a break. But you know Dr. Lulla wouldn't want you to get stuck with needles all day long, so he thinks the best thing to do is to just put a little tubie into your arm."

I motioned along my bicep. "Up here."

The thumb came out of his mouth and Chase sniffed in an injured tone. "Just a little tubie? No more needles?"

"No more needles. Magic, remember?"

That morning, news had traveled around the inpatient ward that a famous cellist would be visiting the hospital later that day. Knowing Chase's love for music, I begged the staff for him to go. On this day of all the days, he needed something wonderful. They had to say no and rightly so; cancer patients were not supposed to leave the floor, and Chase should not be in a large crowd right before his surgery. However, a member of the staff who heard about my request, found me, and with a smile and a wink, he said, "I'll see what I can do."

A short while later, the transport team arrived. As we walked through the halls, I fought eye contact with the nurses. I could feel the tears pressing too close, and I knew if I looked into another pair of eyes, I wouldn't be able to stop the sobs. It wasn't even a big surgery, but the point was that it was *another one*.

Where was God in all of this? I knew He must be there because everything I have ever read promised that He would be, and I had felt His peace again and again, but I couldn't help but feel alone now. My heart cried "Not again," even as the wheels of the surgical gurney carried us down the halls and out of the ward. I wished for something that I didn't even know, something . . . anything, to make this feel bearable.

While we were on the large elevator shooting down the twelve floors at top speed, my phone vibrated with a text. Chase, who loved the staff elevators for their speed, shot a fist into the air, yelling, "To infinity and beyond!" as I pulled out my phone.

The text was from Judi. She could not be with us this day, but a friend of hers, a goddaughter who was a nurse, worked on the floor where we were headed, and actually had been assigned to Chase. And in that moment, Jen, this woman we had yet to meet, became precious because she felt like family through Judi, and as they would cut through skin to find and prepare his veins, Chase would have family in the room with him as he slept.

When we got to pre-op, there was a nurse with dark hair and a beautiful smile waiting for us, dressed for surgery. She offered her hand. "Hi, I'm Jen. You must be Ellie and Chase."

Jen saw to our needs as we waited for the final confirmation. Chase clutched his friend Matthew's stuffed animal to his chest as we turned on the hospital's in-house channel to see if the cellist had started to play, but before we knew it, they were ready to take Chase.

The snap and click of a Stryker bed's wheels unlocking is a sound I equate with good-byes, and as I kissed Chase, his voice was hoarse. "Do not cry for me, Mom. I will be so brave, and I'll be back in a minute."

Jen stood next to the bed, promising me that she would be by his side the entire time.

Chase turned to me. "Mom, can you ask Miss Jen if I can bring Maffew's dog in there with me?"

Overhearing, Jen leaned over the bed to answer Chase herself. "Chase, don't you worry about this guy, okay? I will watch out for him the whole time you're sleeping." She paused. "Does he have a name?"

Chase nodded solemnly. "Scout."

"Scout, okay. Well, how 'bout if you and Scout come with me, and I'll take care of you. Are you ready?"

Chase nodded as I leaned over the bed and kissed him one more time. "Be brave, sweet boy."

His eyes were already fixed on the hallway and what waited. "I will. I am *so* brave."

For reasons I'll know on a future day, God didn't stop all the cancer side effects when I told Him I couldn't handle any more. But in His gracious way, He had sent Jen to stand alongside the angels who watched Chase as he slept. God didn't have to give me something tangible that day to cling to, but He did. And suddenly, even though the weariness remained, for the first time all day, the anger lifted and I felt deeply thankful.

I rode the elevator back upstairs alone and reentered Chase's empty hospital room—the nurses would call me when Chase was in the recovery area. As I breathed in thankfulness and Chase slept surrounded by the staff and angels, I turned on the TV and watched the great cellist step to the microphone in the beautiful sunlit atrium several floors below me. Before a note was played, I heard the cellist say, "This song is for a new friend who wanted to be here with us now but couldn't make it. Chase, this song is for you." And for just a second, the beauty of the music ripped at my heart in the separation. *Chase should be here to experience this.*

When I was called to join Chase in pre-op, Bob had finally arrived. Chase was still asleep, and his entire chest was washed orange with something to keep germs away. The left part of his chest was purple from where they had marked and then cut for the port just a few days prior. On the right side of his chest were the wounds still healing from the last time a line had been placed there, and a bandage was still covering the bruising and scabs on his right arm from the most recent tube. The backs of his hands were covered in tiny red needle marks and spreading dark bruises, and even his heels were bruised from when they had to resort to the veins in his feet. His body was a tablet of his suffering, telling the story of the last few months by all the scars, and it was both heartbreaking to think of the pain and glorious to behold his intense resilience.

After another day or more, Chase was discharged for a while, but that whole spring and summer, as people around us did normal things like go to the beach, the park, or on vacation, we went back and forth to the hospital, often barely connecting with our other children, and it hurt. It was hard not to feel envious of others. We'd drive up Lake Shore Drive en route to the hospital and see people enjoying the lake and the beauty, but we lived that summer behind glass windows on the seventeenth floor of the hospital. It wasn't that a day at the beach would have turned everything around. It was that we couldn't get there and we missed our other children, and we really missed what we felt *normal* should look like.

One particular summer day, when Chase was back in the day hospital for a transfusion, he made friends with another small girl in the playroom. He couldn't remember her name, so he called her "Girl." He'd tap the Connect 4 box with his hand on the table and say, "Hey, Girl, come here and play this game with me!" Understandably, "Girl" quickly tired of his dictatorial ways, at which point, Chase tired of the playroom and we wandered back to the room. As we passed staff members on the way, they'd call greetings to him—he was very loved in that place.

We settled back into the room for what would undoubtedly be two more minutes of watching a movie before another jaunt to the playroom, when I realized that there was a drop of blood on the sheets next to Chase. Quickly pulling back the sheet bunched around his legs, I realized that it wasn't a drop, but a pool. Chase was sitting in a pool of blood. When he realized it a second after me, Chase began screaming, "Blood! *Blood!*" at the top of his voice as I hit the call button.

It turns out that the sound of a three-year-old voice screaming, "Blood!" is an excellent way to get the attention of a large group of hospital staff. Our little area became standing room only as the charge nurse determined that the blood wasn't Chase's, but the transfusion blood that was leaking from a loose cap in his central line. Once the cap was replaced, the transfusion continued without a hitch. We all put our eyeballs back in their sockets and took a few deep breaths. Chase was then cleaned up, and we were ready to go. On our way out, Chase sauntered to the playroom to find the girl, and as she sat at the play table, he leaned nonchalantly against the wall with one foot crossed over the other as if he were thirty-five.

"Girl, I have a problem. I have to go home now, but you will be all right, okay?" And without giving poor "Girl" a chance to respond, he pushed away from the wall and walked away as if he owned everything he saw. Life with Chase is never dull.

That day would not be the only time the new line gave us trouble. Within a few weeks, I came into the bedroom in the early hours of the morning to check on him as he slept, but instead of being curled into a ball with his favorite blanket and the IV bag, he was standing in the crib. As I stood in the doorway of the room, his white pajama shirt turned red at an alarming speed. The line had gone again, and this time it wasn't a transfusion that stained his clothes. For the second time in too few weeks, he stood in the center of the room, screaming, "Blood!" My mom was in Maine with my sister, and while ladies from our church came nearly every day to help me, it was too early in the morning, and I was alone with all four kids and too much spurting blood.

Sometimes caring for people in situations like Chase's gives you a strange set of second nature skills. For me, those skills came with experiences like failing central lines and blood-soaked shirts, which came into play on this morning. Going shopping and sitting in traffic—those things seem stressful to me. But troubleshooting a central line with one hand while dialing the hospital with the other, all the while trying to keep one small child from panicking and calmly reassuring the other three that their brother was fine and that Mommy would be out to fix breakfast in a few minutes and get her first morning cup of coffee . . . now, *that* I can do without breaking a sweat. And as the kids finally ate their breakfast, while we waited for Phyllis, the home health nurse, to arrive and help with Chase's line, I put the bloody shirt on the sink, snapped a picture despite my hands still shaking from the adrenaline rush, and texted it to my mom with the caption, "I might need a cup of coffee."

The chemo-compromised port had been cleared for use within a few weeks, but it kept sticking or leaking and we began to replay the old, weary game of how long we could stay out of the hospital. These times were measured by hours because there was no concept of days anymore. We'd be out and back in sometimes as quickly as two or three hours. And as we became increasingly worn out and Chase became known as a hospital "frequent flyer" again, the staff became less comfortable with Chase's port.

After one twenty-hour turnaround, I stood in the hall outside Chase's room with Dr. Lulla and described what had happened. Putting a hand to his temples, he sighed. "This central line stuff with Chase . . . this is just crazy. You guys must be exhausted. When this is done, you and Bob seriously need to take a vacation."

I laughed because his statement was so true that it struck me as both funny and hard to imagine. *What's a vacation?*

"Okay, as I've been reviewing this and thinking through where we are in his treatment plan and all that's been happening with his central line and now the port, here's what I think we need to do. I had really hoped to save that port and keep Chase from another surgery, but at this point I think we can all agree that even though Chase stabilized after the chemo infiltrated, something still isn't right with that port."

He leaned against the wall as he talked. "I want to talk to surgery first, but my gut instinct is to remove this port entirely, maybe wait for a few days and let him recover, and then we'll put another PICC in his arm and then, when he's stronger, we can place another port if we need to."

Dr. Lulla's gut instinct proved true; the port removal went smoothly, and within twenty-four hours, Chase was back up on the oncology floor riding a big wheel bike at top speed down the hallway while I tried to keep up with his IV pole. When he broke through a crowd of residents gathered for rounds, Chase shouted, "Gentlemen, start your engines!"

Twenty-four hours after his bike race, he was back in an operating room for the PICC line to be inserted in his arm so that we could go home and he could get nutrition once again.

During this season, we began to work with a new home health nurse named Joanna, who was unique in her understanding of Chase and our family. Not only was she a longtime nurse of pediatric cancer patients, but she was also a cancer mom herself. Her oldest child had beaten cancer once and for all, with her very life, several years before we ever met. As Joanna sat in our living room, sometimes multiple times a week, patiently working with Chase in his stubbornness and fear, she talked about how her beautiful daughter would have been in high school if she were alive.

I marveled at Joanna's resilience. She had not only survived something I could not imagine, but she'd walked back into the cancer world with its many memories in order to keep helping others, pouring out grace to those in need. Her gentle strength was a visible example to me when I was so exhausted.

After another three weeks of living with the line in his arm and more hospital admissions for chemo and then re-admissions for fevers and transfusions, Chase was finally strong enough to have surgery. Yet another surgeon performed the procedure, and while Chase slept, they removed the tube from his arm and did his routine spinal tap to check for cancer cells.

It was Chase's eighth and last central line and the longest procedure. They took him in the early afternoon, and the time seemed to stretch forever as Bob and I read, talked, and kept glancing at the flat screens against the wall in the entrance of the waiting room. We had been given a 5-digit number that corresponded to Chase and instructions for how to follow its progress through the stages of the day. Right then, the 5-digit number on the screen was a piece of my heart lying on an operating table yet again, and the status was marked OR for what seemed like far too long.

I stirred in the chair. "Bobby, it's been a long time."

He looked up from his computer, removing the earpiece from his ear. "Hmm? Did you say something?"

I leaned toward him and gestured to the screens on the wall. "It's been a long time, and he's still in the operating room."

Bob nodded. "I know."

It was a routine surgery, but what if something had happened to his chest wall when it was opened? What if he only did well under anesthesia sixty-seven times and the sixty-eighth time was the moment his heart gave out? What if all the stress of treatments and side effects this summer had proved too much for one more thing?

The phone at the concierge's desk finally rang and it was clear she was getting instructions for a patient's family. She put the receiver down gently. "Ewoldt?" We raised our hands like eager schoolchildren answering a teacher, and she came over to us. "Are you Mom and Dad?"

We nodded.

"Okay, that was a call from the OR. Chase is still in surgery but they wanted you to know he's doing well. She said the port was difficult to place, but they got it working fine now, and they're almost done. They'll call again as soon as he's in recovery."

It was finally over, and we would learn the full story much later. The new port had been placed, but despite perfection from a surgical standpoint, they couldn't get fluids to go through the line when they'd tested it before closing his chest. The surgeon had told the team that this was Chase's eighth line and his last option, and everyone had agreed that no person would leave the room until there was a working port. For the sake of Chase, they'd pressed on and fixed and replaced it until at last it was perfect and his chest could be closed again.

How I hated these central lines and the struggle to keep them working and the pain they put Chase through. Yet nearly a year from that eighth and last line surgery, in June 2014, when he went under one last time and they removed the central line forever, I cried. Chase sat up in post-op with the stitches on his chest, sighed, and said, "Mommy, I'm free!"

For the first time in two years, he had no tubes surgically attached to his person. There were no pieces of plastic on which his identity was being formed. It was just his body, his own skin and bones now, and we rejoiced. But I also cried a little because that awful, stupid line had become my friend. We'd fought each other over Chase, and we'd fought together to keep Chase going, and it had become a symbol of the struggle.

This life road and even the road through Chase's cancer has rarely, if ever, looked as I imagined. And yet God continues to put me in situations where I am driven to realize again and again that even though He doesn't always give us our way or follow the plan we would have chosen for our children, our family, or anything else, He has always faithfully equipped us to do what He sovereignly ordained. God gives us the strength in our moment of weariness and need.

It's what author and pastor John Piper describes so well.

Life is not a straight line leading from one blessing to the next and then finally to heaven. Life is a winding and troubled road. Switchback after switchback. And the point of biblical stories . . . is to help us feel in our bones (not just know in our heads) that God is for us in all these strange turns. God is not just showing up after the trouble and cleaning it up. He is plotting the course and managing the troubles with far-reaching purposes for our good and for the glory of Jesus Christ.[7]

24

LEARNING TO PERSEVERE

During all the central line troubles, the reality that Chase's cancer was known for recurring started to push into the daily difficulties of the current treatment. As we grew so weary from all the complications, I couldn't keep the fearful thoughts contained: *You might have to do this again. This probably won't be the only time he'll fight. He'll survive only to get knocked down again.*

One day, while we were in the hospital for chemo, Bob and I talked about this while Chase rested on the bed. It was a clear, blue day. The lake was beautiful, and warm sun flooded the room. I stood by the window, my eyes closed against the glare.

"I feel like I can barely make it through this now . . . let alone do it again."

"I know. Me too."

"And even if he survives this, there are all sorts of secondary cancer concerns. I just feel like it's never going to end, and any end there could possibly be is just unthinkable." Even in the darkest days, I'd always been sure that Chase had a purpose and that none of this would be wasted. But the thought of doing it over again and watching Chase waste away and suffer again just to try to beat something that was statistically likely to win in the end seemed purposeless and meaningless.

Bob looked up from his work. "El, I think this is one of those times when you just can't go there. If it comes to that, we'll face it."

Since Chase was resting, I took the rare opportunity to leave the room and walked down the hall to the huge picture window that overlooked the lake. I called my friend Jean. "I don't think I could do this again if he were to relapse."

Just saying the words out loud released some of the pressure. "This first time through treatment is pushing me to the edge of my sanity and anything more is just inconceivable to me."

Jean listened to my words without comment, but at the moment I moved into self-pity, she gently interrupted with words from Revelation 21.

> He will live with them, and they will be his people. God
> himself will be with them. He will wipe every tear from
> their eyes, and there will be no more death or sorrow
> or crying or pain. All these things are gone forever. And
> the one sitting on the throne said, "Look, I am making
> everything new!"
>
> REVELATION 21:3-5

"Ellie, there may be no explanations or relief here and now. There will be some days where your only paradigm is going to be this picture and promise. The day is coming. I really think this is where you need to stay with Chase."

Later that day I was able to reflect on Jean's words. Yes, the day is coming when God will speak over us that we are His people and He is our God. The day is coming when there will be no more pain or tears because He will take the hurt away and wipe every eye and it will be more glorious than we can ever attempt to imagine! But it is not that day yet and so the seemingly mindless, meaningless suffering will continue. Chase is sick, but the day is coming. He grows weaker, but the day is coming. He may one day die from this illness . . . but the day is coming. So, we must persevere.

That summer, in a rare moment when Chase wasn't admitted, our whole family and a few friends attended a run to benefit the brain tumor program at the hospital. The run was named in honor of a small boy who'd perished many years before Chase was diagnosed, and it took place on a path along one of the lake's harbors. The July heat almost sparkled on the crowds of people gathered. These people gathered because they were connected to brain tumors. Parents and friends ran alongside doctors, nurses, and hospital staff.

Those who were running the 5K had signed up throughout the summer, but there was a small children's course set up, just a few yards long, that you could enter that day. Though Chase was attached to an IV bag and sporting a giant lump on his head from a fall out of bed several weeks prior, he wanted to run.

"Mom, can I please, please, please run?"

"Chase, sweet boy, I just don't know. You have your IV bag on, and you still have the bump on your head." These were the spoken reasons I gave him; the unspoken one was that I wasn't sure if Chase had the balance or stamina to run.

But he stopped me as he frequently did, and said, "No, Mom, please. Let me run. I *need* to run."

And he did. We removed his IV bag, and because Chase was weak and off balance, Bob walked with him. As they approached the finish line, Chase clung to Bob's hand, and he full out ran. It was the most beautiful sight.

This last summer, I was walking with Chase in a park. The gravel path we were on was wide and beautiful, bordered by large stones—markers—that were spaced a few feet apart. Rather than walking along the path next to me, Chase insisted on jumping to the top of each stone, jumping off, taking the one or two steps in between at a gallop, and at times, trying to jump directly from one stone to the other without touching the grass. Maybe it's silly, but I saw a picture in his movements. He will always run, will always endure, and it will almost always be the road less traveled.

This is what we were all created to do. Persevere. Press in and run. Life is hard and often includes the road less traveled—with many more miles than we'd bargained for—but the prize is better than we can imagine.

Forgetting the past and looking forward to what lies
ahead, I press on to reach the end of the race and receive
the heavenly prize for which God, through Christ Jesus,
is calling us.

PHILIPPIANS 3:13-14

25

WE CAN'T PROTECT THEM

On a Saturday night, late in the summer, right before school started, I sat on the couch next to Chase, attaching his IV bag to his arm, while Darcy sat across from me and talked about her day. I started the IV pump, strapping it into the bag and closing it, and laid the black satchel at his side. Suddenly, Chase grabbed his stomach. "Mommy, I don't feel very good."

"What hurts, buddy? Do you feel like you're going to throw up?" I tensed ever so slightly at his words. Bob was upstairs getting Karsten ready for bed, and my parents were nearly an hour away at a wedding. *Oh, please, Lord. No complications tonight.*

Darcy hopped up. "His bucket is right over here." Darcy had a sixth sense about when Chase was going to vomit and she was often the one who caught it. "Mom, want me to get his 'nice-warm'?" She was referring to a clean gym sock stuffed with uncooked rice that, when warmed in the microwave, made Chase's stomach feel nice and warm.

"Sure, Sister. Can you heat it up for me?"

But the makeshift heating pack did nothing for Chase, and within a few minutes, he was moaning, burying his head into the couch cushions as if trying to get away from the pain. Grabbing the thermometer, I ran it across his forehead: 99.5. *Great.*

"Darcy-girl, can you get your daddy?" She took the stairs at a run, calling his name like the house was on fire. "Daddy! Daddy! Mommy needs you *right now!*"

Sensing her panic, I called after her. "Darcy, settle down! It's going to be okay. Just slow down and take a breath, okay? No yelling in the house, please."

But as I turned back to Chase, his teeth had started chattering. "Are you cold, sweet boy?" He shook his head rigidly. Within another minute, his whole body was shaking, experiencing what I'd heard the doctors clinically refer to as "rigors" so many times—a teeth-chattering, full-body shake like he was cold, only his skin was getting warmer. Something was happening, and whatever it was moved rapidly.

Bob came down the stairs quickly, carrying Karsten, with Aidan trailing behind, and everybody huddled around the couch. Aidan tried to touch Chase's face. "What's happening to him? Why is he shaking?"

Darcy stepped up behind Aidan. "Is he having another seizure?" I could hear the terror in her voice.

"Okay, kids, that's it." Bob interjected. "Give us a minute. Darcy, you go get a book. Aidan, you sit here on the couch," he motioned Aidan to the far end, away from Chase. "Darcy is going to read to you. You guys just need to stay quiet for a minute so Mommy and Daddy can figure out how to help Chase." Karsten, who didn't care about fevers or rigors, had toddled off to the bedroom to find his toys.

As Darcy and Aidan held up a book, I could see they were only pretending to read, their eyes still focused on Chase while Bob and I talked in low tones.

"What happened?"

"I have no idea. I started the pump, and he started crashing within ten minutes. It started with stomach pain."

"Did you check the line? Is everything working?"

"Yes and yes. There's no swelling or discoloration, and the pump hasn't alarmed once, so I don't think he's in distress that way."

"His counts should be okay right now." Bob stood, hands on hips, clearly as puzzled as I was. "Did you check the rest of his body? Any swelling or rashes anywhere else?"

"None. But the shaking . . . that," I lowered my voice completely, only mouthing the words in the presence of small children who would take their cue from us, "*is freaking me out.*"

Bob nodded. "Okay. Make the call."

"Do you think we're okay to take him by ourselves?" There was a small part of me that wondered if he'd stay stable on the drive.

Bob remained calm. "It'll be fine. If he starts seizing, I'll pull over and call 911."

Call the doctor, arrange the bags, make sure the ER knew Chase was coming, etc.—this was all becoming much too routine. And because my parents were gone, I stayed with the other children while Bob took Chase ahead to get him stable until somebody else could come and be with the kids. In our preoccupation, it never dawned on us that most of Chase's urgent moments happened either in the hospital or late at night, times when neither Darcy nor Aidan had seen Chase this compromised. It had been since the early July morning when they watched me hold an oxygen mask to Chase's face, telling them it was all going to be okay.

As the door closed behind Bob and Chase, I hugged Aidan and Darcy close. "Thank you so much for your help and for being so brave. I'm sorry Daddy and I were rushing around like that. Chase is going to be okay. We just needed to move quickly."

Aidan pushed out of my arms. "Okay. Mom, can I go play LEGOs?"

I nodded as he went on his mission, but Darcy moved away, sat down on the couch, and started to sob. "Mommy, I thought he was going to die! He was just shaking and shaking, and it was like that time in the bed when he had the seizure. Did we do something to hurt him? Is Chase going to die?"

Sitting down next to her, I just rubbed her back, unsure of how to respond other than to start crying myself. "Oh, honey, no, no he's not. Chase is sick from a fever right now, and that's how his body handles a fever. As far as we know, Chase is doing really well. And I promise we will tell you if that changes."

She looked up, sniffing and wiping her eyes. "But what if he is really dying and you don't know it?"

My young daughter was asking the secret, scary questions that occasionally popped into my own head, but I tried my best to answer. "Sister, the truth is, we're all dying." Her eyes grew wide.

"Not like Chase, not everybody has cancer, but everybody is going to die at some point." I stopped for just a minute, trying to collect my thoughts.

"But the doctors have said that Chase is doing really well, and he keeps having MRIs that show them what his brain looks like, so they aren't just guessing . . . they really are pretty sure. And, Sis"—I could feel myself choking back the tears as her eyes welled up again—"if . . . if something were ever to happen to Chase, I promise you Daddy and I would tell you. And Jesus would give us strength."

She put her arms around me, squeezing as hard as she could. "I love you, Mama. Thank you."

I looked at her face. "Are you sure you're okay?"

She nodded. "I just got really scared when he started shaking."

Chase was fine after he received antibiotics and other medication to reduce the fever. It was not the end of that story as we were readmitted to the hospital downtown the next day, and the fever went along with the ongoing central line issues. But, that night in the ER, when I joined Chase and Bob at the hospital, we made paper airplanes and sailed them across the room, then sent pictures home via text for the kids to see so they would know Chase wasn't shaking anymore and that he was going to be okay.

The heartbreak of putting death into words defies everything. I had felt it with Chase when we sat under the Christmas decorations after radiation, and I felt it again now. The ugliness of death and separation seemed so inappropriate for children—they should not even know of these things at such a young age, let alone experience them on some level. I was supposed to protect Darcy, but instead, she was being exposed to the most awful things just for being in our family, in our house. She stood in a room and watched her brother shaking uncontrollably, sure that he was having another seizure and was about to die.

I wanted to rip those images from her mind and give her more joy and less fear than the adults around her. I wanted her experience to be better and easier than mine. But we were part of a family, and a family, just like a body, hurts together. Just as I could not separate myself from Chase's pain, neither could I separate her from it. It was and is awful, but it also holds beauty around the edges because as we sat and cried together, we talked about it more openly than we ever had. And though I could not protect her, the very same grief I would choose to take from her allowed us to connect and has subsequently strengthened her in ways I wouldn't have imagined. Once again, I had underestimated the amazing and surprising good in the hard things. There in the fevers, pain, and fear was the tiniest glimpse of the promise that God will make all things new.

26

PRACTICING ENDURANCE

The sun was low over the city when Judi visited Chase and me in the hospital one late afternoon. While Judi was there, Chase began vomiting all over the hospital bed. After I paged the nurse for clean sheets yet again—a frequent request during chemo—I wiped Chase's torso around his IV tubing while Judi and I talked and tried to keep him distracted. A moment later, Courtney, our nurse, entered with armfuls of starched white linens, and I lifted Chase gingerly off the bed. Although his retching was sad to witness, there was virtually no odor in the room because Chase's nutrition went into his body through his veins and not his stomach.

As I held Chase close, he backed away so he could see my face. "Mom, can I go to the playroom now?"

Shaking my head, I glanced at the clock on the wall to verify my answer. "I'm so sorry, Son, it's closed now."

Rearing back in my arms, his face turned red as he began to screech in a high-pitched tone. "But I want to go now!"

"Chase, I'm so sorry, but it's closed. We can go for a walk if you want, but the playroom is closed. You have to be patient, Son." My arms tightened around him as he fought the hold, but I could not release him as his thrashing jeopardized the stability of the cords attached to his body. And then it started. He slapped me once and then a second time. I closed my eyes as the blows from tiny, weak hands rained down on my face and shoulders; he grabbed my glasses and threw them against a cupboard on the far wall of the room. His screaming was so close to my face that my ears were ringing.

"No-o-o-o! Let go of me! Put me down! I want to go to the playroom now!" I wanted to snatch his arms away from my face, but keeping him safe with the cords was the first priority.

I was protecting him and couldn't protect myself, a powerless and frustrating place to be. Judi stood at my shoulder, trying to get Chase's attention and defuse his anger by talking to him sweetly, but in that moment, he was consumed and showed no sign of stopping.

Courtney signaled in my peripheral vision. "The bed is done. You can put him back down now."

I nodded. "I know. I'm just terrified he's going to pull the cord."

I turned my attention back to the crazed boy in my arms. "Chase, please stop. You're hurting me, Chase . . . Chase." On some level, I hoped even the repetition of his name would pull him out of the rage.

I could sense Courtney wanting to respect my role with Chase even as she wanted to protect both of us. "Chase, you shouldn't hit your mom."

The admonition from a member of the hospital staff was enough to give Chase pause, and he immediately dissolved into ashamed tears, the fight completely gone, leaving his body limp and sweaty.

Courtney checked the bandages around his central line as Chase whimpered self-indulgently, his tone indicating that he still held the fact that the playroom was closed against every adult in the room.

Gently, I kissed his smooth forehead. "Chasey, I love you, and I'll always love you no matter what, but you can't do that. It's okay to be angry, but it's never okay to hit people. Ever."

He sniffed as he looked up at me, his face suddenly contrite, the intensity gone almost as quickly as it had come. "I'm so sorry, Mommy. You're the best mommy in the whole world, and I'll never, ever hit you again."

I nodded. "Remember what we've been saying? You need to be . . ." I paused, wanting him to understand the universal nature of his struggle. "Actually, not just you; *me* too. We need to be quick to hear, slow to speak, slow to anger. . . . Remember to use your words first, and if something is making you feel angry, let me know that you need a minute by yourself. I will help you, okay? I love you."

As I hugged him close and worked through this latest issue from a slowly building pattern of behavior, fearful thoughts whispered. *What if this is who he is? What if this is how his brain will always be?*

The fight in the hospital was not the first. In between admissions, while we were home, Chase would often have days when he seemed to fight every action at every turn. Whether due to our personalities or the fact that I was physically around him more often, Chase seemed to fight me more than he fought Bob, and that often made my parents frustrated and angry as the aggressive behavior affected both their child and grandchild.

Many times, after Chase had calmed, my mom would gently approach him as he sat crying on my lap, her heart's instinct to protect mirrored in her eyes, and quietly tell him, "Chase, that makes my heart so sad when you hit your mommy. She's my daughter, I'm *her* mommy, and I don't want people to hurt my children."

The layers of family dynamics were fraught with intensity, stress, and guilt.

One day, after an especially trying episode, when I finally got him quieted down and in his bed for a nap, I dropped onto the step stool in the corner of the kitchen—a place I often sat to talk to my mom while she prepared a meal. I fell into the comforting routine and aired my concerns to her.

"I don't even know how to handle him when he's like this. What's chemo, what's damage, and what's Chase?"

Her expression was troubled. "Have you talked to his doctors about this?"

"I have, but there are so many factors. This could be a side effect of one of the medicines; part of damage from treatment or surgeries, or it could simply be a really aggressive response to having his entire life be so out of control right now. It all needs to be addressed but mostly after treatment is done. Until then, we're just trying to maintain boundaries and make sure he's safe."

I rubbed my eyes and forehead with the palms of my hands as if the stress could be massaged away. "Here's the thing. I can handle him *now*. He weighs less than thirty pounds. What happens if this doesn't stop? What happens when he starts taking it out on siblings? What happens if he grows as big and tall as Bob and he still can't control himself? That really freaks me out!"

My mom listened quietly as she stood at the stove, taking it all in. "Did you know about the behavior aspect at the beginning . . . ?"

I curtly cut her off. "Of course we did! We absolutely knew it was a possibility. Before the brain surgery, the doctors mentioned the possibility of emotional changes taking place, but we didn't know what it would look like."

I sighed and rubbed my face again, my voice calming. The question was legitimate. "I'm sorry, Mom. We would still make the exact same decisions. It was treatment or his life. He went in with

a six-centimeter tumor, he had midline shift, and he was a mess!"
Somehow, the rehearsal of details we both knew by heart helped
the reasoning.

"In a lot of ways, it couldn't have been more simple. It's just that
the day-to-day feels like it's crushing me right now. I can't imagine
handling Chase like this forever, and I feel so guilty. Outside of you
and Bob, I can't really talk about this with anyone, and I definitely
can't write about this right now. At the end of the day, we don't get to
complain. Chase is alive. To freak out about his care, his moods, all
that kind of stuff—that just seems ungrateful, you know?"

She listened to me pour it all out and then she spoke quietly.
"But it *is* a big deal and it *is* hard, and people don't have any idea
what a day in your life looks like. You may not be able to say much,
but there have to be even little ways to discuss it. I don't think it's
wrong to be honest. People need to know how to pray for you,
sweetie." She used the pet name she'd often used when I was a small
child, and her words energized me to keep facing forward in this
newest battlefield. As we neared the end of treatment, in a moment
not unlike the first clear scan, the story was shifting again. Once
again, we were moving from a position of fighting death to fighting
the complications of life.

Chase's personality and behavior were fast becoming one of the
hardest seasons to address because his struggle had become our personal challenge. It is universally acknowledged that having a child
with a life-threatening illness is hard for everyone. But while people
around us celebrated that Chase was alive and that treatment was
about to end, we were left with the quiet knowledge that his care
and special considerations were nowhere near ending—and possibly never would. And sometimes, the quiet, isolated feeling of this
emerging, more private struggle was overwhelming.

Incredibly, it had actually been easier to talk about a child dying than to talk about the collateral damage—damage that largely stemmed from the treatments we had voluntarily chosen. I had expected to feel many things but not guilt. One thing was certain: Chase's normal was not everyone's normal, and as long as either of us had breath, this life with him would not be for the faint of heart.

Chase had always had a uniquely strong personality (remember, he stared down a truck!), but it had seemed to develop on an increasingly polarized level as he progressed through treatment. What he felt was what we saw. If he was disappointed, he'd weep; if he was frustrated, he'd often respond with instant fury. Joy brought giddiness and love for anyone near him—known or unknown. At times he'd even ask to give the nurses a kiss.

Trying to help Chase work on controlling his feelings required removing him from the situation until he could calm down and we could dialogue on an appropriate response, a task that was nearly impossible in a crowded, busy hospital. For some months now, we had witnessed this struggle inside Chase, and as hard as it was to deal with, we knew the energy in all those scenarios was probably being muted by illness, low blood counts, and numerous chemotherapies. *What would a fully energized, healthy Chase look like in our home?*

This question and so many others weighed heavily on our hearts as we looked to the end of treatment. It felt as if Chase had been a house set on fire, and the fire had now been put out, but we had no idea how to rebuild, especially with the existing foundation looking so different than anything before his diagnosis. And to add to all of it, as we'd read many times, Chase's cancer is not known for staying away, so we would be rebuilding in the constant shadow of relapse.

The last of the summer days passed quickly into fall, and my calendar showed there were four rounds of chemo, and then three, and then two, and then, suddenly, it was almost the middle of October and there was only one more round of chemotherapy ahead of us.

On some level, we'd been waiting for this moment since we started, but as it came closer, we faced it with both relief and horror.

The hospital had become our home away from home when everything we'd known was ripped away, and the staff had become like a family, sharing our joys and sorrows. All of it, the building and the people, had been rolled into a giant safety net under us that was about to be taken away. They would still be there if we needed them, but we didn't even know what we'd need. It was slightly sickening to realize that Chase's treatment, the very thing we'd fought against as "not normal" for so very long, was suddenly the only place that felt right or safe.

"Hi, Ellie. It's Lauren. Are you ready for this?" The voice of Chase's neuro-oncology nurse sounded unusually encouraged in our first of the twice-a-week calls to discuss Chase's labs. Heart pounding, as it always does when somebody asks me if I'm ready for something, I heard the news. "So, we got the results, and Chase's counts are stable. His platelets are good, his hemoglobin is strong, and his absolute neutrophil count is really great."

Pacing as I listened to her words, I was shocked at how quickly both his red and white blood cells had rebounded. "Lauren, do you realize? I think this is the first time in his entire treatment that his counts have rebounded without a transfusion!"

"You're right. Wow."

"It's as if his body knows he's almost done."

I heard her laugh on the other end of the phone. "Quite possibly, yes. Just so you know, he's been cleared to restart chemo next Monday. The spinal tap is already scheduled, and they'll call you to confirm the procedure time." The last chemo was finally here. Chase was almost done.

Early the following Monday morning, for the last time, we laid Chase on a gurney for his sixteenth and final spinal tap. I knelt over the bed for a second before they ushered him from the room. "I love you, my Chasey Bear. Have sweet dreams."

He nodded, his thumb in his mouth, and his eyes little more than slits as he anticipated the unconsciousness that was nearly upon him.

I stroked his arm. "Do you want me to hold your hand?"

The shake of his head was ever so slight as he began to feel the effects of the medicine in his body.

I leaned so my head was against the rail of the bed. "Are you so brave, my son?"

Chase nodded as the last of his liquid "sleepy medicine" entered his body. He sighed in peace as his eyes rolled back in his head and closed for his last "nap" with the doctor. After he woke from the anesthesia, for the last time we were admitted to the inpatient floor. The chemotherapies ran for three days while our hospital family, the nurses and doctors, came in and out to congratulate us and say good-bye, making Chase promise to visit whenever he came back for neuro-oncology clinic.

Even though treatment was ending, the truth was that we never outgrow or move past the need for that moment-by-moment grace. Such grace was not left at the side of the hospital bed or in the surgery waiting room, but would continue to follow us and be our salvation for every moment of every day. As I fussed and fretted about what *normal* would look like for us as we ended chemo and how people would understand us as we moved past treatment, a dear friend had smiled kindly, looked into my scared eyes, and said "El, *normal* is just a setting on the washer, you know."

So many of the things that we consider vital for quality of life have turned out to be so unnecessary. I firmly believe—and have to relearn nearly every day—that my standard and goal is "Christ and Him crucified," to bring the gospel to my children and myself. And then there is everything else. My average day doesn't look the same as yours, and yours probably won't look the same as the person next to you. All that matters is our individual callings before God.

I love the expression "there are only so many hills you can die on." In fact, I've seriously considered painting that on a canvas and hanging it in my house; although, at the rate I'm going, I should write it on a piece of paper and tape it to my forehead. There are so many times that I try to plant my flag and feet strongly in the dirt of a hill I should never have climbed in the first place. And the factor that keeps me real on those days when I'd like to come off all spit-polished and pretty is almost always a small cancer child. Because there's nothing to pull you out of a fake world and test your priorities like a sensory-overwhelmed boy in the middle of a knock-down, drag-out screaming fit on the floor of the church lobby over an incorrectly placed name tag.

As the finality of this treatment chapter sunk in, the choice was clear. We could fight for normal or fight for Christ and trust Him to give us strength when the days ate us alive. There would be no moment when life snapped into an easier place after chemo stopped flowing, and we were on this cancer road because it was where God put Chase and our family.

Some days I forget that God knows what I need more than I do. He knew I needed Chase. We'd been led this far, and God had always been faithful. Time and again there'd been proven purposes in the hard days, and He would not leave us now, whatever post-treatment life held, whatever complications or relapse unfolded. And so in the late afternoon, on Wednesday, October 16, 2013, fourteen months to the day from the start, the last infusion of the very last therapy sounded that it was done. On the IV pump monitor, one word scrolled across the message screen again and again: "COMPLETE." For better, for worse, or for normal, treatment was done.

27

FINDING PEACE
WITHOUT BEING FREE

"I think we need to start thinking about moving out." Bob sat at my parents' dining room table as I hunted for some school papers in the cluttered piles on the shelf in the corner. The only part of the shelf that didn't immediately make me want to cry at the lack of organization was the last two sections, where box after box of medical supplies were stored neatly in labeled rows. This had become our life—everything medical was in order; everything nonmedical was cluttered and stressful.

"Bob, I know this is something we need to work through, but it feels like Chase just finished treatment. I understand that we can't stay here with my parents forever, but can we just have one minute in time where there isn't a fire to be put out? It feels like we've gone from thing to thing to thing"—I stopped to catch my breath—"for years now, and I just don't know how much more I can handle. Also, it's the holiday season. We've got the boys' birthdays, Christmas, family coming in—can we please not do this right now?"

Bob nodded, and I could see my forward-thinking husband trying to wrap his mind around being still for my sake. "Okay, but it's something I'd like us to start thinking about in January. We need to do this for our family, so we really need to start thinking about the next step."

I saw his concession for a slower time frame as the olive branch it was intended to be. "Okay. January. I'll start figuring that out when I start all the evaluations for Chase's therapies." I exhaled deeply, feeling the stress piling up from the many projects ahead.

He smiled. "It's going to be okay."

"You're just saying that because you won't have to live with your in-laws anymore," I shot at him.

His smile grew. "Hey . . ."

My mom's voice filtered in from the kitchen. "I heard that!"

Bob raised his voice just loud enough to make sure it carried. "And like I was saying . . . I have the best mother-in-law in the world!"

Listening to my mom's laughter, I rolled my eyes and smiled at him as I walked away. I was going to miss all of us being under one roof like this.

It had been sixteen months since the paramedics had wheeled Chase and me out of our condo. Since that time, our family had become nomads. Some of our possessions had remained in the condo while the rest had been transported on an "as needed" basis to my parents' house. Much of what we'd brought over was in boxes and laundry baskets—a picture of picking up and leaving in a rush. The only place we'd learned to call "home"—the hospital—was a facility in which our rooms, status, and neighbors were always changing.

By November, Chase had begun to eat again, taking his first real bites of food from a piece of pumpkin pie at Thanksgiving dinner, about five weeks after his chemo had ended. My brand-new 2014 calendar had started to fill up with evaluations and appointments for physical therapy, speech therapy, and occupational therapy. Our family relationships began to solidify as we all grew used to being under the same roof again after months of more separation than togetherness. Slowly, we were rebuilding our lives.

In January, as I'd promised Bob, I prepared to list our first little home and faced the wisps of sweet memories as I packed baby clothes, pictures, and long-forgotten first hospital bracelets from when we welcomed the children into the world—back in the days when a hospital meant joy and not chemo. Most of the packing sessions included friends from church, but one evening, while the kids slept under the watchful eyes of their grandparents, Bob and I worked alone.

Closing and labeling a box on the bed in front of me, I turned slightly to face him. "Do you think there's a part of us that wants to move so that we don't have to come back here and restart at "ground zero," where it all started to go wrong?"

Bob halted, holding the suits he had just pulled out of the closet. "On some level, maybe. And I think that's something that we need to address, maybe even seek counsel on. Practically speaking, we've outgrown a two-bedroom condo, and right now, with Chase being so immune compromised, we really can't be in a place where people are permitted to smoke or have pets. It's a logical move, but I think we definitely need to look at our motivation."

I nodded. "I want to be at peace in this place. I don't want it to hurt to look around, and I don't want to leave because of that. No running away."

The February MRI was clear again, and for the first time ever, we really began to look ahead and plan more than a few days into the future. And one damp, foggy night, as the rain hit the snowdrifts and froze, we sat around the dining room table and signed papers to list the condo.

Life continued and about a week before each MRI, our heads would remain clear, knowing that God was in control, but our hearts would grow increasingly heavy. The whispered fear of relapse was always right on the edge of consciousness. *What if it's back this time . . . ?*

The weight of worry would grow heavier until Chase was carried into the MRI chamber. Then there would be momentary peace before the wait for results would hit. And after the call and the relief that he was once again in the clear, we would spend the following days meeting with lots and lots of "ologists" —checking the cancer cells, his hearing, his heart, his endocrine system, his development, and on it went. We would come home weary and set up to do it all again in three months.

Chemo had ended quietly, and in the middle of continued MRIs, doctors' appointments, therapy appointments, and selling our house, we needed a moment to not be so quiet, and so the week before the May 2014 MRI, we planned a "Chase Party" and invited everyone we knew to convene in the church gym on a Saturday afternoon. We celebrated Chase's life and got to publicly thank so many people for seeing us through the long months of treatment. They had taken our struggle and made it theirs, and we finally got a chance to show our gratitude and celebrate God's faithfulness to us with them. They had not only prayed for us, but they'd brought us meals, folded our laundry, cleaned the house, packed boxes in preparation for moving, and one spring day, one dear woman spent the afternoon showing Aidan and Darcy how to plant flowers in containers for the front porch because I was too weary from a hospital run to do that small task with them. As we gathered and decorated cookies and a magician passed through the crowds of people with enthralled children following his every move, a small place in the back of my mind whispered that it wasn't the greatest timing to celebrate right before an MRI, but we did it anyway.

God knew it was time to celebrate. The May MRI was clear, and in July the condo finally sold.

And so we came to August. One Saturday morning we decided to surprise the kids and take them to see the new property we'd put an offer on. We listened to questions and guesses about our destination as we turned onto our street. Even from a few blocks away, I spotted the blue siding of the house nestled in the trees and the multicolored sign still pitched in the front with the words of great expectancy: under contract. Small voices filled the back of the van as all four children craned their necks for the first glimpse.

"Where is it?"

"Are we almost there?"

"Will there be a backyard for me to play in?"

"Will there be a bedroom for me to sleep in—and not have to share it with my brothers?"

"Is there room in the yard for a swing set?"

"Here we are!" Bob's voice announced into the mayhem as we pulled into the driveway. "We can't go inside today as we won't be signing the papers for a few more days, but kids, this is going to be our new house." And cheers erupted in the backseats.

Just as Bob had predicted to the children, a few days later we sat in yet another conference room, closing on the new house, and thinking through the beginning of a new school year in a new place. We would finally be in a place where the urgencies of cancer could be more of a memory than an everyday reality. We were finally moving forward.

As we sat around the large oak conference table in the appointed office, and all the interested parties looked on, Bob signed the most papers we'd signed since agreeing to a brain surgery. He looked up. "What's today's date?"

"August 13," someone responded.

I turned to Jeff, our real estate agent and friend, and whispered, "Today is the thirteenth, which means that Chase's MRI is in the morning. The implications of what we're doing are . . . wow." I shook my head half in wonder, half in fear. "We're pretty much signing up for the idea that everything is as normal as it's going to be. We're committing to this being what our life is going to look like."

Jeff smiled as he watched Bob sign, "Well, this is where taking it one thing at a time is best. This is the moment by moment."

The next morning the MRI occurred without a hitch, and after Chase broke his post-anesthesia fast with a hot chocolate, Bob and I dropped him off with my parents and headed over to the new house to begin cleaning, painting, and keeping ourselves as busy as possible while we waited for the call with the results.

Dropping me off to begin wiping down the walls, Bob left to find paint supplies at the hardware store up the street when my phone started ringing. Hands shaking, I answered. "Hello?"

"Ellie, it's Rishi." Dr. Lulla's familiar voice meant one thing: MRI results. As if sensing the direction of my thoughts, he continued, "I have the results here. Let me start off by saying that his spine looks clear, and overall, his brain looks amazing . . ." The words he spoke were good and encouraging, but there was a hesitancy in his tone that made me feel heavy all over—something else was coming. "But there appear to be several small growths in the original tumor site."

Old feelings I'd nearly forgotten resurfaced as I tried to process his words. Twenty months and eight MRIs since that first clear scan after radiation ended, and suddenly everything was changing. *Why now?*

As I stood in the emptiness of a kitchen that didn't even feel like my own yet, all I could think was that I needed to find a pen and some paper. Frantically searching through my purse, I found an old receipt. Flipping it over, I began to take notes.

"There are about four growths, and they aren't very big at all, but they weren't there on the last scan, so they've come up rather quickly."

"Rishi, Chase's initial tumor grew quickly too, right? Can you tell me what you're thinking about this? Is the cancer back?"

The momentary silence on the other end of the phone only added to my fear. I knew he needed to choose his words carefully because so much was still unknown, but I wanted to know what he thought. I felt the urge to know the same way I had when we'd sat around the conference table with Dr. Becca so long ago and talked about percentages of survival. I didn't know what the words would be, but my heart was tied to them all the same. Once again, I wished Bob were with me.

"There are a couple of things that this could be. It could be the cancer, but it could also be something from radiation. It's not uncommon to see scar tissue or 'effects' in children like Chase who have undergone radiation."

"Is that what you think they are?"

"To be honest with you, statistically speaking, we often see radiation effects coming up within a certain time frame after the treatment. Chase finished in August, right? So it's been a year?"

I interjected. "No, Rishi, December. His birthday."

"Oh, that's right! His birthday!"

"His birthday in 2012. It's been almost two years since radiation ended."

"Wow, okay. We don't commonly see effects crop up this late, but you need to keep in mind that the word *commonly* in the pediatric field . . ."

I cut him off. "I know, I know, Rishi. You know I'm listening to all of this with an open mind, and even if you could be completely sure, I probably wouldn't believe you because . . ." and here, I couldn't help the slightest smile, "it's Chase. You know he always finds his own way through these things. What do you think the chance is that they aren't from radiation and that it's actually the cancer?"

"I really can't say right now, but I can tell you that there are a couple of things I don't like about these growths. They seem to have grown very quickly, which is a shared characteristic with the initial tumor. Also, there is a cyst-like component—as you may remember, that was also a characteristic of the initial tumor. That being said, there's still so much we don't know about this, so let's not go down that road quite yet."

"Okay." I could hear the shakiness in my voice. "So, what's next? Tumor board?"

"Yes. The next step will be presenting this to the tumor board and seeing what the recommended course of action is going to be."

I knew doctors generally hated being pushed into supposition, but I just couldn't help myself as I asked question after question. Fear of the unknown was already accelerating my heart rate as my brain bounced across every possibility I could imagine.

"Can you tell me what your recommendation is going to be to the tumor board?"

"The possible options are surgery to remove, obviously, but that is the most invasive and least likely action right now. There is also the possibility of doing a biopsy to test for cancer cells and to get a better idea of what we're up against here. But I really think I'd prefer to wait on a biopsy or surgery until absolutely necessary. Chase is doing so well right now in terms of not having seizures, and opening up his head, even for the biopsy, could greatly increase his risk of starting to have seizures again. So, the biopsy is definitely an option, but there is another one. We could always wait and scan again in, say, six weeks and see if anything has changed."

I glanced down at the paper where I'd scribbled a single word: *Biopsy?*

"This point that we're at with Chase . . . we've already utilized every curative option, which means that our decision now would potentially be the same as it is in six weeks in terms of what is available to us for any type of treatment. But Ellie, ultimately, this is up to you and Bob. If you're both like, 'I just don't think we can go through this again. We need to know what this is now,' we can definitely discuss the biopsy."

Even though Dr. Lulla's voice remained even, the words "curative option" jumped out as if he'd shouted it. If this were the cancer again, whatever we did, whenever we did it, we'd only be buying time. "Oh wow, I need to talk to Bob, but as much as I'd love to know, Rishi, I can't see putting Chase at risk for more seizures. I can't see putting him into procedures that open his skull just so I can sleep at night knowing what we're up against."

"I know, but just think about it. And talk to Bob about it—see what he thinks too. Let's plan on you coming to the hospital with Chase tomorrow, and by then, I will have talked to the board and we'll figure things out from there. Does that work for you?"

I had no idea what my schedule was, but the response was in my gut. "Of course."

"Okay. You and Bob discuss it and if you have any questions, let me know. Also, if Bob wants to talk to me about this, have him call me, okay? Try to get some rest tonight."

"Okay, thanks, Rishi."

I put the phone down and stared out the bay window at the far end of my new kitchen. The window looked out into the side yard where a flowering crab apple flourished and a line of evergreens on the border of the property made the yard feel secluded and cozy, but I looked at it all unseeingly. It had taken me months to be able to walk into our condo without flashing back to the moment Chase had his seizure. My parents' house was full of our medical supplies and our cancer memories too. But this house, this new house had finally been a fresh start—a symbol of turning a corner—yet in the first twenty-four hours of it being in our possession, the very first phone call I'd gotten within its walls was a devastating cancer call.

As I stared blankly out the window, I felt like God was reminding me that I couldn't run from the cancer. This new space had now been baptized by it, and I would forever associate our first day here with the old threat. Once again, I'd been looking for normal and had been let down.

I picked up my phone again, not even wanting to wait until Bob came back to the house to tell him. "Hey, what's up?"

"Bobby, Rishi just called. There's something growing. . . ."

After we talked and I made some phone calls to friends and family who had been waiting on the results with us, neither Bob nor I felt like talking anymore or working on the house. Instead, we desperately wanted to go back to my parents' house and be with our children. It had been so long since we'd heard news like this that I forgot how it radiates like a physical blow to the body. We'd stayed standing for the initial conversation, but the pain and weight of it radiated in waves and hurt more the longer we knew.

I came out of what would be the boys' room where I'd been preparing walls and found Bob on a ladder in the living room.

"Bob, would it be okay just to go home tonight? I really want to be with the kids."

He nodded. "Me too."

"Hey, we're going to get asked what the next steps are. How do you feel about it?"

He absently brushed paint on the wall in front of him, not making eye contact as he spoke. "I've been thinking about it, and I want to know what this is but not to the point where that's the only reason we'd put Chase into a procedure or surgery. I feel like we should only do that if there's something that we can stop right now that will change the outcome." He spoke the last two words quietly but they resonated loudly. *The outcome.* We were suddenly and freshly aware of something we hadn't seriously considered in months other than the brief hours around each MRI—this cancer diagnosis was potentially terminal.

An hour later we were back with the kids, and even though on the surface it looked like a wonderful summer evening, my mom's eyes were sad and pained as she worked in the kitchen. I'd watched it happen enough times to know that my dad was in the backyard with the kids because he always made extra time to play with them when there was a hard thing coming.

Greeting all the kids with hugs, we asked Chase to stay inside for just a minute so we could talk to him first. Anxious to play outside with his siblings, he remained standing in the kitchen, shifting from one foot to the other. The most common reason for holding a conference like this was a behavior issue, and the confusion was written on his face—he hadn't hit or pushed anybody.

I looked at Bob and he nodded, signaling that I should be the one to explain. "Chase, we just needed to talk to you for a minute about your MRI."

His head tilted. "My MRI?"

"Yes. Dr. Lulla said there were a couple of bumps or spots where your tumor used to be."

"Is it *cancer?*" The question wasn't so much asked as screeched with a visible recoil in his small frame.

"Hey, hey, it's okay. He and Dr. Alden . . ."

"Alden!" Again, the screech came.

"You know Dr. Alden. He's your friend." I searched for anything to help him make association. "He's the doctor you see after the MRIs who always makes you touch your nose, remember?"

He relaxed and giggled. "Dr. Touch-Your-Nose."

We all smiled. "Yes, him. Anyway, Dr. Lulla and Dr. Alden . . . sorry, Dr. Touch-Your-Nose . . . they're both going to talk to all the other doctors and see what they need to do about the spots. And they're probably going to want to see you for a while. I know we haven't had to go to the hospital very often, but we might need to go see them a lot, okay?"

Chase held up his hand to stop me. "Okay, but Mom, stop. Don't tell me anything else. Can I go back outside?"

"Of course, but wait just a second. Are you sure you don't have any questions for us? Is there anything you want to talk about with this?"

He shook his head emphatically. "No. Don't tell me anything else. I'm going to go play now." His siblings would react much the same way. In the resiliency of childhood, they saw no reason to worry until the threat moved from conceptual to real. The backyard on a warm summer night was far more alluring than thinking about their brother going back to the hospital.

This cancer thing never ceases to turn life upside down, and I replayed Chase's words over and over again: "Don't tell me anything else." Like a child, weary of rehashed concepts and hard days, I needed to put my hand out to God in faith. *Don't tell me anything else right now. You know what comes next, so I don't need to. I trust You.*

With the new house, each new scan, and every change, I kept seeking to be free. I felt like I'd barely come up for air after treatment before sinking again, but as I stood in the kitchen that night with the words "don't tell me anything else" ringing in my ears, I realized that I'll never be free of the cancer. It will always be with me whether in memory or reality. But just because Chase may never be free of it or our family may never be free of it doesn't mean I can't have peace. I remembered sitting cross-legged on that ICU bench in the early hours before Chase's brain surgery when I wrote him my good-bye, writing the words that I needed so desperately. *There is no normal, there is only Christ.* For surely, if I ever stand on anything else, I am destined to fail. Christ's sacrifice is my ultimate freedom; His love is my always-and-forever peace. I don't need anything else.

28

THE MOST PERFECT IDENTITY

Two days later, we sat in one of the hospital's many small conference rooms. All these pivotal moments somehow came down to a conference room. While Dr. Lulla sat at a small desk to pull up the scan images on a computer screen, Bob and I sat closely with Chase, who was bored with the length of time the conference was taking and alternated between sighing loudly and throwing himself across my lap. Encouraging him to sit quietly for just a few more minutes, we viewed this newest threat to his brain and put together a plan.

Rehashing the same conversation we'd had over the phone, we discussed surgery, having a biopsy done, or waiting six weeks, with the official recommendation of the tumor board now being to wait if we could. It was up to us as Chase's parents to decide.

As we talked and looked at the screen, for the first time in a long time, I felt it all again. My head felt calm, but I could feel my heart beating hard as a wave of dizziness hit. My body was absorbing heartbreak and stress on a level I couldn't even articulate.

Bob took point. "Let's wait. If there's nothing we can do right now that we can't do in six weeks, let's wait. I think that's best for Chase."

Dr. Lulla nodded in agreement. "Okay, we'll schedule another MRI, and while he's under anesthesia, we'll do a spinal tap too. Probably on Monday, October 20."

The date broke into my thoughts. "Oh my word, Rishi, my sister is getting married in Tulsa on Saturday, the eighteenth. We'd been planning on driving down for the wedding, but should we still go?"

"Absolutely. You should absolutely still go. Being with family is probably the best possible thing right now. And you guys know . . . we've talked about this before . . . make the most of the time. In fact, we should all be doing that all the time, but especially now. If you guys haven't done your Make-A-Wish yet, now would be the time to make sure it gets done."

I glanced at Chase to make sure he wasn't listening in as I lowered my voice slightly. "We did. I mean we're going to. Chase wants a swing set and a fort, and we just closed on our house, so now that we have a backyard, those will be going in within the next few weeks."

"Excellent! That's great to hear. Congratulations on the house, too. That's wonderful."

Bob and I smiled at his kind words, both thinking how much things had changed in such a short time.

"Rishi, with the trip to Tulsa . . ." I struggled to find the words. "If this is the cancer and it keeps growing, Chase could be at a higher risk for breakthrough seizures. I don't know if you've ever been through southern Illinois and Missouri, but there are long stretches of road where there's nothing for miles. What do we do if Chase starts having a seizure? Are you sure this is safe for him?"

"Absolutely. That's a good question, by the way. You would do exactly what you'd do around here. If he started having a seizure, pull off to the side of the road, call 911, and they'll get you to an area hospital. From there, we'd work to get you back here as quickly as possible."

We nodded, taking it all in. It felt like we were dealing with a time bomb instead of a small boy.

"It's going to be okay. You'll be with family, and you'll have his seizure medications with you."

"Thank you, Rishi."

Chase stirred. "Are we done yet? Can we go?"

Dr. Lulla laughed. "Yes, Chase, we're almost done. You're doing a great job letting your mom and dad talk for a while." And then he directed his attention back to us. "I don't anticipate anything, but you know what to look for . . ."

"The usual, right? Changes to speech, gait, sleep, etc.?"

"Yes. Call me if you guys need anything—seriously, anything at all. Otherwise, we'll see you in six weeks."

"Thank you."

As we left, I marveled how far we'd come from the first time we'd sat in a room and talked about cancer. Then, I'd needed Dr. Lulla to know us. Now, he was a part of our family. Then, he'd had to tell us every little thing. Now, we knew so many of the basics of care and neurological benchmarks that he only had to hit the highlights. Our family had grown so much in these hospital halls, and now, even though the subject of our conversation was grievous, our words were comfortable. I didn't know whether to be thankful or deeply horrified that the discussion of terminal relapse felt so calm.

As we unfolded the news of Chase's poor scan and our plan to wait to those around us, the response was overwhelmingly supportive, but there was a sentence that kept popping up in many forms. *You've already been through so much.* Quietly, it fed my fear and anger as we waited the six weeks. It wasn't just that Chase had had a bad MRI but that he'd had a bad MRI on top of dozens of MRIs and surgeries and treatment complications, oh, and a life-threatening brain cancer. Quietly, I felt my heart hardening around the edges again. Once again, I pleaded: *Please, no more . . .*

The week before Carrie's wedding, I sat at my kitchen table with my mom and my sister Abby, whose family had flown in from Kenya for the occasion. After sharing her own harrowing stories of missionary life in a third-world country, Abby wanted to know—really and truly know—how we were doing.

I fiddled with the coffee cup in my hands. "The wedding terrifies me. Being that far from Chase's hospital . . ." I shrugged.

Abby is the most compassionate in the family, and at my few words, her eyes welled up with giant tears that rolled down her suntanned cheeks. "I wish I could have been there for you."

I stopped her as I pushed the tissue box in her direction, and we shared a smile. Where the Poole women gather, there also shall a box of tissues be. "Don't even . . . We've been fine. You're here now, and I'm so glad. You'll be stateside when we get the news—whatever it is. I just feel this shadow as we wait, and I hate the thought of taking that with me to Care's wedding. This is her happy day, and we're going to walk in there with our cancer shadow and ruin it."

My mom, who was sitting between us, had been listening quietly, but now she broke her silence as she touched our arms. "No, it's going to be okay. This is what family does. Nobody can take Carrie and Jared's joy, and nobody will take your sorrow either. We're family. We'll get through both."

The following week, we took what felt like a huge leap of faith and drove to Tulsa. When we crossed the Mississippi River, the

"Welcome to Missouri" sign made me smile—it marked the first time we had left Illinois since Chase was diagnosed. In addition to Abby and her family, my sister Meg and her husband, who were expecting their first child, and my parents were all converging to celebrate Carrie. It would be the first time in a long time that we'd all be together, and although nobody had the courage to say it aloud at such a happy moment, we were all thankful that we had these moments in the shadow of Chase's most recent scan.

A little voice from the backseat ended my reflections. "Hey, Mom? Um, remember back there when we crossed the Mississippi Ocean?"

The query was quickly followed by an older, more knowledge-able sibling's correction. "Ocean? It's a *river*, Aidan. The Mississippi River."

I heard Aidan's sigh of annoyance. "Okay, fine, the Mississippi *River*. But, hey, Mom, when we crossed it, does that mean we're almost to Auntie Care's wedding?"

Before I could answer him, Chase interjected eagerly. "Mom! Is there going to be cake? Will Auntie Care share it with us?"

Bob and I exchanged silent smiles. "No, we aren't to Tulsa yet, and yes, Chase, if there's cake, I'm sure Auntie Care will share it with you."

Chase growled. "But I bet she won't share and that makes me *so* angry because we're supposed to share! What if Uncle Jared doesn't let her share the cake?"

"Chasey Bear, Auntie Care and Uncle Jared will want to share the cake with you, I promise."

"Okay, fine. But hey, Mom, is Karsten allowed to eat crayons?"

Clearly, there would be plenty of distractions this weekend before the next scan.

On October 20, 2014, with Carrie and Jared wonderfully married and their wedding cake duly and appropriately shared, Chase went in for his much-anticipated MRI, talking all the while about how his Auntie Care had been a princess. Though the small spots had grown, the growth was minimal. So with a huge sigh of relief, a continued concern for relapse, and the consensus to keep waiting, we set up another scan for December, right before Chase's fifth birthday. This scan, a very brief look at his ventricles, was Chase's first "awake" MRI and his first scan in an outpatient building of the hospital. If he made it through this next round without too much growth, the likelihood of it being cancer would drop again.

As Bob waited by the door that would take them to the machine, Chase hung back in the pre-op area. "But I'm so scared, Mom."

I put my arms around him. "I know you are, sweet boy, but you can do it. Daddy will be right there with you, and it's only going to be for a few minutes."

He whimpered as he drew closer. "But the beeping hurts my ears."

"I know, sweet boy, I know." I felt powerless to comfort him. It would be hard, but it was something we needed to do. "I'll stand as close to the machine as they'll let me stand, so I'll be with you too. We can do this. Are you brave?"

He smiled as much as he could muster. "I'm so brave."

Within minutes of the MRI, we walked down the hall to meet with Dr. Alden and heard the same thing we'd heard six weeks prior—that the spots were growing, but slowly. Another six weeks went by and we did it again with the same results, and sometime around the end of January, it was decided that Chase's neurological status was stable enough to go back to MRIs every three months.

At the same time as these meetings, we collected a small stack of paperwork for blood work to check Chase's system and confirm the truth of what we thought we were seeing—the treatment damage was affecting Chase's spine. In the long days of winter, Karsten and Chase, nearly two years apart, stood at roughly the same height. If it wasn't the cancer, it was the side effects of treatment, and once again the sad and true whisper came with hints of bitterness: *You've already been through so much and now it's one more thing.*

In April 2015, as Chase answered his anesthesiologist's questions in preparation for yet another MRI, I secretly wished I had his answers in writing to pull out and remind him on the days that the request to make his bed was treated like a crime against humanity.

"Are you married?"

"Ew! Gross! No way!"

"Do you have a job?"

"Yes, my job is to make my bed and clean my room."

The results of this MRI were much the same as they'd been for months now. The spots were growing, but so slowly that continuing to monitor them was the optimal solution. The passage of time alone seemed to point less to cancer and more to treatment effects.

Gradually, it began to feel like the cancer shadow was once again lifting. Having the MRIs every three months now seemed like a luxurious time span after every six weeks. Chase had grown a little taller, and though his skin remained very pale, he'd begun to fill out and grow eyelashes again. We were as close to normal life as we'd been in a long time.

Two days after Chase's April MRI, as my mom sat in my kitchen, she got a call. Her routine mammogram had been irregular, and they wanted her to come back in for a more in-depth test. I knew the feeling of waiting for results, and a part of me was in denial that this was on my mom now. "Mom, they're probably just doing this to cover their bases. It's probably nothing."

She shrugged. "I know it's probably nothing. But after the last several years with Chase, nothing ever feels like nothing. There's always this chance that it's something."

"I know, but just . . . this is where we need to stay, like we did with Chase. The 'moment by moment' always applies."

"I'm really nervous about this," she said. "My heart feels peace, but I can't even focus on anything."

I couldn't contain a small laugh. "Welcome to my world."

She looked at me, an incredulous laugh escaping her lips as she entered a different understanding of the struggle we had been enduring with Chase. "Wow."

"The need for 'moment by moment' never goes away. And like you said, we're family. This is what we do. We'll be right here with you every step of the way."

Within the next weeks, tests led to biopsies, and one afternoon, as I called to check in on how she was doing, I could hear the thickness of stress and sadness in her voice.

"Mom, what's wrong? Are you okay?"

"I just got off the phone with the doctor who did the biopsy yesterday." Her voice was hesitant. "It's not what they hoped for, El. It's cancer."

I felt like I was being crushed, even as practical and coping words came out of my mouth. "Okay, okay. What's the next step? What can I do to help you?"

"Honestly, I have no idea. I just got off the phone with the doctor right before you called. I haven't even wrapped my mind around it or told anyone yet. I'm going to meet with a surgeon in a couple of days. But El, I haven't even . . . I need to talk to your dad. I need to go, okay?"

"Of course. I understand. Go do what you need to do. I'm here if you need anything. I love you."

"Love you, too, honey. Bye." Her voice was distracted and I wondered if the shock had set in.

Immediately, I called Bob. "Hey, what's up?"

"Bobby, it's Mom. She has cancer." Somehow, saying the words aloud made them real, and I started to sob on the phone.

"What?"

"Yeah, I don't know anything else and nobody else knows yet, so please don't say anything to anyone, but it's true. She just found out."

"Are you going to be okay?"

"I don't know. She's always been so careful about her health. I don't understand it, Bob."

"I don't either. The most we can do is be there for her, whatever happens."

"I hate this wretched disease."

"Me too. I'm sorry, love. I'm here for you. Call me if you need me."

And just like that, I stood alone in the room, facing cancer in someone I loved once again. And even though it wasn't my health in jeopardy, I heard that quiet thought creep up. We'd already been through so much, and now this. *God, I can't do this again . . . I just can't.*

A little less than four weeks later, leaving our children in the care of a friend from church, Bob and I sat in yet another hospital. I stayed next to my mom in the presurgery bay, and as they wheeled her away, I stood with my dad in the hall. With hands clenching and unclenching powerlessly at his sides, he desperately tried not to openly weep as the large white double doors closed behind his bride of forty-three years. The fear and fight against separation that we had battled so many times with Chase was in my dad's eyes now as he stood under the TV monitors in the waiting room watching the status of Mom's whereabouts on the screen. It was as if he were certain that standing near her ID number on the monitor would somehow keep him closer to her.

That night, after a successful surgery that took away part of her chest and gave her "clean margins," I held the familiar pink vomit bucket as the aftereffects of anesthesia and pain medications did their worst, and I helped my dad keep her comfortable as a tube at her side drained where they'd cut into her. In those moments, I felt like a mother taking care of my child even though the person in my care had always cared for me.

My identity in those moments was not the same as it had been before. I was mothering my cancer mother the same way I'd mothered my cancer son. And over the long months, I'd let the idea that "once through a cancer journey was enough" sink so deeply into my identity that I felt like I didn't know who I was anymore. Especially when it threatened the people I loved not once, but twice within a very few months.

My son, my mother, a friend, another child; surgeries, treatments, standing with tears and empty arms after a long and weary fight—it feels like it happens all too often. These have become the moments that I weep for human brokenness and my weakness in it all and the need to identify who I am again. I am a child of God. He loves me. I have the life that I do today because He's given it to me. I may never escape cancer around me; in fact, I know I won't, but ultimately, my life is for His glory. When everything else around me shifts and tilts, and security is ripped away again, come one cancer battle or ten, my perfect identity—the one that comes with a limitless supply of the moment-by-moment grace and strength—is safe in the hands of the One who made me.

29

LEARNING TO LOVE

Once again, August came. A year had passed since I'd stood in the kitchen of our new house with the phone to my ear, hearing words about growths on Chase's brain. Despite the ups and downs of it all, the news had remained much the same. The growth was bad, the slowness of the growth was good, and the MRI every three months was monitoring everything. It had been nearly three months since my mom's surgery, and she was on the road to making a complete recovery. Miraculously, the surgeons and oncologists believed that they'd been able to remove all the cancer with the surgery and that at this time, no further treatment was needed.

Chase was selected as one of five 2015 national ambassadors for St. Baldrick's—a wonderful cancer research foundation—and we had spent the year sharing his story on a number of levels, including with a reporter, where Chase informed him that not only did he have cancer but that he left his dirty socks around the house whenever he wanted to because "my Daddy does it too."

One of my favorite encounters was during the summer when we were at the hospital. Chase had brought some St. Baldrick's cards that had pictures of him and Dr. Lulla on them to hand out to people. As we were preparing to leave, we passed one of several check-in stations with a security guard. Chase paused, looked at the tall, burly man in his uniform, and then looked back at me.

When I nodded, Chase boldly approached the man, holding out a card. "This is for you. You can keep it because it is for you because I'm an ambassador." His words tumbled out over themselves, but the effect was immediate. With a huge smile on his face, the guard crouched down to Chase's level. He explained that he pastored a church in the city and that his congregation had been after him to shave his head for some time. He didn't specify why, but I wondered if his church had felt the pain of cancer too.

"I wasn't so sure, but I'm gonna do it, Chase. I'm gonna do it for you!" he exclaimed. They hugged, becoming instant friends. It was just one of many treasured, precious moments that Bob and I witnessed in a place we never would have been if not for Chase's cancer.

One day, I got a call from my friend Sarah. "Ellie, how would you and your family like to see Matt Redman in concert? Do you think that would be something that Chase would like?"

Her words were incredible. "Sarah! Are you serious? 'Like' doesn't even begin to describe . . . he would freak out!"

I could hear the smile in Sarah's voice as she passed on the details for the upcoming concert. "This is such a joy. I can't wait to hear all about it."

That night, Bob and I gathered the kids to hear the news. "Hey, Chase, do you have your iPad? Can you turn on your song?"

Chase ran to the ottoman. Lifting the lid and pulling out his tablet, he typed in the code and pulled up the music video for "10,000 Reasons."

"Mom, it's my song! It's 'O My Soul!'"

We all crowded around. "Hey, Chase, what would you think if we all got to go and hear Matt . . ."

He interrupted, pointing to the screen. "Which one is Matt?"

Immediately, several hands pointed to the dark-haired singer in the center of the screen.

"Him! That's Matt? I'd get to go see him?"

Bob nodded. "What would you think about that?"

As the kids started dancing around the room in pure joy, Chase suddenly halted. "Do you think he'll sing my song?"

"You bet he will, sweet boy."

The day arrived, and after years of feeling like his music had been written for us because it reflected what was on our hearts, after years of watching the music video on the iPad—sometimes dozens of times in a row—Chase was going to get to see the singer of "his song" face-to-face.

Before the concert began, we were ushered to a back hallway by the tour manager. "Please wait here," he said, smiling. Our whole family stood, backs against the wall, almost as if we were in a lineup, while my mom and other friends lined the other side of the hall, waiting and watching for this special moment to unfold.

Chase stood next to me, and he shifted his weight from one foot to the other, unable to stand still in anticipation. I looked down at him and smiled. He was deep into his Spider-Man phase, with red superhero shoes and a red shirt proclaiming that Spider-Man was "amazing." Secretly, whenever he wore his favorite shirt, I always imagined the word pertained to Chase Ewoldt and not Peter Parker.

"Are you getting excited to meet Matt Redman?" He nodded emphatically, looking in both directions as if the sound of his name might make Matt appear in the hall.

Chase looked up at me, asking the same question he'd been

asking nearly every day since he'd found out about the concert. "Is he going to sing my song tonight?"

"I'm sure he will, sweet boy. I'm sure he will."

I looked down the row and winked at Darcy, bringing a small smile to her face. I could tell that she was nervous the boys might misbehave in this big moment—how I cherished her sister heart toward the boys.

There was no fanfare or announcement, just quiet and humble joy as Matt was suddenly standing in front of us. He gave each one of us a hug and quiet words of encouragement. "I've heard so much about you."

Then he knelt down by Chase and Aidan. "You must be Chase. Hi, I'm Matt."

Chase nodded quietly, and as he often did when he needed a talking point, he turned to his shoes. "Do you like my shoes? They have Spider-Man on them."

Playing along, as the experienced father of several boys himself, Matt affirmed that the shoes were pretty cool, and addressing both Aidan and Chase together, he said, "Here's a question for you . . ."

The boys leaned closer, intrigued. "If Batman and Spider-Man were in a fight, who do you think would win?"

Their eyes growing wide, the boys pondered this most serious and philosophical of questions. Clearly this man spoke their love language of superheroes and epic battles. The adults among us chuckled quietly at the stymied looks on the boys' faces. The question is debated in our house to this very day.

Matt stayed with us a moment longer, and then it was time for him to go, but before he did, he spoke once again with Chase. "We're going to sing '10,000 Reasons' at the concert tonight. That's the song we close the show with. Are you going to stay for the whole thing and hear the song?"

Chase's eyes lit up. "Yes!"

Matt smiled and shook Chase's hand. "Good. It was great to meet you, Chase."

Chase nodded in agreement.

A little while later, in the darkened auditorium, we joined hundreds of people standing shoulder to shoulder, singing and worshiping in so many words about abiding in God and finding Him good even in the worst of our circumstances.

It was time for the last song, and Matt stepped up to the microphone. "Before we started tonight, I had the chance to meet a family, and the kids are all firecrackers." A quiet ripple of laughter whispered along our row. In just a word, he'd captured the essence of the Ewoldt children.

"But that's not what I want to tell you about tonight. I want to tell you just a little about one of their sons, Chase. In fact, I think we may even have a picture of him here." Turning from the mic, he looked up at the large screens, where a picture of Chase had appeared, almost as if by magic. Chase sat up straight on my lap and exclaimed, "That's me!"

My eyes began to tear up as Matt finished his introduction. "Chase was diagnosed with a brain tumor and has gone through treatment and so many things, and he's here tonight to hear this song we're about to sing. And we aren't going to sing this song for Chase; we're here to worship, but we join Chase and sing it with him tonight because we are the church and this is what we do for one another: We bear each other's burdens."

And as we sat among hundreds of others, and the familiar piano chords began, the echo of voices singing filled the room with the same words that had echoed off the walls of hospital rooms, surgery bays, radiation rooms, and dozens of other places in between. When everyone stood to their feet, Bob and I held Chase up on a chair so he could see, Darcy and Aidan tucked in close, and Karsten cuddled with my mom. We reached for each others' hands as we voiced the prayer of our hearts—Oh, to be able to bless the Lord for ten thousand years and then forever more. And as tears rolled down my cheeks, I could hear Chase's voice close to my ear: ". . . singing when the evening comes."[8]

This is the heart of it: We never know what the evening is going to bring. Each day is a new challenge full of long and weary marathon running, but something Matt Redman said stuck close to me as we left the concert that night. This gathering together, holding each other up, this is the heart and soul of what we do for one another. I tell Chase's story and you listen; you tell your story and others listen. We carry the struggle for each other because this is what God made us to do. This is how we learn to love one another just as God loves us.

All too often the trials and shadows of cancer don't go away, but we hold to the truth that God is with us no matter what. He gives us peace against all reason, and as we speak to each other and come alongside each other in our sufferings—life or death, cure or not—we chase the cancer away.

AFTERWORD

November 8, 2015

The sun rose slowly in the late fall sky as Bob slipped the small tracking chip through the laces of his left running shoe. Eleven months of training and it would all come down to this cold morning—his first marathon.

"Is the sign ready?"

I nodded as I clutched a warm coffee mug close, feeling the excitement even as I wouldn't have minded more sleep. "You're all set."

Suddenly, we could hear the sound of small feet hitting the upstairs floor at a near run, and then Chase was coming down the stairs in his signature metered gait. Chase always rose with the sun and this morning was no different.

"Dad, are you still here?"

Bob held his arms open for a hug. "Of course!"

Chase hugged him tightly and then took his most authoritative stance. "Dad, here's the deal . . . you have to run fast. Don't slow down." He gestured emphatically with his hands. "Dad, you have to run like me, okay?"

Bob glanced at me over the small, bossy person in front of him, and we smiled at each other.

"Can you get me the sign?" Bob gathered up his gear, preparing to walk the half mile to the starting line.

"I'll help! I want to help!" Chase bounded ahead of me to the garage door where the poster board, still wreaking of permanent marker, had spent the night.

Opening the door, I handed him the wooden dowel that held the large white sign. His small hands still had faint scars from so many IV needles that he'd had to endure.

"Mom, I can read the letters!" he exclaimed. "That's a C for Chase! I know what this sign says!" He smiled proudly, sounding out and pretending to read the words he already knew by heart. "Ch-ase A-way Can-cer—Chase Away Cancer! That's me!"

It was hard to imagine that a large tumor had ever decimated his brain's language center and I still found myself in awe of how his brain clung to the memory of letters and sounds when he shouldn't even have been able to speak. "Good job, Chasey Bear!"

He growled. "M-o-o-o-m . . . I told you not to call me that anymore. I'm a big boy now. My name is just Chase."

I smiled again and kissed the top of his head where fine infant-like hair swirled sweetly. "You'll always be my Chasey Bear, no matter how old you get." And even though he protested, he didn't pull away from the hug.

As Chase gave Bob the sign, I asked the same question I'd asked several times in the last few weeks. "Are you really going to hold the sign while you run?"

Bob's face held a familiar determination, not unlike the small look-alike at his side. "Yes, I am."

"Okay, but if you get tired, you can always pass it off to me when we see you at the checkpoint."

"I'll be fine."

Chase tugged at the edge of Bob's running shirt. "Dad, don't forget to run fast like me."

And then Bob was out the door. After waking the other kids, all of us—grandma and grandpa included—bundled up for the weather and walked to the first checkpoint at the end of my parents' block. The marathon wove through the heart of their city.

We made a mismatched and funny crew as we huddled together, wrapped in blankets, adults with coffee mugs. Chase stood next to Bapa, his winter hat pulled down nearly to his eyes, clutching the poster my dad had made that proclaimed "Sweat is liquid awesome."

We cheered the hundreds of runners as they pounded the pavement in front of us. As they ran east, we looked west, scanning the participants for a familiar gold shirt. Suddenly we saw the white sign above the sea of bobbing heads: Chase Away Cancer.

The kids began jumping up and down. "Can we run with him? Please, can we run with Daddy?"

I nodded as the clouds broke and the sun streamed down onto the crowded street. "Stay on the sidewalk. You can take this down to the end of the street. Here he comes! Are you ready?"

As we screamed for Bob, Darcy began to run, pacing herself to her father. Karsten stayed tucked in the blanket at his grandma's side, but Aidan followed closely on Darcy's heels. And a little distance behind them came Chase—his head down in a determined posture, legs pumping and arms bent with fists clenched tight, all his energy going into his sprint. The look on his face was sheer delight.

Some five hours later, as Bob crossed the finish line, he still held the sign high over his head, having carried the mission and his heart for the whole 26.2 miles. Minutes later, Chase was in his father's arms, examining the medal that hung around his neck and smiling. "Good job, Dad! I told you to run like me because I'm a survivor."

The final image in this book is not one of resolution, but rather one of pure joy. Our hearts long for healing while acknowledging we may never see it the way we'd like in this life. Though Chase's progress over these last three years has been shocking and wonderful, at the time this book was being written, he was still having MRIs every three to four months.

Many children who go through what Chase has been through are at increased risk for secondary cancers, sometimes even as far out as a decade from diagnosis. Because so many pediatric cancers lack funding for optimal research or treatment, we have always felt like Chase and his generation are pioneers. Statistically, Chase's future could be quite difficult. To the best of our knowledge, he will never fully be free from the threat of relapse, but if you've read this far, you know quite well that Chase tends to blow through statistics like he blows through medical residents on rounds. He takes his own route through everything—and it almost always includes running.

Some days, the cancer shadow is dark over us as we prepare for appointments, deal with brokenness, or even come alongside one of Chase's hospital friends who may be sick or dying. And other days, if you were in the middle of our house, you'd never know Chase from the other boys if you didn't see his bald head and the scar. There are peanut butter sandwiches to be made, sibling squabbles to be resolved, the great stress of math homework, and the fact that nobody wants to take responsibility for the lightsaber dent in the family room wall.

In a way, this book ends before Chase's story does, but I don't want to wait until the end of whatever may come to share with you what has already passed. No matter what unfolds next, if I know Chase, it will be interesting. And this is the heart of the story: to prove God good and true even when we don't get the resolution we so desperately desire. Moment by moment, in this story without an ending lies our need for grace.

When you hold this book in your hands, you hold pieces of the hard, messy, and unfinished life that is being knit into a beautiful creation by a Master with an intricate plan that is still very much unfolding.

So read these pieces of our story, and then gather your own jagged and beautiful pieces—for we all have them. Write them down on paper, on your computer, in your heart, wherever you must, and remember that He is good, that His ways are good, all the time, no matter what.

Moment by moment.

PHOTO GALLERY

*I've heard it said that pictures are pieces of heart and soul, and
I know for myself they are worth many handfuls of words. So here,
on these pages, see the pieces of our hearts laid out and moments
in seasons that, at times, defy countless words. I hope by the end
you will know our family a little better.*

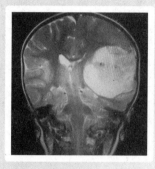

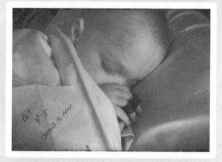

JULY 31, 2012. *Chase's first MRI. The
tumor is the giant white ball on the
right. You can see that the middle of
the brain is bowing to the left under
the pressure of the mass. The pressure
from this midline shift is most likely
what caused Chase's initial seizure.
To say he was in distress is an
understatement.*

JULY 31, 2012. *Diagnosis day. His cheeks still rosy
from the steroids, Chase sleeps peacefully with Pastor
Dave's wonderful reminder close by.*

LATE SUMMER 2012: *"Bring
Your Brother to Clinic Day."
Aidan has always been able to
make Chase laugh, and his
presence during a full, long day of
hospital appointments was such a gift.*

AUGUST 2, 2012. *Laughing about gorillas and smelling the strawberries, Bob captures us in that final moment before surgery.*

DECEMBER 12, 2012. *It was his third birthday, and Chase whispered, "I'm so brave . . ." as he lost consciousness against my forehead before he collapsed onto my shoulder, and then I laid him on the table for his final radiation treatment.*

Chase's "one of a kind" graduation signature on the wall of the radiation center—the somewhat legendary three-fingered handprint.

CHASE
12.12.12

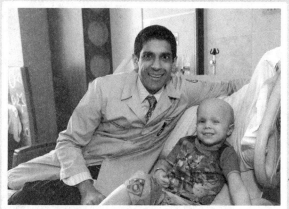

Chase and his attending neuro-oncologist and St. Baldrick Foundation's researcher, Dr. Rishi Lulla, spend some time hanging out for an early-morning photo session with the hospital.

Chase laughs with one of his favorite hematology and oncology nurses, Ashlee, whose many gifts include being an expert hide-and-seek player. This amazing moment of joy was captured during a particularly terrible chemo infusion.

WINTER 2013. *Whatever Daddy does, Chase has to do too. The "boys" pass the time waiting in clinic.*

WINTER 2013. *After five long days of chemo infusions, Chase is exhausted and glad for the support of Grammie (my mom) and sister Darcy as he awaits the final dose. Less than twenty-four hours after this picture was taken, Chase was readmitted with fevers and central line issues.*

JULY 2013. *Bob and Chase participate in the "Run for Gus" at Diversey Harbor in Chicago, which benefits the pediatric brain tumor program at Ann & Robert H. Lurie Children's Hospital of Chicago. The event was named in honor of Gus Evangelides, a little boy who succumbed to a malignant brain tumor in the spring of 1995.*

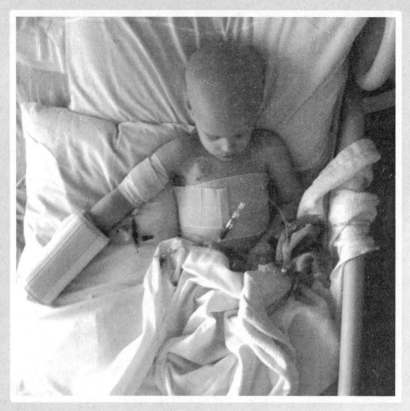

SUMMER 2013: *The summer of "tubies" and "tacos" and too many cords. Caught in between surgeries, Chase has three separate access lines in his body.*

AUGUST 2013. *Nurse Jen gets final instructions on the care of Scout, a borrowed pet puppy, before Chase goes in for yet another "nap" to replace his central line.*

AUGUST 2013. *Chase and Aunt Carrie celebrate the placement of his final port.*

JULY 19, 2014. *Nobody's making faces and nobody's running out of the shot—it's a minor miracle. Our official family portrait for St. Baldrick's. [l. to r.] Bob, Karsten, Darcy, Aidan, me, and Chase.*

ver may pass, and whate fore me... Let me be ving he evening comes...

3 years

JULY 31, 2015. *Chase sitting on the lawn and promising to smile nicely. Three years earlier to the hour, Chase and I were in an ambulance being rushed to Chicago. God is good.*

AUGUST 12, 2015. *Chase spends a few minutes discussing cancer, his bravery, and of course, Spider-Man with his friend, "Mr. Matt" (Redman).*

ACKNOWLEDGMENTS

If I could speak the name of every person for whom I'm deeply thankful, the names alone could fill a chapter, for truly, behind every one person and one story told in the pages of this book, there are dozens more people with handfuls of stories to go along.

So thank you, dear family. The family I was born into, the family I married into, the family with whom I go to church, the family we have gained at Lurie Children's, the family we've been blessed with just through the word *cancer*, and the family we've been gifted with in the process of publishing this book.

You have seen us at our best and worst. You have held our weary bodies up with generous acts of kindness as often as you've held us up in prayer. You've listened to us without judgment. You've spoken life and love to us when we felt without hope. You've comforted us even in your own sorrows. And you've taken on Chase's struggle as your own.

Thank you for being the hands and feet of Jesus to us in so many tangible and precious ways.

We would not be where we are today without you.

Oh, how great are God's riches and wisdom and knowledge!
How impossible it is for us to understand his decisions and his
ways! For everything comes from him and exists by his power
and is intended for his glory. All glory to him forever! Amen.

ROMANS 11:33, 36

SOURCES OF COMFORT, STRENGTH, AND INSPIRATION

Every person's path through this journey of pain is different and precious, but I wanted to share a few of the resources that have held me up and revived my spirit throughout Chase's cancer journey. And because music is like breath to our family, and reading a book was at times put aside in favor of flying paper airplanes in a pediatric ER, I've also included some of our favorite songs. I hope these pieces of other sojourners' journeys encourage you as they've sustained us.

BOOKS

John Piper: *Don't Waste Your Cancer*
C. S. Lewis: *A Grief Observed*
Nancy Guthrie: *Hoping for Something Better*; *Holding On to Hope*;
The One Year Book of Hope
Ann Voskamp: *One Thousand Gifts*
Linda Dillow: *Calm My Anxious Heart*
Kara Tippetts: *The Hardest Peace*

MUSIC

Matt Redman: "10,000 Reasons (Bless the Lord)"; "Abide With Me"
Lecrae, featuring Anthony Evans: "Boasting"
Meredith Andrews: "Not for a Moment (After All)"
Sovereign Grace Music: "All I Have Is Christ"
Matt Papa: "Joshua 1:9 (Be Strong and Courageous)"; "I Will Trust In You My God"

Chris Tomlin: "Whom Shall I Fear (God of Angel Armies)";
    "Sovereign"
Casting Crowns: "Glorious Day (Living He Loved Me)"
Shane and Shane: "Though You Slay Me"
Rend Collective: "My Lighthouse"; "More Than Conquerors"
Mark and Stephen Altrogge: "Whatever My God Ordains Is Right"

NOTES

1. The signs and symptoms of pediatric central nervous system tumors overlap in many ways with common and "benign" conditions in children. This issue is often compounded by a young child's inability to articulate his or her symptoms. In a significant majority of cases, children are seen and diagnosed (sometimes multiple times) with another condition prior to the discovery of a brain tumor.
2. Horatius Bonar, "Calm," http://www.gutenberg.org/files/28591/28591-h/28591-h.htm.
3. Gungor, "Beautiful Things," from the album *Beautiful Things*, Brash Records, 2010.
4. Matt Redman, "10,000 Reasons (Bless the Lord)," from the album *10,000 Reasons*, sixsteprecords/Sparrow Records, 2011.
5. Ibid.
6. Michael W. Smith, "Gloria," from the album *Christmas*, Reunion Records, September 1993.
7. John Piper, *A Sweet and Bitter Providence* (Wheaton, IL: Crossway Books, 2010), 101–102.
8. Matt Redman, "10,000 Reasons (Bless the Lord)."

ABOUT THE AUTHOR

Ellie Poole Ewoldt is married to Bob, the mother of Darcy, Aidan, Chase, and Karsten, as well as a daughter, a sister, and a friend. With a lifelong love of reading, writing, and history, she has a degree from North Central College in early modern European history with a minor in art history. Currently, her skill set includes being able to keep several plates in the air while talking to small children about not throwing plates, labeling the "weird stain" on the rug correctly, and being able to navigate an entire playroom without stepping on a single toy.

In 2010, Ellie started a small family blog as a way to share her daily life, child-related anecdotes, and the continuous discovery of God's goodness as she and Bob raised four children in an eleven-hundred-square-foot condo. Writing the beautiful, silly, and hard became a way of practicing thankfulness and seeking "stones of remembrance."

On July 31, 2012, the family's lives changed forever with the words, "*There's a large mass*," catapulting them on a deep, complex journey through pediatric cancer. Ellie began to chronicle the life and fight of their third child, Chase, and the effect of the disease on their family as they continued to search for joy in the worst of times.

Today her days are spent caring for quickly growing children, walking alongside Chase in his cancer diagnosis and resulting special neurological needs, and continuing to chronicle God's faithfulness in the big and small things alike. Ellie and Bob have shared Chase's story on behalf of Ann & Robert H. Lurie Children's Hospital of Chicago, and his story has been featured in venues such as Lurie Children's, Children's Miracle Network Hospitals, the ACE Foundation, All for Hope, Cal's Angels, Young Associates Board's Run for Gus, and the St. Baldrick's Foundation.

To learn more about Ellie and her family, visit www.chaseawaycancer .com.

D0101233

Kids are special.
WE TREAT THEM THAT WAY.

EVERY THREE MINUTES, A CHILD IS DIAGNOSED WITH CANCER. In the United States, one in five won't survive.

But for kids like Chase, survival is just the beginning of the story. Many of today's best cancer treatments are toxic and can cause damage to kids' growing minds and bodies, triggering long-term effects, including loss of hearing or sight, heart disease, secondary cancers, learning disabilities, infertility, and more.

The St. Baldrick's Foundation exists to change these realities.

What started as a single head-shaving challenge in 2000 has grown to become the world's largest volunteer-powered charity for childhood cancer research and the largest private funder of childhood cancer research grants.

Together, we're funding the most promising research so kids with cancer can get back to what's important: just being kids.

St. Baldrick's
FOUNDATION
Conquer Childhood Cancers

To learn more, please visit us online at
StBaldricks.org and
StBaldricks.org/conquer

CP1090